Praise for

IN AWE OF BEING HUMAN
A Doctor's Stories from the Edge of Life and Death

"These luminous stories show how doctors and patients alike step forward to meet the most daunting challenges life can bring, demonstrating beautifully for the rest of us what it means to be human. Read this book—it will nourish your soul!"
—ANDREW WEIL, M.D., author of *Why Our Health Matters, Spontaneous Healing, Healthy Aging,* and *Spontaneous Happiness*

"*In Awe of Being Human* is a book of inspiration and renewal. At this challenging time in American medicine, doctor/healer Betsy MacGregor reminds us of the powerful calling that doctors have and the intention to serve that brings us to this work. It is impossible to read these beautiful stories without remembering that, at its core, medicine is not a work of science but an act of love."
—RACHEL NAOMI REMEN, M.D., author of *Kitchen Table Wisdom* and *My Grandfather's Blessings*; Clinical Professor, Family and Community Medicine, UCSF School of Medicine

"*In Awe of Being Human* is a brilliant, inspired work. It is the view of a physician who can marvel at the spectacular ways the human condition displays itself in health and illness. As these sparkling stories reveal, Betsy MacGregor is the kind of physician everyone wants. If you can't have Betsy as your doctor, do the next best thing: read her magnificent book."
—LARRY DOSSEY, M.D., author of *The Extraordinary Healing Power of Ordinary Things, Healing Words, Power of Premonitions,* and *Reinventing Medicine*

"Betsy MacGregor has been a wise and compassionate guide for critically ill children and for the dying. The beauty of her soul is reflected in this wonderful exploration of healing and medicine. Don't miss it."
—MICHAEL LERNER, founder of Commonweal; cofounder and president of the Commonweal Cancer Help Program; author of *Choices In Healing: Integrating The Best of Conventional and Complementary Approaches to Cancer*

continued on next page . . .

"One of us is a writer involved in public health who has worked with eminent physicians around the world, from Nobel Prize winners to those toiling selflessly to serve people in dire need. The other has a career in the helping professions that has brought her into contact with renowned clinicians, the kind of people who have helped shape modern psychiatric practice. But without doubt the most profoundly wise doctor we have encountered is a physician we first met on the morning of our first child's birth. As she reviewed a constellation of troubling anomalies, Dr. Betsy MacGregor was candid about both the import of what we were discussing as well as the limits of medical science in predicting how these factors would affect our newborn child's life.

This was not merely humility, but a rare wisdom that proved enormously significant to our family's future. In the weeks and months that followed, we consulted with a variety of New York City's most sought-after specialists, from Geneticists to Developmental Pediatricians, who authoritatively declared that our son would be profoundly retarded.

The fact that we rejected this view, removed him from the N.I.C.U. and took him home to raise a vivacious, warm and wise human being had everything to do with a pediatrician willing to acknowledge feelings as well as findings. Betsy was and is a clinician in touch with her heart as well as her head, a person deeply intuitively wise about a view of brain and body that has emerged in the decades since that time.

Betsy was far more than our son's doctor. She was our family's partner and counselor, a scientist who helped us manage a variety of serious issues without ever being less than a kind friend. Her gifts as a writer mirror her abilities as a doctor who de-mystified medical concepts without ever over-simplifying.

Betsy personifies the ideal of medicine as a social engagement, a thoroughly modern scientist who is as much a student as a teacher, deeply respectful of the families she worked with and always unfailingly kind. And not only is she a doctor who has been willing to learn from her patients, she is a writer who tells wonderful stories that have a great deal to teach us all."

—DANNY AND PATTI ABELSON, parents of a young patient

"There is no better way to summarize *In Awe of Being Human* than to quote from the very first sentence of the prologue: this is indeed a collection of 'gut-wrenching, heart-expanding, soul-uplifting stories that chart the human journey.' These stories reflect the author's extraordinary compassion, insight, sensitivity and humility. They are a joy to read—though, like most joys, complemented by great sadness as well. That, after all, is the essence of being human."

—ROBERT G. NEWMAN, M.D., former president and CEO of Beth Israel Medical Center and president emeritus of Continuum Health Partners, Inc.

"This is an extraordinary book that reminds us of the preciousness of life and the mystery of death. Written by a compassionate clinician whose humanity shines through every word, Dr. MacGregor gives us a view of living, illness, dying and death that is remarkable in its hopefulness and wisdom."

—ROSHI JOAN HALIFAX, founding Abbot, Upaya Zen Center; author of *Being with Dying: Cultivating Compassion and Fearlessness in the Presence of Death*; founder and director of the Being with Dying Project, committed to educating health-care professionals in the contemplative care of the terminally ill

"Betsy MacGregor is a physician who brings x-ray vision into the tension between our growing health technologies and our growing sense of humanity. Are we machines to keep alive or souls to bless on a larger journey? Everyone should read this book before they die—or before someone else they love enters the dying process in today's medical industry. This is a tender and moving book, filled with grace. You can catch sight of heaven by entering the gripping, raw, and powerful world of Betsy MacGregor—a skilled doctor and compassionate soul who offers insightful and often surprising stories from the edge of existence."

—DUANE ELGIN, author of *Voluntary Simplicity, The Living Universe,* and *Awakening Earth*

"In these tender, powerful stories, hurt yields to healing, and despair flowers unexpectedly into hope. Page after page, tears filled my eyes as my heart opened and my spirit soared. Betsy MacGregor is the loving, life-affirming physician all of us want, the wise teacher every doctor needs."

—JAMES GORDON, M.D., founder and director, The Center for Mind Body Medicine; author of *Unstuck: Your Guide to the Seven-Stage Journey Out of Depression*

continued on next page . . .

"The becoming of Enso House Hospice had a lot to do with Betsy Daishi MacGregor. Her experiences as a doctor in New York City where she saw many people at the moment they were on the edge of dying, and her astonishment at how bright and shining this was, had great meaning in Enso House's development—a meaning which is beyond measure. I have seen this too, and so this hospice was our mutual vow. I have profound gratitude to her for this."
—SHODO HARADA ROSHI, Abbot of Sogenji Monastery, Japan;
founder of Tahoma Monastery, Washington State;
co-founder of Enso House Hospice, Washington State

"Dr. MacGregor's book is about mystery and compassion and presence, and, thankfully, she is not afraid to talk about these issues. It is also a story about becoming—becoming a medical student, a resident, a young pediatrician, a skilled pediatric pain expert, a palliative care physician, and finally a patient. Throughout this long career, Dr. MacGregor has not hesitated to confront the suffering of her patients and her colleagues, and she shows us how these experiences have shaped her personhood. She learns to be tolerant and to manage uncertainty. We see her grow—emotionally, intellectually, morally.

She demonstrates great authenticity and generosity of spirit as she takes her own experience and dissects its impact on herself and her learning and maturing as a doctor and a person. Her stories are compelling and some very challenging to imagine, and yet she stays with each patient and their family, no matter what befalls them. She walks the last mile with them, and she is there both to help them and to learn from them, while always respecting their dignity. She is a doctor who has taken her patients into her heart, sharing with them the wonder, terror, and exultation of being on the edge of being. We can all benefit from her experience."
—KATHY FOLEY, M.D., Chair of the Society of Memorial Sloan-
Kettering Cancer Center and Attending Physician in Neurology;
Professor of Neurology, Neuroscience and Clinical Pharmacology,
Weil Medical College of Cornell University;
Medical Director, International Palliative Care Initiative,
Open Society Foundation

IN AWE OF
BEING HUMAN

IN AWE OF
BEING HUMAN

*A Doctor's Stories from the
Edge of Life and Death*

by

Betsy MacGregor, M.D.

Abiding Nowhere Press
Greenbank, WA

Published by Abiding Nowhere Press
Printed in the USA
www.abidingnowhere.com

Learn more about
In Awe of Being Human:
A Doctor's Stories from the Edge of Life and Death,
upcoming events, and Betsy MacGregor, M.D.
at www.betsymacgregor.com

ISBN-13:978-0985496777 (Abiding Nowhere Press)
ISBN-10:0985496770

Cover design by Christine Nyburg
Book layout design by Sandra J. Welch

Photographs on back cover:
author's photo by Joe Menth, Fine Balance Imaging Studios;
photo of author in surgery and author as an intern with young patient,
from author's archives

To my patients and their families,
who showed me
the full spectrum of human strength and vulnerability

Contents

Draw your chair up close to the edge of the precipice,
and I'll tell you a story.

—F. Scott Fitzgerald

Prologue

ONE OF THE WONDERFUL things about being a doctor is that you are privileged to witness amazing stories: gut-wrenching, heart-opening, soul-uplifting stories that chart the human journey, the epic process of challenge and growth in which every one of us is engaged. For nearly thirty years, most of them spent working at a major medical center in New York City, I witnessed a great many such stories, far more, in fact, than I can possibly remember. And still, there are more than enough that I will never forget, fierce and tender ones that carved out a permanent niche in the marrow of my bones, and these I feel compelled to share.

These are stories of my patients and their families—people I cared for and worked with every day, people I loved and learned from. These stories come from my years as a medical student, intern and resident in clinical training, and then as a hospital-based inner-city pediatrician and adolescent medicine specialist, and finally as a research physician in charge of a three-year research project entitled "Dying and the Inner Life," investigating what people with terminal illness can tell us about the experience of feeling the end of life approaching. The stories span the arc of the human journey from the beginning to the very end. They lead from the arrival of new life in the hospital delivery room through episodes of illness and injury and the ever-present hope of healing, all the way

1

to the bedside of those who are in their final days. They tell about moments when ordinary people seek help in facing extraordinary trials, and they reveal the many ways in which triumph and transformation can prevail amid the harrowing circumstances of hospital life and the hi-tech, sometimes Stone-Age-like practices of modern medicine.

At the same time, these stories shed light on the inner life of doctors. They provide insight into the long, grueling path of training that doctors must undergo and the soul-stretching experiences we endure as we seek to help people whose lives are at stake. It is a life I have loved. Being able to help people who are ill and suffering has been a privilege. To see life become better for many of them has been a wonderful reward.

I have loved the profession of medicine for another reason as well: being a doctor has made me appreciate life's enigmatic nature. This mystery of life—the miracle that surrounds us at every moment but is so easily taken for granted—stands out more clearly in times of urgency or crisis like those encountered in an emergency room or intensive care unit or delivery suite. When you feel life is at risk of slipping away, you become very aware of how precious and irreplaceable it is. And because these places of urgency and crisis are where I spent much of my time, I felt the wonder of human existence on a daily basis.

These stories contain that wonder, each in a different way. Some relate the experience of parents, like Saul and Rebecca, whose first child died in their arms from a brain tumor at the age of two, and whose second child came into the world bearing a gift that made all of us in the delivery room gasp. Others describe the experience of infants, from the snuggly wrapped newborns lying safely asleep in their bassinets in the well-baby nurseries to the other little newcomers in the Neonatal Intensive Care Unit down the hall, the not-so-lucky ones who clung to life by a thread.

Still others concern remarkable children, such as four-year-old Isabella, an impish child with AIDS whose wisdom reached far beyond her years; and young Bobby, who taught every person he knew that being "different" means nothing more or less than being exactly who you are; and little Angel, who had the gentlest dying of anyone I have ever known. There are also adolescents, like Migdalia, an angry sixteen-year-old whose inner strength allowed her to survive a devastating accident and find a goodness in it that changed her life, and Leo, a terminally ill, thrown-away teenager in foster care who discovered the power of forgiveness and generosity all on his own.

Some of the stories concern older people too: James, a longtime drug dealer with AIDS whose near-death experience showed him that his wasted life had more good in it than he had imagined; Randolf, a proud patriarch of the theater world who made peace with a monstrous self-doubt in time to savor a gentler view of himself as he waited for death to come; and ninety-six-year-old Hildie, who, despite her toothless, debilitated condition, insisted that being grateful is one of the most important things one can do in life.

My aim in telling these stories is to offer a riveting glimpse into the world of hospitals and doctoring where so much intensity and depth exists. It seems to me that many people today are hungering for this—hungering to taste the unadorned reality of joy and pain, of life and death. I have done my best to see that the stories contained in the following pages provide that opportunity. They are intended to plunge readers into the sometimes unsettling but ultimately uplifting drama of life and leave them in awe at the miracle of being human.

ONE

Beauty & Brutality

THE COEXISTENCE OF BEAUTY and brutality creates a paradox that you cannot escape in the practice of medicine. Such a seemingly terrible mismatch is not easy to confront if you happen to be a young doctor just beginning your clinical training. Coming upon these two apparent opposites standing starkly side by side can challenge and stretch you incomprehensibly. For myself, many years went by before I began to accept how thoroughly beauty and brutality could sometimes intertwine, simultaneously filling my heart with reverence and causing it to cry out in anguished protest as together the two carved out in me a fuller capacity for being human.

I recall the ice crystals that decorated the outside windowpanes of the Pediatric Special Care Unit on one particularly cold winter day. They sparkled with a touch of bright New York City sunlight. Inside the unit's spacious room, fifteen-year-old Julia lay unconscious in her bed, a white hospital blanket lying neat and smooth over her unmoving form, while the quiet beeping of the cardiac monitor still testified to the beating of her courageous heart. Julia was coming to the end of her long struggle with a brutal illness: childhood leukemia. As valiantly as she had fought to stay alive, she rested now in a tranquil sleep as the rapidly multiplying leukemic cells that had infiltrated her brain proceeded to shut it down.

Julia's parents had been preparing themselves for this day, and they sat together at the foot of Julia's bed, hand in hand. For the time being they shared a quiet space, a lull in the exhaustion of their grief. After three grueling years of seeking the best possible care for their daughter, partnering with her oncologist in making every medical decision, they had arrived at a place of silence. No words were important enough now to speak. The nurses instinctively knew this, too, and they moved on noiseless feet about the room as they checked the IV drip line and watched Julia's breath come and go.

Julia's younger sister, Lily, age nine, was the only one in the room who was truly busy. She had assigned herself an important task, and she was tending to it with calm and certain skill. Sitting in a chair that she had pulled alongside the head of Julia's hospital bed, she had hairbrush in hand and was carefully brushing her older sister's silky brown hair. Of course, it was only the wig that Julia had liked to wear when she had still felt well, for the uncaring potency of chemotherapy had stolen her own precious hair long ago. Lily had accompanied Julia the day she selected that wig from among many others in order to hide her baldness from the sideways looks of strangers. Today, Lily had begged her parents to put the wig back on Julia and now was treating it with loving care. She had been at the task for some time, and her strokes had spread the hair out evenly all across the pillow, like a soft, tawny halo around her dying sister's head.

As she proceeded with her project of smoothing and brushing, brushing and smoothing, Lily paused occasionally and tilted her head this way and that, as if to view her work and assess the merit of the gift she was giving to Julia, her much more grown-up sister who almost certainly had never allowed her to do such a thing before. And all the while, Lily accompanied herself with a tune that she hummed in time with the strokes of her brush, while her sister lay still and patient and accepting of her sibling's gift.

I chanced to see this scene when passing by the door of the Special Care Unit as I went about my intern work on the adjacent ward. Julia was a private patient of an important attending physician in our department who specialized in pediatric oncology. The house staff played only a peripheral role in her care. Still, we were all acutely aware of her presence and her imminent passing, and an unusual quietude tempered the normal hustle and bustle of the ward that day.

The attending, Dr. Kaplan, was a temperamental man given to outbursts of anger if his orders were not followed to the letter, and many a member of the house staff had felt the bite of that anger. Yet we readily forgave him in light of the uncommon devotion he had to his patients. He fussed over all of them like a mother hen clucking over her chicks and oversaw their care with a sharp and unwavering eye. He knew every nuance of each one's illness and was rarely fooled by the wily twists and turns that childhood leukemia or cancer can take. Years of experience had honed in him, too, a hard clarity that could discern when hope of healing was real and when it was not.

Therefore, Dr. Kaplan had been frank with Julia's parents, explaining that she would not recover from her coma and that it was time to let her go. As he instructed the house staff that we were to forgo all measures aimed at prolonging her life any further, I felt compassion for the man. His was not an enviable job, holding the scales of living and dying in his hands.

As for me, I felt drawn to Julia's room as surely as a moth is drawn to a window through which light is shining on a dark night. Each time my pressing chores caused me to hurry down the corridor past the partially curtained window of the Special Care Unit, the intimate scene I glimpsed within beckoned to me like a quiet eddy in a rushing river. My feet slowed of their own accord, and my busy thoughts fell temporarily quiet as my heart took in the enormity of the event transpiring there: the passing away of a beautiful soul far too early, a treasured soul who would be sorely missed. Some instinct in me yearned to stand guard over that little sanctuary and shield it from the never-ending buzz of the ward's more everyday affairs. Yet I had not been assigned such a role, and thus, each time my feet began to slow, I reluctantly made them carry me on my way.

Nevertheless, that day on the ward is one I will never forget. The simple sight of a nine-year-old girl brushing the hair of her dying sister—the sound of Lily humming as she bent lovingly to her labor—these remain deeply etched in my memory many decades later. I will never forget the exquisite intertwining of tenderness and sorrow my eyes beheld that day, and I continue to cherish that scene, with its poignancy that only certain human acts can have.

As for Lily, I have no doubt she, too, still remembers what happened on that chilly winter day. I suspect it will remain forever with her as the day she helped her sister look beautiful, just before her brutal illness took her away.

* * * * * *

In the beginning I was surprised to see that such a contradictory combination as beauty and brutality could happen, though some of my colleagues appeared to take it for granted. I was still a medical student, doing my third-year surgery rotation in a hospital up in Harlem, when I encountered the strange occurrence for the very first time, one unsettling night while I was on duty in the ER.

All the medical students knew this particular hospital as a very busy place where good "action" was to be had, and "action" was highly valued among any who were contemplating surgery as their career, and even some who were not. Assigned to night call with the surgery team, I was waiting restlessly for something to happen when the surgery resident suddenly walked over and clapped me on the shoulder, announcing that he had a case for me. A tall, lanky guy with a lopsided smile and slight swagger to his step, he jerked his thumb over his shoulder toward an approaching stretcher.

On the stretcher lay a heavily sedated figure. A pair of uniformed police officers walked stiffly alongside the stretcher as a nurse guided it unerringly through the noisy ER activity toward my curtained cubicle. According to the resident, the patient was a victim of violence. No witnesses had been able to say exactly what had happened, nor was it known what part the man himself might have played in the outbreak of the violence. Victim and perpetrator were sometimes hard to distinguish on the streets of the inner city. To many, violence was simply a way of life.

The surgery resident apparently found no thrill in treating yet another bullet wound. This was Harlem, after all, and shootings occurred all too frequently back in those days. With a detached shrug, he parceled the case out to me, probably thinking it would do no great harm for me to hone my infant surgical skills on this poor bloke. Maybe he even derived a little amusement out of plunging a green-around-the-gills female medical student into the gutsy protocol of Bullet Removal 101. He handed me the man's chart, instructing me to read what the triage nurse had written in her notes as well as the reports filed by the paramedics and police. Clearly, he had no interest in the incidentals of the case. His only concern was supervising the surgical procedure I was to do and seeing that I did it well.

As the nurse flipped the white sheet off the stretcher with a perfunctory sweep of her arm, my breath caught unexpectedly in my throat. Beauty lay visible there. The muscles of this person's chest and arms curved with graceful power, his deep-toned skin lustrous and smooth, his regal face completely at peace as he gently snored under the influence of a powerful sedative. He looked the picture of fine health and luxurious relaxation but for one small flaw, which became visible when the nurse removed the pressure dressing from his right leg: an ugly hole in the front of his thigh.

The hole measured less than an inch across but had a grizzly implication: buried somewhere in the flesh below was one of modern man's cruel inventions, sent into his perfect body with brutal intent to hurt and harm. The beautiful brown skin puckered away at the edges, exposing a pink circle of under-flesh that oozed a steady stream of blood diluted with spilled cellular contents. The sight struck me as gruesome, and the questions it raised about the circumstances of this man's life discomforted me.

With mechanical precision the surgery resident doled out his instructions for preparing the surgical field. "Put on surgical gloves," he said. "Swab the wound and surrounding skin with antiseptic . . . Now drape a sterile shield around the perimeter . . . Now lay out your instruments, and select a scalpel and forceps."

Once I had dutifully accomplished this, he briskly instructed me to begin digging for the bullet, a painstaking process of teasing apart torn muscle fibers and poking my finger ever further into the patient's thigh, tracing the path carved by the mean little missile. The resident's watchful eye noted my every move.

I gritted my teeth. My breath came in abbreviated gulps, and the faint odor of my own nervous sweat hung in the air. To wiggle my finger deep into the flesh of another human being went against every instinct I had. I could not convince my senses that I was not doing harm, and I half-expected the wounded man to howl in pain at any moment.

But the steady drone of instruction from the resident left no room for hesitation. By the time my probing finger finally found the destructive little ball of metal and my forceps reached in to claim it and bring it forth in triumph, I was ready to cry with relief. Instead, a brittle little laugh popped out of my throat, bringing a wry smile to the face of my watching superior.

"Want to do another one?" he snickered.

"Not just now, thanks," I croaked, as I cleaned up a pile of bloody gauze sponges and tossed them into a waiting bucket. I did not care to have another such macabre experience that evening. Instead, I wished I could have spoken to the man, could have introduced myself and called him by his name and asked why this terrible thing had happened to him, such a decent-looking person who should have had a lot going for him.

But, I argued with myself, at least he was alive and would return home, unlike others brought to the ER. Perhaps this collision with a bullet would even deflect his course away from further harm, and his regal face would smile at life on some other day.

Still, such reasonable thoughts did little to allay my discomfort, and disturbing questions prowled about in my mind the rest of that night. Why did life let such wasteful things happen? Why was beauty allowed to be marred by such brutality? No matter how I looked at it, it did not seem right.

*　*　*　*　*　*　*

The practice of medicine is rife with opportunities to learn that life does not always conduct itself in ways one would regard as right or reasonable. The emergency room demonstrates this daily, sometimes with stark intensity. There I first witnessed dying in the medical setting, and the frenetic activity that engulfed that particular ending of life made it easy to miss any intimation of a softer, gentler side of things.

I was in my fourth year of medical school, immersed in a rotation in Emergency Medicine when it happened. An ambulance pulled into the emergency bay with sirens blaring and unloaded its human cargo with the requisite speed. Orderlies whisked an obese elderly man, red-faced and anxious and securely strapped to the ambulance gurney, into the ER suite. He wore an oxygen mask and had an IV already running, started by the emergency medicine technicians for delivering medications en route. As he flapped his hands in agitation, the EMTs reported to the receiving medical team that he was complaining of acute chest pain. From the look of things, the attending ER doc said, the unfortunate fellow was having a heart attack.

Before another word was spoken, the on-duty team sprang into full-blown action. They rapidly stripped away the man's clothes, attached cardiac monitor leads to his chest, inserted a second IV, drew blood for testing, filled syringes with medication, and ordered a STAT chest x-ray. The ER attending physician was asking the agitated man if he had ever had heart trouble before when things took a turn for the worse. The man's head slumped to one side, and his color rapidly went from flushed red to dusky blue. Simultaneously, the alarm on the cardiac monitor began beeping wildly, showing that the line tracing the rhythm of his heartbeats on the monitor screen had gone flat.

"He's coding!" someone shouted. A cardiac arrest was happening before my eyes.

Controlled pandemonium immediately broke loose. Someone slammed a manual ventilating bag over the man's mouth and started pumping air into his lungs, as someone else prepared to intubate him for more effective oxygen delivery. A junior resident whisked the fire-engine-red "crash cart" with all its resuscitation implements into place beside the stretcher, and a senior resident readied shock paddles to jump-start the man's failed heart back to life. His body gave a quick, heavy, upward heave as the electrical current coursed through his chest.

The resuscitation procedures moved forward with a strange beauty, like some dark ballet wherein the dancers whirl through their steps with fierce and focused grace. Everyone had their assigned task to perform (mine being to run quickly for more supplies as they were needed), and all worked with one intention: to save this man's life. No doubt he would want that to be done, though he had never actually been consulted. If he sustained a broken tooth or two while being intubated, or a cracked rib from the chest compressions being conducted with concentrated precision by a muscular second-year resident, what did that really matter? Patient permission was not considered necessary when a person's life was at stake.

As we labored on, however, the minutes lengthened, and a subtle change began to take place in the rhythm of the effort. The heroic outpouring of energy was waning ever so slightly. Not from tiredness—there was still plenty of adrenaline pumping through each of us—but from something else. Perhaps our hope grew dull. People were starting to shake their heads. There should have been some response by now. The cardiac monitor should have picked up a rhythm again. The man's chest should have started to expand with breaths of air, his skin to begin regaining a healthy pinkish hue.

Eventually, the ER attending heaved a reluctant sigh and called the end of the code. The right endeavor had been made, the opportunity offered, but life had not taken it up. Life had turned away. Then the medical staff did as well. Every one of them turned their backs and walked away as if on cue, quickly becoming swept up into other ER busyness. Only I stayed, off to one side, staring at what remained behind.

The body of the man lay where it had been abandoned on the stretcher, bare-naked except for his boxer shorts, the intubation tube still sticking awkwardly out of his mouth, surrounded by the aftermath of the furious exertion made on his behalf. The floor was strewn with discarded gauze pads and spotted with blood. IV poles stood solemnly by, lonely attendants no longer needed.

This sight struck me as more disturbing to witness than the resuscitation attempt itself. The sudden poetic loneliness of the scene stood out sharply amid the surrounding hubbub of ER activity that clamored on insistently. Perhaps that was why the resuscitation team had walked away so quickly, leaving the nurses and nursing assistants to do the work of cleaning up. They found it too hard to assimilate.

The intense focus of the past forty-five minutes lingered in the air like a lonely ghost. A short time ago this man had been rushed in, clinging to life, only to have life desert him as the heroic efforts of the emergency room team to make it otherwise came to naught. Yet something else lingered there, too, something besides the aftermath of failure. A small area of quiet remained: a fertile stillness, which, for a while, stood apart from the commotion of the rest of the ER that was hard at work, as if beauty was refusing to let brutality have the final word.

*   *   *   *   *   *   *

Life has many different kinds of beauty, and some lie behind such a rough exterior that you have to pay close attention to appreciate them. Brutality, too, may assume a more subtle form. It may lurk in the very things you are trained to do as a doctor, the things you are taught to regard as helpful and correct. These were the paradoxes in Katherine's case, or at least how I saw it as a still-wet-behind-the-ears third-year medical student.

I was doing my month-long rotation in Internal Medicine when I met Katherine, and she won me to her cause immediately. A slender, probably once attractive woman in her late thirties, Katherine lay confined to bed in Room 301A on the medical ward with the most disturbing disease I had ever seen. Her diagnosis was far-advanced scleroderma, a condition in which a person's immune system becomes confused.

Instead of producing antibodies that defend against outside invaders, it produces antibodies that attack the person's own connective tissues, those strong and marvelously flexible tissues that give our skin its supple quality and that form the bulwark of our muscles, our blood vessels and all our internal organs. The attacking antibodies rob these connective tissues of their marvelous elasticity, making them grow stiff and hard and resistant to movement. Unfortunately, modern medicine has not yet learned how to stop this grim process. Once started, the disease can progress slowly or more rapidly, affecting its victim in merely a few isolated places, or spreading throughout the person's entire body, as it was doing in Katherine's case.

Katherine had begun to develop the early signs of scleroderma a decade earlier. A feeling of tightness in her skin, together with a shiny appearance, developed first on her fingers and toes; then it also appeared on her elbows and knees. She had seen other patients with cases more advanced than hers in her specialist's office, and she had known what was coming. As time went on, the disease progressed, steadily gaining ground with its leathery unyieldingness, eventually closing in so fully all around her that she could do nothing but lie stiff and motionless in bed. She was encased in a body that would one day become her own coffin.

To look at Katherine required a certain amount of courage, or else a defensive denial of feeling. She lay inert but fully present, like a tortoise pulled into its shell. Only her eyes moved as she gazed out from her fortress at the world going by. Her arms and legs were nearly useless, and her face could no longer smile. Talking and swallowing were very difficult. So, too, was the act of breathing, for the disease was increasingly claiming critical respiratory muscles and robbing her lungs of their ability to fill with air. Meanwhile, her tired tissues still registered pain all too well. Seeing her made my mind writhe in protest. How could life create such an awful fate for a human being, and why had she been selected to be one of those made to endure it?

Yet, for all the horror of her predicament, Katherine was not lost. Her steady, alert presence gave no hint of anger or self-pity or any other recriminating emotion I might have imagined a person would have under such daunting conditions. One way she could still express herself was with her eyes, and out of them poured an unjustified patience. For three weeks I visited her room nearly every day, going out of my way to spend time with her, touched by her equanimity, drawn by her strange contradictions: the softness that lay buried under stone, the openness behind the hardened encasement that enclosed her.

One Friday afternoon, the senior resident announced that Katherine needed to have a new intravenous line inserted, as her old one had stopped working. The line provided her with essential fluids and pain-relief medications. Accomplishing such a task in most patients was only modestly challenging, but for Katherine, replacing a nonfunctioning line would be no small matter. Locating the usual blood vessels under that tough skin would be nearly impossible. The resident said we were going to have to aim for the jugular vein, the largest vein in the neck and one that lay conveniently close to the surface. We gathered up the necessary supplies—syringes and needles, bags of IV fluid and plastic tubing, gauze pads and antiseptic solution—and marched to her room.

As the senior resident explained the procedure to Katherine, her eyes widened and she glanced at me with a look that made my throat catch.

"I'll be with you," I said and put my hand on her rigid arm, keeping it there while the residents surrounded her bed and placed white drapes across her chest and over her shoulders. As they set up their sterile field and laid out their instruments, she clung to me with her eyes.

What happened next can only be called gruesome. The vein proved exceedingly difficult to locate, and the senior resident's needle pierced Katherine's neck again and again as he searched for it. Having been edged away from Katherine's side by the laboring residents, I stood nearby with eyes glued to the tip of the needle, begging life to cooperate. Eventually Katherine began to moan and attempt to turn her head, prompting one of the junior residents to lean over and subdue her with the pressure of both arms until the probing needle finally hit its mark.

As Katherine's blood began to flow into the plastic tubing, the senior resident slipped the indwelling catheter forward from the needle into her vein and carefully stabilized it against her neck with surgical tape. He then connected the other end of the tubing to a bag of IV fluid, which he hung on the IV pole—only to reveal a new problem. The fluid was flowing into Katherine's vein far too slowly, a sign that the catheter was not situated properly. It would have to be adjusted. As the senior resident tinkered with the catheter in Katherine's neck, another resident suggested putting the IV bag in a higher location in order to get more gravitational pull on the fluid. I was immediately elected for the job and instructed to climb on top of the bedside table and stand there, holding the bag with arms stretched up as far above my head as possible.

Reluctantly, I left Katherine's side and did as requested, standing for the longest time in the strangest pose, like a supplicant atop a pedestal, extending an offering upward to the higher realms in exchange for clemency toward one who was suffering below. It may have made no difference, or it may have been exactly what was needed. In either case, success was finally achieved. The fluid commenced a steady, reassuring drip into Katherine's neck.

As soon as I climbed down from my perch, I leaned close to Katherine's expressionless face and asked if she was all right. She gave a tiny nod and closed her eyes. Whether it was from exhaustion or from a desire to shut everything medical out of her awareness was not clear, but I took her closed eyes as a sign that she wanted to be finished with us.

"I'm sorry that was so hard," I whispered. "I hope you can get some rest. I'll see you on Monday."

I then rejoined the little troupe with which I had come, and together we collected the various paraphernalia we had brought. With the room neat and tidy once again, we withdrew, leaving Katherine to recover in peace and quiet from what we had done to her.

On Monday morning when I returned to the ward, I headed straight for Room 301A to see how Katherine had fared over the weekend. She had been in my thoughts, and I was eager to learn if the new IV had provided her with a little respite.

As I stepped into the room, what met my eyes was anything but what I had expected. Where Katherine had been was a freshly made bed, its white hospital sheets and cotton hospital blanket tucked tight and perfectly smooth. Not a single wrinkle indicated that a body had ever lain there.

I stopped dead in my tracks, and my mind churned around in confusion, looking desperately for a rational explanation. "Surely there's some mistake," I thought. "Am I in the wrong room? Is she off having a test, or has she been transferred somewhere else?"

But the bed was imperturbable. No, it answered with cool indifference. I am empty, not just temporarily vacated. She is gone.

I hurried to find someone who could explain. The first person I encountered was the head nurse, sitting at the staff workstation. As I blurted out my question, she looked up with a sigh from the chart notes she was writing and confirmed what the empty bed had said. Katherine was gone. Her heart had given out Saturday night.

Hearing the nurse's clearly articulated words did not make any difference, however. Katherine's absence was simply more than my mind could grasp. Feeling strangely numb and not knowing what else to do, I went off to begin my morning chores, which were rapidly piling up, telling myself that I should be happy she had finally escaped from her terrible imprisonment, glad she had no further need for our well-intentioned but lamentably harsh attempts to be of help.

Not surprisingly, as true as these thoughts were, they did nothing to revive my spirit. Instead, a bleak sense of hollowness crouched along with me everywhere I went, all that day and the next.

Yet that was not the end of the matter, because a deeper truth lay behind those rational thoughts, waiting for the initial shock to pass before revealing itself, and it took me by surprise when I discovered it on the third day. It was simple. I greatly missed the gentle presence that had peered out from the depths of Katherine's landlocked eyes. The world seemed an emptier, more lonely place without the person in Room 301A whom I had grown to know and care about.

As that recognition sank in, some very human part of me finally opened to the pain of Katherine's passing. Like a dark flower blossoming in my heart, the sorrow of knowing I would never see her again spread it petals open wide. Then, at last, I shed the tears that wanted to come for not having been able to say good-bye to such a beautiful soul and tell her how much she had meant to me.

* * * * * * *

Some patients for whom you develop a fondness as you go through your training may weave in and out of your life over years as you play a role in their ongoing journey. Saul and Rebecca's journey began when their son Sammy was diagnosed at age two with neuroblastoma, an aggressive type of early childhood cancer. By the time the cancer was discovered, it had spread widely in his body. By his third birthday, he had been given as much aggressive treatment as modern medicine could provide—surgery, chemotherapy, and radiation therapy—and as much as his little body could endure.

Sadly, it was not enough. Sammy's neuroblastoma shrugged off the effects of the cancer treatment and grew steadily, until, with an ever-increasing appetite, it began to gobble the young boy up before his parents' horrified eyes. Malignant cells invaded his liver, swelled his belly, caused his eyes to bulge grotesquely, stole all his energy, and filled his bones with pain. To see their son dying hurt badly enough, but to see his beautiful body being ravaged by the killer as it claimed him was completely overwhelming. Saul and Rebecca closeted themselves in their private room on our ward, together with their precious child and their grief, permitting entry only to a necessary few. They wanted no eyes but their own to see what they were seeing. It was far too personal, and sympathy was too great a burden to bear on top of everything else.

Nevertheless, the day that Sammy died, every one of us on the ward knew instantly, for an agonized wailing began in Sammy's room. The dam of Saul and Rebecca's grief had broken. The foreboding waters it had been holding back were rushing free.

The senior resident, Mark, had been one of the few whom Saul and Rebecca had permitted to tend to Sammy in his dying days, and he stood in the hall outside their room, waiting. Suddenly the door to the room was flung open, and Saul came crashing out like a pain-crazed animal blindly seeking escape. He ran straight into Mark, who engulfed the crumbling man with both arms. And there, in the safety of a fellow human being's grip, Saul poured out his pain, pounding Mark's chest with both fists and sobbing uncontrollably.

Following some deep human instinct, Mark did not attempt to quiet Saul, but silently absorbed the impacts of Saul's clenched fists, continuing to hold him until exhaustion came and took him over. Meanwhile, all around them, the ward was utterly still, as if every other activity had halted in mid-stride with the sound of Saul and Rebecca's pain. Very few eyes were dry that day among those of us working on the ward.

But Saul and Rebecca's story was far from finished. The young couple left the hospital looking haggard and defeated; then, several months after Sammy's burial, they returned for a surprise visit. They had taken refuge in their synagogue's strong sense of community, they told us, and with deep faith in the goodness of love, had decided the most important thing they could do was to have another child. They had come back, they said, to share with us the good news that they had been blessed with pregnancy nearly immediately. Their intention for this pregnancy, they explained, was not to replace Sammy, for that would never be possible, nor even to lessen the pain of his passing, but rather to make good use of the great unspent love they had to give. As they spoke, the young couple's eyes shone with such happiness that it spilled over all of us, and we readily joined them in their rejoicing.

Rebecca's pregnancy went well, allowing time for healing and preparation. When her due date drew near, she was scheduled for a cesarean section. Her first delivery had required a cesarean section, and repeat cesareans were standard practice then for women who had already had one. As the resident assigned to attend the delivery, I was delighted at the opportunity to participate in the couple's joy.

On the elected day, Rebecca bid good-bye to Saul, who remained in the waiting room, and was wheeled on a stretcher to the operating suite. Her face was flushed with anticipation, and she smiled as the nurses helped her lie down on the operating table, her belly bulging under the hospital sheet that covered her. The anesthesiologist stepped forward to put a mask over her mouth and nose and guide her gently into sleep with his merciful drugs, while I stood, gloved and gowned, beside the warming table where I was prepared to place her newborn baby for his or her first examination.

The obstetrician, Dr. Mendez, had performed so many cesarean sections that he probably could have done one with his eyes closed. With skill and precision, he had Rebecca's abdomen open within what seemed like minutes and was reaching in with both hands to retrieve her child, when the course of events made a sudden change of direction. As Dr. Mendez withdrew the slippery bundle from its resting place in Rebecca's womb, he uttered an involuntary gasp.

A stunned silence fell over the operating room as all eyes turned toward Rebecca's baby. Every one of us—Dr. Mendez, the anesthesiologist, the OR nurses, and I—knew full well how much these parents were anticipating the birth of a beautiful, healthy baby. But the baby who had just entered the world could not be called either beautiful or healthy. She had multiple red and purple bruises on her body and deformed arms with lobster-claw-like hands.

How easily I had been lulled into thinking I knew what to expect. A mere hour ago I had been anticipating jogging down the hall to the waiting room after Rebecca's delivery to give Saul good news: *Congratulations, you have a beautiful new baby!* I had been imagining that the most exciting part of the news would be whether the child was a boy or a girl. Instead, I found myself placing Saul and Rebecca's newborn baby gingerly in an incubator and wheeling her with aching heart to the Neonatal Intensive Care Unit, leaving the still-anesthetized Rebecca unaware of what was happening.

I returned quickly to speak with Saul in the waiting room, but only to deliver a message of uncertainty: there was a problem, but we were not yet certain of its nature and would speak further with him and Rebecca just as soon as possible. In the meantime, I said, it would be prudent to keep the baby in the Neonatal Intensive Care Unit. There she could be observed and have appropriate tests performed.

But though I touched Saul on the shoulder and asked if he was all right, it was disconcerting to see a blank expression on his face. He would need more news than this, I thought, and for his sake it should be soon.

Meanwhile, in the NICU, the baby's evaluation was under way, and the answers came quickly. On the basis of her physical examination that showed characteristic bruises and deformities, and on the results of blood tests, we established the diagnosis. She had TAR syndrome, or thrombocytopenia-absent-radius syndrome, a rare disorder that manifests during gestation and causes abnormalities in the blood, in the skeletal system (including the missing radius bone in the lower arm), and sometimes also in the heart and kidneys and other parts of the anatomy as well.

The most serious part of the condition that Saul and Rebecca's little girl had, by far, was the problem with her blood—the thrombocytopenia, or paucity of platelets—which was life-threatening. Her body was producing far too few of these tiny but essential blood cells. Having an insufficient number is dangerous because the job they perform is so critical. Basically, they plug up the holes that develop in our tissues from minor or major injuries and also from the everyday wear and tear of living. They mastermind the blood clots that stop our nosebleeds and staunch the flow of blood from wounds. Without them, even minor bleeding would never end.

The blood test quickly performed on Saul and Rebecca's little girl showed that her platelet count was critically low, putting her at risk for spontaneous internal bleeding that could lead to death. She would have to remain in the NICU for close observation and would be given platelet transfusions if the count fell any lower. She would also need to be evaluated by specialists for possible internal abnormalities known to be associated with TAR syndrome. Bad news indeed.

Even though I was still in my residency training, I knew that delivering bad news to patients and their families is one of the most difficult things to do in the practice of medicine.

In many medical schools today, students are helped to prepare for this. They have practice sessions with actor-patients with whom they hone their communication skills, and they are given valuable feedback by both their professors and the actor-patients themselves. In my time, however, no one said a single word about the challenging task of facing other human beings and telling them that something was seriously wrong. Young doctors had to learn that skill by trial and error, at the expense of the patient or the patient's relatives. Often, patients and their families reeled in shock, too frightened, bewildered, or overwhelmed to ask a single question or even remember clearly what was said to them.

Delivering bad news to Saul and Rebecca would be especially difficult. Life had already given them too much bad news—still more seemed unconscionable. The entire NICU staff was distressed by what had happened, and though they dealt with disasters on a daily basis, all the staff members nevertheless shuddered at the brutal blow dealt to this young couple, still raw from their recent loss. How could life possibly be so unfair, so callous and unkind?

Thus, with some trepidation, I walked side by side with the chief resident to the hospital room where Rebecca was recovering from her surgery, Saul by her side. When we entered, two pale faces turned toward us expectantly. As gently and carefully as possible, we explained the situation, acutely aware that we were addressing two people who understood what it was to fight for a child's life and what it was to lose that fight. We told them everything we knew about their baby's condition and the uncertainties that still required investigation, about what the danger to her was and what we were proposing to do to protect her, and they both listened intently.

When we paused to ask if they had any questions, they responded immediately and in unison, asking the one question of uppermost importance to them: "Can we see her?"

Ordinarily, an NICU does not let its patients venture out from under its protection, but in this case the NICU Director made an exception. Saul and Rebecca had to see the child they desired so much, Sammy's sister, who was coming to them in his wake. Since Rebecca could not leave her bed, the baby would need to go to them, and so arrangements were made for two doctors to take her. The chief resident and I volunteered for the task.

Their meeting was simple and beautiful. Saul sat on the edge of the bed, his arm around Rebecca, who cradled their little daughter in her lap. The two gazed adoringly at her, and then at each other, silently brushing away the tears that ran down their cheeks. Then Rebecca gathered up the baby's tiny misshapen hands and crooked arms and stroked them with her fingertips. Finally, she bent closer and held the baby's hands to her lips and kissed them tenderly all over.

At that moment I saw something about Rebecca and Saul's baby that I had completely overlooked before. I saw the sweetness of this little girl, with her perfect puckered lips and button nose and sleepy eyes. We in the NICU had been looking at her through the lens of our professional concern, and her medical problems were all that lens focused on. Her parents, on the other hand, were seeing her as the beloved child they had been awaiting—a blessed gift, adorable and perfect exactly as she was. Seeing her as they did revealed a whole new dimension of her being, one that touched me deeply.

As the ensuing weeks and months went by, Saul and Rebecca held to their perspective unwaveringly, and two years later they made clear to me how well that perspective had served them. It was the last day I ever saw them, and long after their daughter had succeeded in weathering her harrowing entrance into life. For as can happen with the TAR syndrome, their little girl gradually outgrew her life-threatening platelet problem. Her body eventually found a way to manufacture all the platelets she needed, and she made it through the initial danger unscathed. The rest of her evaluation revealed no additional problems, to everyone's great relief, and she had been discharged from the NICU at six weeks of age and followed closely as an outpatient ever since. As for her deformities, she was enrolled in a regular program of physical therapy and would have corrective surgery on her arms and hands when she was older.

Saul and Rebecca came that day to say good-bye. They were moving to a different section of the city and would have to transfer care to another hospital closer to their new home. Their daughter, whom they had named Johanna (which they said meant "God's gracious gift" in Hebrew), was with them. Dressed in a pink smock with her hair pulled back by two matching pink barrettes, and with the perky personality of a two-year-old, she was darling.

I was happy to see the three of them one last time. I congratulated Saul and Rebecca on having come so far, adding that I thought Johanna very lucky to have them as her parents.

Saul shook his head. "We're the lucky ones," he corrected me. "Rebecca and I came this far because of Johanna."

Rebecca nodded. "We were overwhelmed with grief after Sammy died," she said, "but living with that grief was what made us ready to love Johanna as fully as she needed to be loved."

"That's right," Saul added emphatically, slipping his arm around his wife and child. "We saw that Johanna was wounded, just like us. We needed each other in order to heal."

Rebecca smiled. "It may seem ironic," she said, gazing thoughtfully at the child now growing sleepy in her arms, "but I believe suffering can give people a greater capacity to love. And it's the loving we do that heals the suffering we've undergone."

Saul sighed. "These haven't been easy lessons to learn," he added with a grimace, "but we can tell you this, Dr. MacGregor. Learning them has been the most important thing we've ever done."

I nodded, as Saul and Rebecca gave each other a knowing look. Then the two parents whom I had grown so fond of wished me well and headed down the hall with their adorable pink-frocked daughter cradled in Rebecca's arms.

*   *   *   *   *   *   *

If you deal with other people's problems all day long as doctors do, your ability to see the larger picture may falter at times. You may become so preoccupied by the deficiencies confronting you that you almost forget to see the strengths. You may grow so focused on what needs to be fixed that you overlook the parts that do not require any fixing at all but are beautiful just as they are. The day I went to see Denise, by then having been a senior staff physician for many years, I was prepared only to meet the worst, and certainly that is what I saw at first glance.

Denise was born in a part of Harlem where violence and desperation were the everyday fare, as prevalent as the graffiti on the rundown buildings. She knew her mother only briefly, for she died of a drug overdose at age seventeen, when Denise was two. While growing up, Denise bounced from one foster home to another, until as a teenager she took to the streets where her life revolved around abusive boyfriends, petty crime, cocaine and heroin. By the time she turned twenty, she was afflicted with not one but two incurable scourges: schizophrenia and AIDS. By age thirty-five, these two afflictions had taken a heavy toll. Denise was a forgotten person, friendless, penniless and homeless, and suffering from an advanced degenerative neurological disorder that was an aggressive complication of her AIDS. She was steadily losing control of both her body and her mind.

Denise crossed my path when she was transferred from a shelter for homeless women to the hospice inpatient unit in my hospital. After performing her admission examination, the medical director of the hospice service concluded that she was terminally ill and would most likely die very soon. The hospital staff would help her feel comfortable and cared for in the time that remained. I visited her twice in her room before she passed away.

Meeting Denise for the first time was a jolting experience, like suddenly turning off a well-lit, well-kept main street into a dark, foreboding alley. She appeared utterly worn down, ravaged as much by the harsh life on the streets as by the destructive diseases in her body and psyche. She was bedridden, unable to walk or feed herself or even sit up, and she spoke only with difficulty. With her large, baleful brown eyes and apologetic smile, she looked like a neglected child ever hopeful for a morsel of attention. Her pushed-in nose and the scar on her chin, her discolored teeth and the ragged tremor in her hands all gave testimony to a life of disempowerment and loss.

Given her precarious condition, I did not expect that Denise could engage in much conversation. Sitting in a chair at her bedside, I asked her if she could tell me how she thought she was doing.

Closing her eyes, she summoned two words to say what she knew was true: "I'm dying."

I nodded and replied, "Yes, I know. I'm sorry," and we both remained silent for a while, absorbing that stark truth.

After a bit, I asked if she could tell me what it was like to know that she was dying.

She raised her eyes to mine again and murmured, "It makes me sad."

I sighed and nodded my head.

At that she gathered her strength to say more, as if wanting to make sure I understood her meaning correctly.

"I'm not sad just because I'm dying," she said carefully. "I'm sad that I'm dying from all the bad choices I made in my life."

After a pause, she added with painful certainty, "It could have been different."

I could hear the remorse in her voice. "That must be a hard thing to realize," I responded.

She nodded, and a tear rolled down her cheek, making my heart ache for her. It was not easy to see this fellow human being sinking in the quicksand of her failed life. As words seemed to offer little hope of alleviating the kind of pain she was feeling, I took her hand and just sat quietly with her.

One week later I paid Denise another visit. Since I last saw her, her condition had worsened considerably. She was too weak to lift her head and could barely muster enough energy to speak. Yet as our eyes met, her face lit up with a smile. After pulling a chair close and telling her about the beautiful day outside with its warm sunshine and bright blue sky and seeing her eyes brighten, I inquired if I might ask her a question. When she nodded, I proceeded.

"You told me last week about what makes you sad. Is there something about your life that makes you glad?"

Without a moment's hesitation she smiled again and, pausing to catch her breath after each word, whispered, "My . . . daughter . . ."

I knew from having read Denise's medical chart that she had a sixteen-year-old daughter named Serena, who was living with a relative. As I smiled back at Denise, she beamed, and then added, "She's . . . doing . . . much better . . . than I am."

When I responded that this seemed to mean a great deal to Denise, she nodded her head emphatically. Touched by the obvious importance to Denise of this mother-daughter relationship, I ventured another question.

"Do you think your own mother might have something to say to you right now?"

She looked up from her bed with big eyes that were filling with tears and nodded again. In a halting voice almost too soft to hear, she answered, "It's . . . OK, . . . Denise."

Now tears began to moisten my eyes, too, for this did not sound like a person destroyed by the brutality of life. These words could only be spoken by someone whose sadness and regret were being laid to rest, someone who was moving beyond judgment and recrimination and entering the deeper realms of human nature to which dying can provide access, the realms where forgiveness and acceptance reside. Denise was finding her way there.

For a moment, the perfection of the words she had just spoken lingered between us, and then I heard myself saying, as I stroked her head like one would a weary child, "Yes, it is OK, Denise. It's all OK."

After a bit, Denise looked squarely at me again and, with evident effort, spoke once more. "I . . . love . . . you," she said.

I was not expecting these words, and they made me take a closer look at Denise. To my surprise, her eyes were shining. She looked beautiful. This woman who had led a life of struggle and hardship, and now was lying impoverished and dying, was offering a gift to a person she barely knew.

I accepted her gift and offered mine in return. "Thank you, Denise. I love you too."

She smiled the faintest of smiles and whispered, "Love . . . is . . . important."

How amazing. Here in the shadow of death, Denise had arrived at the core lesson of life, and she was inviting me to share it with her. Beyond the roles of doctor and patient, beyond definitions of success and failure, we were meeting, human being to human being, in the most healing of all places, the place of love.

"Yes, love is important," I agreed. "It certainly is." And for a time, we quietly embraced that thought together before I finally slipped away to do my other work.

When I left the hospital at the end of the day, Denise was still on my mind. I was moved by the balance she had found between beauty and brutality as her final hour approached. Their apparent opposition was no longer relevant, leaving nothing in need of fixing. I found myself musing inwardly to her, telling her my thoughts: *Denise, my friend, you may have failed at many worldly things, but clearly not at certain other things that matter greatly, such as love. There you've succeeded against enormous odds. With love, you've found equanimity at the end and showed that the beauty within a human being can continue to shine in the darkest of circumstances. Thank you for that. I bow to your beauty, Denise. May I be wise enough to learn from it.*

TWO

Mystery & Miracles

MANY DOCTORS I KNOW would agree that mysteries and miracles do exist in our world, and that human existence is one of the most fascinating of them all. Doctors have a special opportunity to appreciate this, for the work that we do takes us deep into the drama of people's lives where moments of tension between life and death can illuminate the mysterious and miraculous nature of human existence with a special clarity. Yet such revealing moments do not always attract the attention they deserve amid the hustle and bustle of hospital activity. Life's wondrousness can slip by unnoticed, obscured by more urgent and demanding concerns. Still, when it decides to tap you on the shoulder, you may be bowled over by the force of it.

I remember a moment when I was coursing confidently along, expecting life to proceed in a predictable manner, when it did something wholly unexpected. The words informing me that life had just made an abrupt change of course were ordinary enough, yet my mind could barely fathom them.

"Excuse me, Doctor, but I have to ask you to leave the room!" the nurse was saying. The urgency in her voice seemed to reach my ears from across a great chasm, even though she stood inches from my elbow. In any case, she had little hope of getting my attention; my eyes were riveted on my husband

Charles's face, which only a moment ago had sparkled with life but now sagged, ashen and empty.

The unimaginable had just occurred. My mate and dearest friend had gone into cardiac arrest while I was standing beside his hospital bed talking with him. We had been marveling at how smoothly his carefully planned time as a patient in the cardiology short-stay unit was going and how impressive the achievements of modern medicine were. Just a few hours earlier a cardiologist specializing in interventional procedures had performed a miraculous feat. With skillful fingers and sophisticated monitoring devices to back him up, he had inserted a long, thin piece of plastic tubing into a major artery in Charles's groin and threaded it all the way up to the center of his chest where the tube then pushed a tiny meshed cylinder made of cobalt chromium alloy into a partially blocked coronary artery that ran along the surface of Charles's heart, thereby reestablishing a healthy flow of blood to that vital, ever-beating organ and preventing a future heart attack.

The cardiologist, a cordial and knowledgeable man whose demeanor inspired confidence in his professional skills, had permitted me to don a green scrub suit and attend the highly technical procedure. Having an MD after my name, he had said with a smile, gave me the status of professional colleague rather than merely the patient's spouse. So for two hours I kept a close watch on the real-time image of Charles's heart, projected simultaneously on four overhead screens and multiplied several times larger than life. Watching the catheter worm its way upward from his hip and into the narrow channels of his heart's blood supply was mesmerizing, to say the least.

Now, after his heart had weathered such an unnatural and invasive procedure so well—a procedure that promised it a measure of bionic indestructibility and greater longevity—how could it have abruptly given out? There had to be some mistake. That whole hi-tech undertaking hadn't all been for naught, had it? Charles's heart couldn't be calling it quits right after being given a new lease on life, could it?

I stared dumbfounded at the vital signs monitor mounted on the wall above Charles's bed. Just moments before, the monitor's glowing green line was tracing a steady succession of nicely formed spikes that reflected the electrical activity of his heart. The comfortable rhythm of the beats had not shown the slightest sign of any ill effects. Yet now the line was perfectly, unmistakably flat.

Suddenly the nurse's voice came again, this time with more insistence. "Doctor, we need to make space here. Please leave the room *now!*"

Indeed, there was very little space for the muscular male nurse who had just run into the room to maneuver by me, especially since he was carrying a three-foot-by-three-foot board with both hands. As I edged to one side, he moved forward and slid the board swiftly under Charles' back for firm support, and then assumed cardiopulmonary resuscitation posture and started pumping, stiff-elbowed, on Charles' chest. Nearby, the first nurse prepared to put the rubber mask of an Ambu bag over Charles' face in order to pump oxygen into his lungs. Reluctantly, I turned and headed for the door, just as four more people dressed in hospital garb rushed in, the last one pushing a resuscitation cart bearing all the paraphernalia necessary for advanced lifesaving intervention. As I exited, someone closed the door firmly behind me.

Outside in the hallway, there was not a single soul to be seen. I walked a short distance and stopped to lean against the wall with my eyes closed, hoping that the dizziness I was feeling would pass and allow me to get a handle on things.

After several slow deep breaths, the dizziness did pass, only to be replaced by something else: the realization that a strange kind of quiet engulfed the entire length of the hall. Not only was there no sound of activity issuing from Charles' room or any other room, but there was also an unfamiliar quiet within my own self too. My internal monologue that never ceased its questioning and commenting, pondering and planning, had fallen completely and utterly silent. Even the passing of time seemed to have halted. Around me stretched an endless, empty expanse, deep and still and unfathomable. I floated in a sea of mystery.

Somewhere ahead in that timeless, dimensionless void, I could sense two equally possible but vastly different futures waiting for life to choose between them. If the scales of life tilted in one direction, Charles would return, and the two of us would resume moving along the path we had been traveling. If the scales tipped in the opposite direction, Charles would not return, and life would be inconceivably different from before. I had not the slightest idea about which would come to pass. Yet standing in that empty hallway with no thought of what to do, I felt deeply, inexplicably reassured, as if I were being held in the embrace of a love that had no end. Whatever came next, I would be ready.

I would gladly have stayed longer in the arms of that mystery, had it not been for the hand that suddenly touched my shoulder. Brought abruptly back to the present, I heard the voice of a nurse saying, "Doctor! Doctor! Good news! Your husband is fine!"

And indeed he was, as my quick sprint down the hall and into his embrace assured me. In fact, he was more than fine, for while Charles's heart had teetered between life and death, he had gone on an adventure of his own into mystery. As the nurses bustled about at a respectful distance, straightening the disorder created in his room by the resuscitation activity, he pulled me close and whispered his strange tale.

He had been pulled rapidly through a long, dark tunnel, he said, arriving in a quiet place where a group of people who appeared to be advisers greeted him. They had engaged in conversation with him, and though he no longer recalled their exact words, the tone in which they spoke had put him at ease.

They had then made some kind of adjustment in his heart involving his life's purpose and greater wisdom on which he could draw. Once finished, they sent him swiftly back the way he had come, leaving him feeling deeply restored.

Without a doubt, Charles looked nothing like any person I had ever seen who had just been yanked back from the jaws of an untimely death by the harsh procedures of a resuscitation team. He was positively glowing with life. Suffice it to say, we were enormously glad to see each other, and though we had each suffered a significant jolt that day, we were both left feeling elated by how the arms of mystery had wrapped around us as they did.

*   *   *   *   *   *   *

Becoming a doctor takes a long time and requires great effort, and miracles and mysteries do not rank high on the teaching agenda. After four years of college, you must complete four years of medical school and then three to four years of internship and residency training, with long days and on-call nights and weekend duty as well. I remember wondering if the process would ever end. And though I appreciated advancing in my scientific understanding and learning highly technical skills, the emphasis on the purely mechanical dimension of how the human body functioned, together with the frequent times of dullness and drudgery and profound exhaustion, sometimes made me question whether it was really worth the effort.

Still, life never allowed me to wallow there for long. Exciting moments always came along to more than redeem the uninspiring times. An experience that never failed to leave me in a state of awe was witnessing human birth.

The first time I saw a baby being born was in my third year of medical school during the required month-long clinical rotation in Obstetrics and Gynecology. Having listened to the professors' lectures on the birth process during my second year and having dutifully digested the textbook chapters on birth's anatomy, physiology, and pathology, I marched into my ob-gyn rotation equipped with a solid intellectual foundation. Lists of factors associated with high-risk pregnancy, algorithms for managing fetal distress, and indications for forceps delivery or cesarean section filled my head, together with many gaping holes from lack of firsthand experience. I shivered with excitement then, when assigned to the delivery room for my first night on call, with a chance to see the real thing.

Hospital policy required all personnel in the delivery room to dress as if for surgery, exchanging everyday clothing for a green scrub suit complemented with paper booties pulled up over shoes, a shower-cap-like head cover pulled down over hair, and a surgical mask positioned over nose and mouth. It was an ungainly outfit. The booties made an annoyingly loud rustling noise with every step, the cap gave the impression that a large, puffy mushroom was overtaking the wearer's head, and the surgical mask erased the last of the wearer's individuality. All that remained as a clue to any person's identity were the two eyes peering out over the mask and the muffled sound of a voice. Yet for all its comical strangeness, there was a compelling mystique about wearing such hospital garb, and a powerful thrill swept through me the first time I donned the whole costume and strode into the delivery room along with the residents on call that night.

The woman in labor was an exception to the rule of attire, of course. She wore nothing but a short, white hospital gown, open-backed and printed all over with the name of the medical center in tiny block letters. As was customary at the time, she had been injected with a potent sedative plus a narcotic painkiller, which had quite literally knocked her out. Apparently, the staff regarded the birth process as being far too much for the average woman to endure. Everything would be easier if the woman would lie quietly asleep while the doctors took charge of the hazardous task of getting the newborn down and out of the birth canal. Once the danger passed and the mess was cleaned up, the baby could be presented to the mother, neatly bundled in a spanking-white hospital sheet in the perfect way that only an experienced delivery room nurse can do, with just its cherubic face visible.

As our team assembled in the delivery room, I positioned myself in a strategic spot, close enough to see but cautiously out of the way of those who would soon be very busy. From there I noticed a disconcerting sight: the wrists and ankles of the mother-to-be were fastened tightly to the delivery table by leather straps. I wondered at the reason for such harsh-appearing restraint, yet there was no time to explore the issue, beyond eliciting a clipped, over-the-shoulder comment from the nearest resident: "That's how it's done." For beneath the green obstetrical drapes that covered the woman's now straining body, something momentous was clearly preparing to happen.

Curt orders flew back and forth, and the medical staff's focus sharpened. Close by, a variety of machines beeped authoritatively, informing the staff of the progress of both mother and child. Apparently, giving birth, even with a normal pregnancy like this one had been, was a serious affair laden with potential pitfalls that skilled professionals had to strenuously guard against.

As the uterine contractions intensified under the direction of powerful maternal hormones, all heads bent forward in anticipation. Within minutes the ob-gyn resident announced that the baby was crowning. The moment I had read about and been lectured about had arrived. The top of the child's head appeared in the opening of the birth canal. The miracle of birth was imminent. I edged my way closer for a better view, careful not to interfere with the work of my superiors.

What I saw staggered me. From within the depths of this woman's body, a brand-new human being was about to enter the world. What science fiction writer could have created a stranger scenario? Nine months earlier a spark of life ignited in this woman's womb, and for the duration of those months that spark grew steadily. It gathered vast numbers of minerals, carbohydrates, amino acids, and other essential substances from the woman's bloodstream, slowly but surely assembling them into tissues and organs and other specialized structures, fitting these together to form an intricate whole. The construction process continued without pause until the endpoint of intrauterine development was finally achieved and the full-grown fetus was prepared to separate from the life-support system of the mother's body. The remarkable collaborative arrangement invented by nature—the intricately bonded uterus and placenta that up until this final moment had been delivering all the nourishment and oxygen necessary for the baby's body to thrive, while simultaneously carrying away all the waste products the baby's body produced—was no longer needed. The infant was ready to live in the world on its own.

From within the dark cavern where its creation from a mere spark had taken place, a new human being was emerging, ready to fill his or her lungs with a breath of the earth's atmosphere for the very first time. An independent life was about to begin.

Tears of awe welled up in my eyes, overflowing in joyous rivulets. The door to the source of life was swinging open right there before us, and we green-clad ones, privileged to serve that source, were about to welcome the new arrival. Mystery stood thick around us, or so it seemed to me.

With an abrupt *pop!* the baby's head came out, swiftly followed by arms, and then legs. At the same moment, someone shoved a red rubber bulb syringe into my hands with the orders, "Suction the kid's airway!"

I did as directed, clumsily clearing birth fluids from the little nostrils and throat as quickly as I could. A second later, someone swung the baby upside down by the ankles and gave the slippery little backside a sharp smack, producing a gasp from the tiny open mouth and then a full-throated "Whaaaaaaa!" Meanwhile, someone else clamped the umbilical cord tight and neatly severed it with a scalpel, undoing in a flash the bond that had kept mother and child together as one for nine miraculous months.

As the well-practiced delivery room procedures unfolded seamlessly over the next several minutes, I stepped aside and surreptitiously adjusted my mask, noticing by now that no one was shedding tears but me. Apparently, I was the only one to have been awestruck, the only one wanting to bow my head in reverence.

Fortunately, the surgical mask fit imperfectly, leaving a slight gap at the top, just beneath my eyelids, which allowed the tears to flow down my cheeks behind its convenient barrier, unseen by my much more businesslike superiors. From that day on, I decided, I would have to conduct myself more cautiously. The delivery room was clearly not the place for unabashed appreciation of the marvels of human existence.

In fact, many such occasions in one's training as a doctor caution you to camouflage your sense of awe. For better or worse, you learn to be on guard against excessive exuberance lest it impede your performance and portray you as not fully professional. Your feelings of delight and fascination might still abound in the presence of birth and other astonishing happenings, for it is hard to deny such feelings, but you keep them carefully out of sight behind a reliable mask, be it literal or figurative.

*   *   *   *   *   *   *

Death is a mystery of equal magnitude to that of birth, though it is typically feared rather than welcomed. As many in our modern culture believe, and certainly as most in my profession were taught, I regarded death only as a foe to be fought against until life showed me otherwise.

Just months after I first witnessed human birth, as the third year of medical school was nearing its end, death came to introduce itself to me in a more intimate way than three years of higher education had yet done. Suddenly, in the middle of my hematology elective, a dear friend was diagnosed with leukemia. Having just studied this life-threatening disease, I knew that the road ahead would be hard and the future uncertain. And because my friend Erling was important to me, I decided that becoming a doctor would have to wait.

I went to my dean, a decent and honorable man, and explained the situation, requesting that he permit me to take an indefinite leave from medical school. His response was not surprising. He frowned and shook his head unhappily, saying he was afraid I would jeopardize my career. He urged me not to be impulsive.

But instead of dissuading me, his very words reinforced my decision. The idea that responding to the crisis of a friend would conflict with my career plans did not make sense. To me, the opposite was true. The desire to care for someone dear in a time of need came from the core of my being, the place where my passion about becoming a doctor had its roots. You have to be true to impulses like that, I felt. It is a matter of being true to yourself. When I persisted, the dean reluctantly let me go.

And so began what turned out to be thirteen months of a nonstop duel with a fierce opponent, one with the power to destroy life. But if anyone could stay in step with such an opponent, it was Erling. For years he had been more than a friend to the circle of friends to which my husband Charles and I belonged. He had been our mentor and teacher. A Swede by birth, historian by training, and philosopher and lover of art by nature, he was the wisest person any of us had ever met. Not surprisingly, many of us withdrew from other obligations to spend time with him and help him navigate the aggressive treatment protocols of chemotherapy.

Together our little band of friends rode the fearsome roller coaster of Erling's remissions and relapses, enduring wrenching swings between hope and disappointment and then hope once more as the oncologists wrestled with the disease, continually refining their strategy, trying one thing after another to buy more time. Day after day we watched Erling bear the complications of his illness with unshakable calm and poise even as it claimed his body bit by bit, sapping his strength, wasting his muscles and cutting away at his activities. And still, throughout it all, he encouraged us and guided us, inviting us to accompany him on this journey.

"Come with me to meet death," he said. "It will teach you what it is to be human and show you how to live your lives more fully."

What happened that year seemed to take place outside of time, as if we had stumbled into another dimension and lifetimes were going by. We spent endless hours sitting at Erling's bedside, talking into the wee hours of the night. Even the oncologists were drawn into the adventure, paying Erling lengthy visits, inspired by his indomitable spirit, while bending the usual hospital rules and allowing his chemotherapy and transfusions to be given at home where he wished to remain.

Whenever we despaired, Erling smiled. He explained that death was not what we thought it was. It is not the end. He told us that our existence continues after the body dies, for the body is just a temporary form, like a suit of clothing we don when coming into physical existence and discard when we leave. He said that the purpose of living a human life is to learn, and he assured us that our learning would continue for ages, as humanity and the earth and the universe as a whole proceed to unfold. He urged us to see life as our teacher.

"Life is the greatest teacher of all," he said, and his words gave us courage.

Indeed, life was teaching us overtime. We learned about fatigue and the importance of patience, about pain and the comfort of touch, about bedside commodes and humility, about wheelchairs and mechanized beds and the loss of independence. We learned about the power of hope to keep a person going in spite of exhaustion, about the determination and inventiveness that difficult situations can inspire, about the strength that friends give to each other, and about the sustaining power of love. Above all, we learned that illness can be a hard but deeply meaningful journey filled with treasures only discovered by being willing to go wherever that journey leads.

Eventually, though, we could see that the end was approaching. Erling had become bedridden. His muscles were wasted, his body weak and weary to the bone. His face had grown gray and gaunt, and the familiar sparkle in his eyes was beginning to dim. For thirteen months he had shown us the power of the human spirit to endure pain and suffering and to shine forth in triumph even as the body declined, but it was clear that he could not go on any longer, nor was it right to ask him to. He told us he had stayed as long as he could, holding off his dying with the help of his many caregivers. But he could forestall it no longer; he was being called away. We had reached the hardest point of all. We had to be willing to let him go.

On Erling's last day of life we came together around his bed, in his home where he wished to be, to gather up our grief and say good-bye, each in our own way. We watched as the energy of his life gradually loosed its hold on his body. His eyes became dull, his skin cooled and lost its color, and the momentum of his breathing slowed, like a mechanism whose battery was running down, until the sound of one last breath came from his lips—barely a whisper—and no more.

The silence that enveloped us then was like nothing any of us had ever known. It was not an empty silence. It was full and deep and endless. With serene power it held us motionless, removing all thought and stilling our souls. It was as if in his dying Erling took us with him to the very threshold of death and there pulled aside the veil between the worlds, enabling us to look out into the domain of eternity that lies only a single breath away from this world.

If you have ever stood on the edge of the Grand Canyon and found yourself looking at a landscape whose breadth and depth your eyes cannot measure nor your mind comprehend, you may be able to imagine what I mean. If you have stared down to the bottom of that chasm, carved into the earth over millions of years, and if you have watched the Colorado River winding slowly between its walls until finally passing beyond the reach of sight, you may know what it is for your mind to stop and allow you to meet reality with a deeper part of yourself. You may even have sensed that though our physical life will end, some undying essence of us will continue, much like that ageless river, flowing on and on through landscapes that stretch beyond conception.

That day of Erling's dying wrought a permanent change in me, a change in the substance of my being, as if there had been an energetic shift in the bonds that held my molecules together. As if a thick layer of grime and confusion had been washed away. I felt surrounded by an ineffable presence underlying all of creation, filling it with purpose and meaning. We all felt this. And in the face of such vastness where peace prevailed, not one doubt remained for us, nor any shred of fear, only awe and gratitude.

Though I sorely missed my friend and teacher, still, when I returned to medical school thirteen months after leaving, things were surprisingly clear and simple. I had not jeopardized my career. Rather, I was coming back having received a very special gift. Life had pulled me aside and given me one extra year of training, something that would make all the difference in my work as a doctor, and in the way I would live.

That year taught me that medical care is not just about diagnosing and treating disease, but includes paying attention to the people who have the disease, human being to human being, and accompanying them in their search for healing. I learned that death, like birth, can help us see beyond our preoccupation with everyday living to the truly miraculous nature of our own existence. I had felt the power of human caring, and I was charged by this knowing to bring it into all I would do.

So I was set at the feet of two noble teachers, birth and death, right there at the beginning. They would guide me throughout my years as a pediatrician and adolescent medicine specialist, and later as a researcher with hospice patients, standing like two Arcs de Triomphe at either end of the human journey.

*   *   *   *   *   *   *

When I was very young, I often felt that enticing secrets were lying just beyond my reach, whispering to me, making my skin tickle with excitement. Perhaps we are more open to the subtle dimensions of life when we are young than when we grow older and more opinionated. These dimensions can speak to us easily then, without our questioning whether they are real or not. Perhaps you, too, remember the way that wonder felt when you were young and sensitive to life's limitless possibilities—when you knew that special, juicy moments were happening unnoticed right under the busy adults' noses every day. I was always on the lookout for such moments, could sometimes sense them hovering near, thick with allurement—like in the barn, that enormous old haven that stood on my grandparents' farm in the backwoods of Maine where I spent countless summer holidays with my family as a child. There I knew the feeling well.

That old barn is deeply imprinted in my memory. It lives in my sinews and bones. I still remember the feeling of pushing with my eager child's energy against the massive wooden door, using all my youthful strength to make it open. Still recall the thrill of stepping into the cool, dark, cavernous space waiting beyond the door . . . pausing as my eyes took on the softer seeing needed there . . . breathing in the sweet air of another world.

The barn seemed a secret place with its own reality, set apart from all the goings-on of the world lying just outside. It called to me, inviting me to share its mysterious intimacy and find within myself a gentler way of being. Long before I knew what reverence was, I could feel it washing over me as I entered.

Inside, angling shafts of sunlight shone down from shadowed rafters high above, lighting up the dust motes floating lazily in the open spaces and filling the air with the fragrance of hay and strong, old wood. Curious noises murmured in the dim recesses: soft sounds of scurrying feet and fluttering wings, the occasional creaking of a board or cooing of a dove, all mixed together with the stillness of cobwebs. Like a huge, hushed cathedral, it whispered of secrets lying beyond human understanding, causing me to fall silent, as if at the entranceway to heaven.

But I was not always alone there, and those were glorious times, too, when my three siblings and I would charge into the barn with a rowdy burst of energy. We were two sisters and two brothers with a spread of six years between us, and together we could accomplish anything. We heard the challenge the barn was making to us, the challenge to test our courage against its quiet, waiting strength. Bolstered by our mutual bravado, we would accept the challenge and, with a great deal of shouting and daring, would climb the creaky wooden ladder to the heights of the hayloft. From there we looked down a very long way to the deep piles of hay below.

Next would come a great mustering of courage, a wild run to the edge and, with a scream of terrified delight, the taking of a mighty leap . . . and then, the point of it all, a delicious falling through space, ending up nearly submerged in cushiony heaps of musty-sweet hay. After a satisfying moment of lying still and savoring the reverberating thrill, and then a brief pause to pick out pieces of straw poking uncomfortably into hair or clothes, we would scramble rapidly back up the ladder to the loft, where we would face the challenge of overcoming fear once again.

Those were good days, when joy and awe lived side by side. The barn, dependable and enduring, nourished my soul. It was like a piece of eternity, and I assumed it would be there forever. But everything changes sooner or later, and one hot summer day, some years after my siblings and I had left our childhood behind and started off into the world, our beloved barn caught fire and burned to the ground. In the twinkling of an eye it was gone, and to my forlorn heart, the world became an emptier place.

And yet even with many long years gone by, the barn still lives in me—just as Erling does and many others whom I have seen pass away too. It remains a presence within me that will never die, and it retains its fragrance still, the fragrance of timeless mystery.

* * * * * * *

The forces that shape the paths we choose to follow can sometimes be traced back to the very beginning. For me, my sights were set on becoming a doctor from early on, as early as a child first conceives the idea of having to become anything at all, and life began preparing me to go in this direction right from the start.

Some might say it was because of my doctor-father that the path of medicine drew me; they might believe that he inspired me, his own achievement naturally becoming the goal that his firstborn child would strive to achieve as well. Another view might be that my soul selected him to be my father so that his destiny might help me find my own. However it is these matters work, the outcome was sure.

My picture of a doctor was painted large before me by my father. He was the embodiment of strength and certainty, dedication and success. Coming from sturdy New England stock, he had made his way from farm-boy to Harvard-trained surgeon with fierce, one-pointed determination. In the middle of his residency training, as World War II engulfed the world, he rushed headlong into battle, armed with stubborn idealism and barely tested surgeon's skills, spending two years aboard a destroyer in the war's fiercest fronts. As chief medical officer of his ship, he tended to the frightful wounds of fellow human beings, saving lives when he could and asking forgiveness when he could not, and was awarded medals for the kind of heroism that war calls forth.

The urgency of a war that demanded all he could give, together with the razor-sharp discipline of military life, left an indelible mark on my father. Having thrived on such intensity and finding his sense of purpose in acts of heroism, he could not settle for a lesser way of life on his return. He became chief of surgery and director of Emergency Medicine at a busy regional medical center. There, for over three decades, he daily tended casualties of another kind, continually rescuing people from the brink of devastating illness or injury and earning the lifelong gratitude of many.

A gruff, no-nonsense man with high principles and low tolerance for anything that looked like laziness, he maintained a rigid sense of what was right and what was wrong. He was probably not unlike many men who lived their youth in the shadow of the Great Depression and then went off to war. Miracles were the farthest thing from my father's mind. Instead, what was important was the power of the scalpel to find a problem and decisively cut it out.

Many a time during my childhood, the phone would ring in the middle of the night, leading to a terse conversation and then the sound of my father rushing out into the darkness on a mission of help. Many a time, too, our family's dinner would linger in the warm oven, our stomachs growling with anticipation while we waited for my father to finish his long day at the hospital before we could sit down together and eat.

Life for us revolved around the important work of saving people's lives.

That important work fueled a steady fire in my imagination. When walking home from school, I often went out of my way to pass by my father's office, which occupied the first floor of an ivy-covered, red brick building on Main Street in our cozy New England town. I went there not so much to see him as to brush up against the intriguing power at work there, embodied in the sharp smell of antiseptics, the strange instruments, the focused conversations, the restrained sense of concern—and also to bask in the deference of the office nurses, the way they had of making me feel important just for being my father's daughter.

On one occasion, after I had reached adolescence, my father let me accompany him to the hospital and tag importantly along behind him as he made his rounds, and then follow him to the hospital's busy surgical suite. There he dressed me in a green operating gown and led me into one of the operating rooms where, with held breath, I circled round the operating table with its huge overhead lights, viewing it from every angle; then I stared in fascination at the gleaming surgical instruments my father used, laid out in ominous precision on a stainless steel tray, ready to be summoned into service. From that day on, I wanted to have a place in that world.

Meanwhile, if my father was an oak tree, sturdy, strong and striving, my mother was a willow. Graceful, patient and yielding, she was the glue that held our family together. I should have seen the strength in her that was faithfully tending the nest in which we four children grew, should have noticed how her sure strength quietly replenished my father's spirit, day after day after day. But with my sights set on my father's world, I was distracted from seeing who my mother really was and not ready to learn from the hard-earned wisdom that was hers.

In the glaring light of my father's heroism, my mother remained in the background, as did many women of her time.

The facts that she oversaw a large team of volunteers at the hospital where my father worked, that she ran a very successful gift shop there, and that neighbors regularly came by our house to ask for her advice failed to capture my attention. I was too preoccupied with the idea that, like my father, I would one day stand in a place of power, unraveling great mysteries and doing good, important things.

Many years would have to pass before I could finally see beyond my father's impressive countenance and recognize that my mother's kind of strength was essential too. She knew the power of patience, and she knew how to temper the heroic drive to intervene with an attentiveness that nurtured and comforted. It may have taken time, but eventually I understood the truth. I had as much to thank my mother for as I did my father.

* * * * * * *

One of the things students look forward to the most on entering medical school is the course on human anatomy. It is a highlight of the initial year, the first deep dive you are invited to take into the mystery of the human body, the moment when you actually see its marvels with your own eyes and touch them with your own fingers. You might say it is a rite of passage into the world of medicine, and though you might not be fully aware that it is happening, the experience shapes your understanding of who you are becoming in subtle and potent ways, simultaneously widening your perspective and limiting it.

It was not surprising, then, that nervous excitement rippled through the entire throng of first-year students as we gathered outside the double doors that would soon admit us to the dissection hall for our very first class. Feet shuffled impatiently as our eager, heady self-importance butted up against the uncertainty of what lay waiting behind those doors. Within minutes we would be initiated into an elite society whose closely guarded secrets would become ours.

Precisely on the hour the big doors swung open and the anatomy professor and his lab assistants appeared, waving their arms and beckoning us in. With shouts of "Quickly now, quickly," and "This way, this way," they moved us along and dispersed us among the long, carefully ordered rows of stainless steel tables, each one laid out with a human form shrouded by a black plastic covering. Once having taken our places, four of us to a table, we paused, waiting breathless over our particular shrouded form, poised at the brink of revelation. What mysteries were we going to discover that day and over the coming weeks and months?

At the professor's signal, we all swept back the plastic shrouds and beheld the cadavers that now belonged to us. Anticipation gave way to awe as we gazed upon the once-living bodies that were to be our teachers, from which we would learn the wonders of the human body. Then, as quickly as that moment of awe had come, it disappeared, cut short by the professor's voice booming across the room, briskly instructing us to put on our full-length rubber aprons and surgical gloves and identify our dissection instruments, while the lab assistants circulated among the tables, handing out printed instructions on how to proceed with the dissection assignment for the day.

But how do you pick up a knife and start cutting without somehow acknowledging the person to whom this body once belonged? How do you relate to the absence revealed in her inscrutably blank face or to the anonymity emphasized by the tag hanging from her toe and the donated-to-science number tattooed on her forearm? How do you not apologize to her nakedness lying so rudely exposed?

But never mind, there was no time for thoughts such as these. All around the room, awkward laughter was breaking the silence, and as the morning wore on, voices that had at first been hushed found refuge in a steady stream of meaningless banter crudely punctuated by inane comments that periodically let off steam like the hiss of a pressure cooker.

"Hey, look how much blubber my guy has! How am I supposed to find anything in here?"

"Wow, what's this—a worm?"

"No, dummy, it's a nerve!"

"Watch it, man! You'd better quit flicking those fat globules off your glove at me, or I'll do something worse to you!"

At a loss for words, I pushed my disappointment aside and got down to the business at hand.

During the ensuing weeks, my scalpel pried apart tissues, traced the pathways of arteries, veins and nerves, and unearthed the bones and organs buried inside the cadaver my three classmates and I shared. Shivers of fascination ran down my spine whenever our digging exposed a new facet of our cadaver's anatomy. What a unique experience we were having, I thought. Very few people would ever see what we were privileged to be seeing. Probably few would even want to.

Overall, I found the class fascinating. It certainly fulfilled its goal of teaching us all about human anatomy. By the end of the semester, we discovered how the many parts of a human body fit precisely together by ever so carefully taking them apart. We learned to wield our scalpels well and dismantled our cadavers completely. Yet what was oddly never spoken about amid all the instruction we received was the fact that these bodies were not mere objects created solely for our edification but had once been actual human beings who had moved and thought and lived a life of their own.

Whether due to conscious intention or to a certain kind of blindness, the omission was obvious. And thus, throughout the process, as instructive as it was, a stubborn discontent simmered within me. It sent unanswered questions drifting through my mind. What had this person's life been like? How did it come to an end? What hopes and dreams did she have? What intention or odd twist of fate sent her body to lie here in front of me, finishing its journey on this table, the object of a human anatomy class?

"No," I forced myself to say, "that's not the purpose here." Each time the questions came, I pushed them away and dove into the piercing odor of formaldehyde, those harsh, uncaring fumes that stung our eyes and nostrils, saturated our hair and clothes, and followed each one of us home at night until the semester was over.

I find it comforting to know that times have changed and that anatomy class is different these days, at least to some degree. Now, at the outset of the course in many medical schools around the country, classes of medical students pause and express gratitude to the people whose bodies they will use for learning. They design rituals to mark completion of the course as well, honoring the gift generously given by those who bequeath their bodies to science.

I take heart, too, from the fact that students themselves often initiate these actions. Apparently, more of today's young people perceive the threat that lies in failing to make such acknowledgment than did in my time. They seem to recognize they are in danger of hardening their hearts right at the beginning of their formation as doctors if they let this omission go by unchallenged, and so they are taking steps to prevent that from happening. To me, this is an encouraging sign about the people who will be our doctors in the future. It shows they recognize that more is involved in becoming a doctor than what a scalpel can address.

* * * * * * *

The opportunities offered by the world of medicine to be amazed are many. Your work can show you these dramatically or sometimes with just a simple nudge—like the day I paid a visit to Mr. and Mrs. Ramirez and their newborn baby.

I was making a rapid sweep through the obstetrical ward one morning, visiting all the mothers who had given birth the night before. My mission was to inform each of them about the results of their newborn's first physical examination—in most cases to reassure them their youngster was perfectly fine—and to discuss newborn feeding procedures, upcoming immunizations, and other practical issues considered necessary for new parents to know. I marched along from room to room, confident in my white-coated professional identity, comfortable in my compassionate bedside manner, reassured by the voluminous body of knowledge in my head, until I finally arrived at the last room on my list for the day, the room of the Ramirez couple, who had just produced their first child.

Mrs. Ramirez, the young mother, was lying in bed, resting from her great exertion. Her head was turned on the pillow toward her husband, who sat in a chair nearby, gazing down at the newborn baby in his lap. Her eyes were fixed on the two of them, a smile on her radiant face, peaceful hands resting on her now-empty abdomen.

I caught Mrs. Ramirez's attention, introduced myself, and ran through my encouraging spiel with well-intentioned concentration, reassuring her that her child appeared healthy in all respects and carefully explaining the essentials of caring for a newborn baby, while she appeared to listen appreciatively.

When I was finished, I paused and, with a magnanimous smile, inquired, "Do you have any questions?"

Mrs. Ramirez beamed and shook her head. Then Mr. Ramirez, who had never once taken his eyes off his newborn son, spoke.

"Isn't it a miracle?" he asked quietly.

In an instant, the all-consuming importance of my helpful advice faded, and I noticed for the first time the rapt expression on Mr. Ramirez's face. Presented with such a question, asked from such a place of quietude, I felt the momentum that had been propelling me unconsciously along dissolve, leaving a calm in its wake that shifted my perspective. What need did this man have for a carefully delivered speech when he was sitting with a miracle on his lap? How could his ears possibly hear what I had to say when he and his wife had just shared one of the most wonderful experiences of human existence? They had opened a door through which a child had come into their life, and all three were basking in the glow of the accomplishment, while I had nearly failed to notice. My good advice could wait.

I tiptoed closer and peered over his shoulder.

"Yes, it surely is," was all that remained for me to say, as I gazed along with him at the child who was indeed a perfect miracle.

* * * * * * *

For Florine the miraculous nature of life was crystal clear. Terminal illness does that for some people. It can strip away the veils that keep us from seeing clearly. From the perspective of the medical profession, Florine was a sad victim of a cruel disease, but she did not view herself that way. She was too busy appreciating the time she had left to feel sorry for herself. In the last conversation I had with her, she spoke forcefully about what she saw.

Florine was enrolled as a patient in the hospice home care program of my medical center while I was working with dying patients late in my career. She had grown up in the Deep South and had migrated north looking for work. At fifty-two, she was a proud, gray-haired woman with a devoted husband, six children ranging from ages fifteen to thirty, and advanced ovarian cancer that had spread widely in her body, leaving her with only a little more time to live.

She had been diagnosed with cancer two years earlier. The original growth on her ovaries had already spread its malignant seeds throughout her abdominal cavity, and exploratory surgery found colonies of cancer invading her intestines, liver, and abdominal walls. Initially, chemotherapy bought her time, but three months ago her doctors announced that the cancer was gaining ground despite all their efforts. Exhausted as much from the effects of chemotherapy as from her disease, she decided to forgo further aggressive treatment and instead enrolled in hospice. As a member of a close-knit extended family and a strong community, she had ample loving care, and she chose to remain at home with those she loved while preparing to die.

I was paying Florine frequent visits under the auspices of a research project I directed entitled "Dying and the Inner Life," and I wanted to hear her views on the experience of facing death. I believed that doctors needed a better understanding of the experience of those who are aware they will die soon so that we might know how best to care for people with terminal disease and help them prepare for their inevitable end.

When I arrived that day for my visit with Florine, I found her lying in bed, no longer strong enough to sit up, her face etched with fatigue. Her kidneys were failing, her body was swollen with retained fluid, and pain was her constant companion despite potent medications. Even the oxygen flowing to her lungs through the plastic nasal prongs she wore gave no respite from the effort it took to breathe. Yet Florine managed to give a weary smile as I pulled over a chair and sat down beside her, ready to hear whatever was important for her to say.

We did not talk long, as she was tired and short of breath. She chose her words carefully, glad, she said, to tell someone about the greatest treasure in her life: her love for her family and their love for her. That love had been unflagging over the years despite the harsh trials they had all endured. Trials no worse than other folks had known, she added, and certainly nothing she cared to complain about. Such times had only brought them greater gratitude in the long run.

The most important thing of all, she declared, waving a thin finger in the air as she spoke, was love. No doubt about it, love made everything possible.

When I asked if there were times when the thought of dying made her feel afraid, Florine gazed at me with a quizzical expression, as if uncertain why I would ask such a thing. Then she explained, with the patience one would use with a child, that she had not an iota of fear, for she believed in the goodness of God, in whose care she felt herself to be. On the contrary, she saw herself as blessed, and her serenity confirmed her words. She paused often to gaze into the distance with a light in her eyes as if savoring some indiscernible source of comfort.

As we talked, my eyes were drawn again and again to the terribly debilitated state of her body. Her belly and legs were so swollen and disfigured that she could hardly move. Each breath she took clearly required enormous effort, and she would wince and shut her eyes tight as spasms of pain slipped past the protection of her pain medication. Her appearance seemed to challenge her every word. How she could endure such physical suffering and still manage to smile seemed beyond comprehension.

I could not help but remark that she must have a great deal of inner strength to be able to go on, one day after another, in her condition.

On hearing my words, Florine gave an indignant shake of her head. The expression on her face said she was thousands of miles beyond the need for sympathy, a universe beyond the reach of pity. Focusing a fierce gaze on me, she reached out and took hold of my hand with an unexpectedly firm grip and pulled me close.

"Listen, honey," she whispered in a raspy voice, "don't you waste your time feeling sorry for me! I don't need it. As far as I'm concerned, life is a miracle, and getting ready to die is just helping me appreciate it more!"

Despite her weakness, there was fire in her voice. She studied me closely, and then continued.

"Don't you see, darling? Being alive is a gift—an *amazing* gift—and I don't plan to miss one second of it, no matter what the cost!"

She paused to catch her breath, and then exclaimed, "Why, sure, when my time is up, I'll go, and that's all right. But you can be certain of one thing. Until then, I intend to be here with my eyes wide open for every blessed minute of it!"

She released my hand, but such intensity blazed from her eyes that I remained pinned to the spot.

Eventually, a kindly smile shaped itself on her face, and she settled back with the air of someone who had said all that needed to be said. I thanked her for sharing her perspective with me and, after a bit more conversation, reluctantly said good-bye, knowing full well it might be the last time I saw her.

It was. One week later, Florine died peacefully in her bed, surrounded by all of her family. And though the news came as no surprise, it made me wonder long and hard about what she had said in our last conversation. How had she been able to experience life the way she did, as a gift so precious that no price was too high to pay for it? How might other people learn to fully appreciate the miracle that their own lives are, as she had? What would it take to truly know what she knew *before* standing at death's doorstep?

THREE

*T*enderness
& *T*echnology

W<small>HEN YOUR DESIRE</small> to help ailing fellow human beings partners with medical science and its mechanistic modus operandi, you discover what may be the defining paradox in the practice of medicine. You see that much of what makes the profession so interesting—so dynamic and endlessly new, not to mention stressful and sometimes downright maddening—is the tension created by the uneasy alliance between tenderness and technology.

From my perspective as a young resident, these dual dimensions of the medical world behaved like two oddly paired dance partners—one subtle and sensuous, the other practical and proud—who swept endlessly around the dance floor, alternately wooing and denying each other in a rapt and unsettled relationship. Sometimes they seemed very much at odds, as if the presence of one discredited the other; other times their movements flowed seamlessly together, suggesting that, alone, each one was incomplete. This unlikely couple troubled me, but tantalized me as well. For when technology and tenderness succeeded in dancing in step and offering the gift that was theirs to give, they graced all those around them with a unique perfection.

Patients get quickly swept up into this dance when they enter the hospital. Whether young or old, whether there by choice or urgent necessity, they are all affected by the push and pull of these two dancers. Among the many caught up in this uncertain swirl, one group of patients struck me as being more affected than any other: the youngest of the young, the premature babies, or "preemies." With these most vulnerable of patients, the dynamism of the dance can become unbearably tense.

That tension is palpable in the presence of preemies, for they are clearly fragile things, not finished with the work of preparing to survive in the world outside their mother's womb. Exposed in all their innocence and helplessness, their very existence cries out for care. Whenever I looked upon one of them, I felt touched by something so sweet and tender and simultaneously unsettling that I could not tell whether gladness or sorrow was filling me. Whichever it was, I ached with it.

Holding one of these preemies during the course of attending to its medical care disconcerted me even more. While the infant lay in the palm of my hand, I would gaze, mesmerized, at wavering hands with ever-so-small fingers reaching out, slender legs bravely kicking, and a dainty mouth pursing and puckering beneath a tiny brow that wrinkled. The faint mewing sounds issuing from its throat and the skin so transparent I could nearly see through it baffled my mind. I could barely comprehend that this little creature was a human being just like me. As I watched its diminutive hand grip the tip of my thumb (which suddenly looked like a clunky thing nearly the size of the baby's entire arm), I felt transformed from my normal, petite self into a giant, robust and overlarge, with movements not finely honed enough for handling such delicate perfection.

Faced with the extreme vulnerability of a miniature being like this, my doctor's instinct clamored for the protection that only medical technology could provide. At the same time I wondered how such delicacy could possibly endure being tampered with.

When they are born, babies like this are taken immediately to the Neonatal Intensive Care Unit, where technology designed to be of help abounds. The NICU contrasts sharply with the newborn nursery, which is a place of tranquility where full-term babies deemed to be healthy receive their care and doze peacefully while friends and family gather to beam in proud appreciation. The NICU is like the newborn nursery's dark sister, the one who provides shelter to infants who have come too early to be safe as well as many whose journey into life has gone awry: those who encounter serious difficulties during the process of birth, and those who bring problems with them brooding in their bodies. Under this watchful eye, many of these babies cling to life by a thread. Whether they survive or not, and what the quality of their life will be if they do, is uncertain.

Whenever I entered the NICU, I had to brace myself, for tenderness and technology clashed sharply there. Preemies require highly skilled nursing care and the expert management of dedicated neonatologists. They may also require the help of specialized medications, oxygen-rich air, and high-nutrient feeding, as well as cardiac monitors, apnea monitors, and pulse oximeters to assess their moment-to-moment status, as they continue the vital growth and development they missed the chance to complete in the protective intrauterine environment.

Some of these tiny patients sleep facedown in their incubators, with legs and arms tucked neatly underneath them like little tree frogs, cute enough to wrest a smile from the most serious onlooker. Others, the sicker ones, lie spread-eagled on their backs with IVs inserted in their blood vessels and breathing tubes in their throats, while ventilators assist them with the hard work of breathing in a world for which their lungs are not yet ready.

For many preemies, life in the NICU is a difficult and tenuous existence, a harsh substitute for the nurturing of a mother's womb. Bending over a little one with a stethoscope in my ears, listening to the tiny heart lying so close to the surface and beating fervently at a pace two to three times that of my own,

I wanted to do my utmost to help this defenseless young one hang on to life and thrive.

Yet the line between helping and hurting preemies as they struggle to survive is extremely thin. Their delicate lungs may be at risk of collapsing if not held open with constant pressure from a ventilator that is forcing air into their airways, and finding the right amount of pressure can be a tricky business. If the pressure is not sufficient, the baby will not receive enough oxygen to nurture its brain and other vital organs. Yet if the pressure is too great, the baby's fragile lungs will be damaged, resulting in permanent scarring and impaired breathing for the rest of the child's life. In fact, everything you do in treating preemies requires careful calibration, for the margin of error is small with these tiny human beings.

In fact, so much calibration is needed for their care that I was often at risk of becoming completely absorbed with the demands of managing it. I would be so busy adjusting the ventilator settings, reviewing the results of x-rays or CAT scans, calculating the amount of sodium or potassium flowing into my patients' veins or the dose of digitalis needed to support the function of their hearts that I barely had a moment to appreciate the sweetness of their nature, or to offer them something equivalent of my own. The effort of keeping them alive weighed so heavily on my shoulders that I could nearly lose sight of who they were as individual human beings. Their names seemed far less significant than the numbers computed by the chemistry lab for their blood gases or by the hematology lab for their hemoglobin, and the caring of both the nurses and the infants' parents paled in importance in my mind when measured against the critical work that only we doctors could do.

Working in such an environment sorely taxed my soul. There was something frightfully wrong about the balance between our desire to be of help and the roughness of our efforts to do so. The benefit of the extreme measures we used to keep these babies alive did not seem to justify those measures' desperate lack of gentleness. I wondered if the effort we were making was truly for our patients' sake or for some unacknowledged reason of our own. Perhaps a need to demonstrate our prowess? Or maybe an urge to prove ourselves more competent than nature herself?

Guilt for subjecting our young patients to suffering gnawed at me. As I poked intravenous lines into their miniscule veins and arteries, pushed breathing tubes in place to force oxygen into their lungs, and stabbed their sensitive skin with needles again and again to sample their blood or infuse it with antibiotics, blood pressure boosters, heart stimulants and other necessary drugs, I would wonder if the price they were being asked to pay for survival was not far too great.

When these young ones survived, I told myself it was worth the price, but when they died in spite of everything, I wondered what we had gained for them besides a prolongation of struggle and pain. All I could do was say, "So sorry, little ones, please forgive our ignorance. I pray that someday we'll know better how to assist you, that soon we'll make it a priority to fine-tune our technology so that it can nurture your tenderness without assaulting it."

Thankfully, the care of preemies has changed over time. The dominance of technology in the NICU has yielded somewhat to the persuasiveness of tenderness, and a new and better balance has gradually been emerging. More is now known about the critical importance of carefully holding these little human beings and speaking to them softly, and neonatology nurses are being instructed in the art of gentle touch, while the parents whose visits were once strictly limited out of fear of causing unnecessary stress for all concerned are now being encouraged to spend time with their young ones as they struggle to survive. Mothers and fathers may even be provided with specially designed slings called kangaroo pouches to hold their infants close to their own bodies, in recognition of the tenderness that we now see as essential to their lives. Such changes greatly hearten me. At the same time, I suspect the need to draw a line between helping and hurting will continually challenge the medical profession to search its soul.

* * * * * * *

The medical intensive care unit, or MICU, is another place where the push and pull between human sensitivity and technological management is intense, for adults can become entangled in these issues nearly as easily as infants. I remember how that happened with Rodney, a man in his early thirties who was approaching the end of a long battle with an aggressive form of lymphoma just as I began my rotation in Internal Medicine as a fourth-year medical student. I followed his case for nearly three weeks, although I never truly knew him, since he was unconscious the entire time.

The only information of a personal nature that I ever learned about Rodney was contained in a single sentence written by the social worker in his medical chart. It noted that he had worked in the world of theater performance and that his life companion was an actor and dancer named Balfour. I recall well how Balfour came faithfully every day in the late afternoon to sit by Rodney's bed with a careworn face, holding Rodney's unresponsive hand in both of his. A sense of forlornness always pierced my heart when I glimpsed him sitting there.

Rodney had been doing fairly well until a couple of months before, when he began sliding slowly downhill. The chemotherapy sapped his energy and gnawed away at his ability to eat and sleep. Even worse, it had crippled his immune system, leaving him vulnerable to serious infection. Now the bacteria in his own body were beginning to attack him. The multitude of microscopic organisms living in his intestinal tract and normally performing helpful functions in the process of digestion had escaped from their normal habitat and invaded his bloodstream, producing the deadly condition of sepsis, that is, infection running rampant through his body. His doctors had transferred him from the medical ward to the Medical Intensive Care Unit for the most rigorous treatment possible.

In the hi-tech environment of the MICU, things happened at a rapid pace. The doctors flooded Rodney's body with antibiotics in an urgent attempt to turn back the advancing army of bacteria. They closely monitored the function of his liver, kidneys, heart, and lungs, since any of them could falter in the face of such an onslaught. His disabled immune system could not protect him. A cascade of physiological events that refused to be deterred was sweeping him helplessly along, and a haze began to settle over his consciousness. His doctors hooked him up to a ventilator to prevent respiratory failure. His condition was critical.

The army of microscopic organisms engaged in chemical warfare against Rodney's body, sending toxic chemicals throughout his bloodstream with a ruinous effect. The toxins assaulted the finely tuned balance normally maintained in the blood between coagulation and anticoagulation, and that balance began to deteriorate in a condition called disseminated intravascular coagulation, or DIC. The result was that blood clots started forming spontaneously throughout his body, while many small areas of uncontrolled bleeding appeared simultaneously.

Hope for recovery when patients progress to full-blown DIC is nearly nonexistent. Their bodily systems begin to virtually fall apart. Medical professionals know the dismal prognosis all too well. They say the letters DIC mean, "Death is coming."

Balfour understood none of these technicalities, nor did he want to. He lived in a state of shock and could hardly think. He clung to hope like a shipwrecked sailor would cling to a small life raft in a turbulent sea with no land to be seen in any direction. All he wanted, he said, was to spend a little time every day with his dearest friend and companion, taking one day at a time. The only thing he desired was the answer to two questions, which he asked daily before he left the MICU, stopping at the doctors' station and addressing them to whomever was there.

"He's going to make it, isn't he? You're doing everything you can, aren't you?"

Every day the truthful answer he was given was the same, even though it came from different lips: "We're sorry, we don't know if he'll make it or not. But please be assured, we're doing everything we possibly can."

Balfour would nod and say he was leaving everything up to us, and then walk off toward the door as if in a dream.

Back in those days, patients were not routinely encouraged, as they are now, to designate health-care proxies or to give advance directives about how they would wish to be cared for in life-threatening situations, nor did many hospitals have ethics committees available to offer advice on difficult cases. All treatment decisions were left up to the particular doctors in charge. Without any reason to decide otherwise, the MICU staff continued to treat Rodney with aggressive, high-technology measures that included a triple antibiotic regimen, platelet transfusions, fresh frozen plasma infusions, blood pressure elevators, and ventilator therapy, while he lay unmoving in his bed.

Watching Rodney being treated with so many radical procedures without any sign of improvement troubled me deeply. I wondered what principles were guiding Rodney's care. How much was his treatment based on careful consideration of all options and a foundation of experience about what was helpful? Was there an element of blind obsession about providing every radical treatment medical science had invented, even beyond the point where such treatment was likely to help? Could we discern if Rodney's chances of recovering were approaching nil and conclude that more intervention would only prolong his dying? Was there a point when it would be right to cut back or stop our interventions, a point at which the merciful thing would be to let him go?

These questions continued to plague me until I finally sought out the medical director of the MICU. He was a tall man with intense black eyes and a habit of stroking his moustache as he thought, and he paused before giving his answer. I recall his words clearly.

"I'm glad to hear you asking these questions, young lady," he said. "They're the questions I wrestle with every day, and the day I stop asking them, I won't be qualified to hold this job anymore."

He gave a wry smile, and then shook his head as if to clear it of such a thought and went on.

"To put it simply, the MICU is where we give it everything we've got. When someone is in crisis, how can you do less than that? Occasionally life lets us perform miracles. We bring some people back from the brink of death, and that's enough to keep us doing what you see us doing now."

He paused for a moment, as if considering how best to explain the nuances of the situation to someone new to the problem, and then continued.

"We offer every possibility we can for each patient to recover when they first come here, and we keep going until the patient declares himself, that is, until the person stops responding to our treatment and gets worse in spite of all we do. When that happens, we view it as if they're declining our attempts to help—as if they're turning away from us. That's what we look for. That tells us they've gone beyond the point of no return. And that's when we can think about changing our approach."

He paused again and shrugged his shoulders.

"Of course, the situation isn't always completely clear, and sometimes we may continue to give aggressive treatment even when the patient isn't responding, if the family members or closest friends aren't ready to let their loved one go. We try to give them the time they need in order to prepare for the loss they're going to feel."

The matter made sense to me when framed by this man's wisdom. It was obviously wrought from challenging firsthand experience.

The next day Rodney did just as the director had described. He seemed to turn away from us, seemed to be slipping beyond our reach. His vital signs became unstable, and small reddish-purple spots began appearing on his skin, signaling the breakdown of his blood vessels.

There was a change in Balfour too. He did not take hold of Rodney's hand that day, but sat back at a distance, and he did not stop to speak to any of the staff before he left.

The next day Rodney was worse, and no further transfusions were given. Balfour sat close to the bed with his head on the pillow beside Rodney's. From across the room, I could see that tears were running down his cheeks. The director went over and pulled up a chair beside him, and they spoke quietly for a while. As Balfour was leaving, he stopped by the doctors' station one last time.

"I told Rodney he can go," he announced in a husky voice, his eyes staring fixedly at the countertop. "He's been through too much. It's not right of me to ask him to stay any longer. He's way too tired."

He paused to brush away the tears that were returning.

"He knows that I care about him," he choked out fiercely, "that's all that matters." Then he turned on his heel and left.

Rodney died that night, and when the chief resident called Balfour at home with the news, Balfour thanked him, adding that he had no need to return to the hospital. He had already bid Rodney good-bye.

By the next morning, a new patient occupied the bed that Rodney had been in, yet Rodney and Balfour remained in my thoughts. The physicians of the MICU had fought valiantly with their technology to save Rodney's life as Balfour had asked, and though their efforts had failed, they had succeeded in accomplishing something else. They created a space in which the tenderness of those two friends could linger for a time—the tenderness of their connection and of their parting.

* * * * * * *

The tempo of the tenderness-technology dance rises and falls dramatically in the Pediatric Emergency Room, where the fears of parents for their children can be confirmed or quelled by the information gleaned from medical tests. I recall one dark night when a young mother swept like a human whirlwind into the pediatric ER, so breathless that she could barely tell the triage nurse her name, much less explain the reason for her urgency. But Irina's story, when she managed to recite it, was an ominous one, and it immediately sent her to the head of the line of parents waiting with their sick children to be seen. For Irina's three-year-old son, Niko, lay limp in her arms and afire with fever, only minutes earlier having been overtaken by a grand mal seizure that shook his body like a rag doll before her very eyes.

As Irina laid Niko gently on the examination table and stood aside for me to examine him, she tumbled out the story. It was a typical one for the Pediatric ER.

When she had picked her son up from the day-care center that day, she said, the day-care supervisor told her that Niko had not been his usual jolly, outgoing self. He had been inexplicably cranky and spent most of his time clinging to his blanket and sucking his thumb, as if consoling himself over some unpleasantness known only to him. The supervisor added that two other children were home sick with "a bug" and hypothesized that "something was going around."

After taking Niko home and feeding him dinner, most of which he refused, Irina noticed that his cheeks were flushed and his skin hot to the touch. The thermometer read 103.0 degrees Fahrenheit. As an experienced single mother who had weathered many a febrile illness with her other two children, Irina filled Niko's bottle with cool juice, gave him some Tylenol, and put him to bed.

At midnight she awoke to the sound of Niko crying. She tried for an hour to rock him back to sleep, but he remained restless, twisting and turning, neither fully awake nor asleep. The thermometer now read 105 degrees. She went to soak a towel in cold water to sponge his little body and draw some of the heat away.

She had only been gone a moment when she heard a strange gagging sound and went running back to find her beautiful son lying with his back arched, head thrown back and vacant eyes upturned, his body convulsing from head to toe. The terrible sight lasted no more than two or three minutes, she said, but it left young Niko limp and unresponsive. Terrified, Irina had scooped him up in her arms and run down the stairs from her fifth-floor walk-up apartment and along the street to the nearest intersection. There, in the city that never sleeps, she had frantically hailed a cab.

As Irina came to the end of her story, she gave a sudden gasp. Her attention had been so bound up with Niko's survival, she had not even realized until that moment that she had left her other two children alone and unattended. That was the breaking point for Irina. She started to sob uncontrollably.

The arrival in the emergency room of a very lethargic young child who is burning up with fever and just had a seizure is cause for immediate action. Two possible explanations for this situation exist, and because they have vastly different implications, the relevant one must be identified quickly.

One possibility—the preferable one, because it is far more benign—is that the convulsion has been caused solely by the fever, which is in turn being caused by a passing minor illness. A high fever burning in a child's body from such an ordinary illness can easily overheat the brain and drive it into a state of hyper-excitation. Like a pot of water that reaches the boiling point and suddenly bubbles over in a burst of excess energy, the overheated brain can spontaneously erupt into a fury of disorganized activity, showering the body with a storm of electrical impulses that obliterate consciousness and cause every muscle to stiffen and jerk uncontrollably.

This can be very frightening to witness. The afflicted person appears to be swept so far beyond reach that it seems uncertain whether he or she will be able to return. Fortunately, however, a febrile seizure is a storm that passes, and most such storms manage to leave their victims unscathed.

On the other hand, the second major cause of fever and seizure in a young child is meningitis, an aggressive infection that passes from the blood to the meninges, the membranous lining of the brain, where it can proceed to cause lasting neurological damage or even death. We needed to know which of these two roads little Niko was on, and we needed to know it quickly so that proper treatment could be started if necessary.

Niko's physical examination did not provide any clear-cut answers. The most valuable information would come from his blood and from his cerebrospinal fluid, or CSF, since meningitis usually leaves a trail of clues in both these places as it secures its hold in the body. So after explaining what would come next to the anxious Irina, I summoned an intern for assistance and promptly subjected young Niko to the unpleasant process of taking blood from his chubby arm and extracting CSF from his spinal column. Fortunately, this was less of an ordeal than it would otherwise have been, given Niko's lethargic state and the lack of resistance he offered, and in very short order, I had obtained the required amount of body fluids for testing.

When I had something as important as blood and CSF samples from a sick child in my hands, I did not like entrusting them to the hospital's usual methods of delivering samples to the labs for processing. The pneumatic tubes that whisk such samples through the walls of the hospital have been known to get stuck or cause the samples to break, and sometimes the people who act as couriers make errors, too, and precious specimens get lost. In a critical situation, I preferred to deliver specimens myself. Thus I headed to the uppermost floor of the hospital where the hematology and chemistry laboratories were housed, Niko's precious body fluids tucked safely in the pocket of my doctor's coat.

Venturing out of the world of direct patient care into the domain of laboratory testing was always an interesting experience. To my clinician's eyes, the labs were foreign territory whose highly specialized technology inspired fascination while simultaneously compelling meek acknowledgment of ignorance. Occupying several cavernous rooms were long tables laden with microscopes, centrifuges, coulter counters, spectrophotometers and other exquisitely precise instruments, as well as a multitude of tubes, beakers, and bottles filled with various substrates and reagents, plus mechanized conveyer systems that conducted a plethora of tests in carefully regimented sequence. The place was as unfamiliar and mysterious to me as the body of a sick patient would be to the technicians who worked with these exacting machines and testing procedures.

Paying a visit to the labs located on the twelfth floor of my hospital in the middle of the night added an interesting twist to the experience of medical technology. It brought me in touch with a very particular culture: the culture of the night owls, those hospital employees who did their work during the wee hours, while the rest of us were at home asleep. Living their lives in a diurnal rhythm that was the reverse of most people's lives and spending their work hours in solitude gave the lab technicians on night duty a slightly eccentric air, yet they could be of immense help when the results of lab tests were urgently needed. I had discovered that placing specimens directly into their hands at 2:00 a.m., along with words of profuse gratitude, was sure to shorten the turnaround time for results and save precious minutes or even hours.

Jimmy and Franco, two regulars who worked the night shift, were both hard at work when I arrived at their respective doors. Jimmy, a fastidious man who worked in the chemistry lab and wore two gold earrings in one ear, rolled his eyes in feigned exasperation at being asked to do a favor yet again, even as he accepted the tubes from my outstretched hand. In the hematology lab, Franco twirled the tips of his black handlebar moustache and swept an imaginary wide-brimmed hat from his head with a lavish bow, pronouncing himself the humble servant of Señora Doctora. Neither asked me for any details of the case I obviously felt was so urgent that I had left my post in the ER to bring the specimens all the way up from the ground floor myself. They knew well enough that the information they could glean from the specimens was vital. I quickly returned to the ER where more patients awaited me.

A short time later Jimmy and Franco each called to report their results. Even before they told me what the exact numbers were, the tone of their voices made the outcome clear. For although laboratory technicians rarely encounter patients face-to-face, they still feel pain at having to report bad news, and any sound of discomfort in their voices is a nuance that physicians quickly discern. In this case, however, there was none. Both Jimmy and Franco sounded pleased to report that Niko's values were completely normal. Neither his blood nor his cerebrospinal fluid showed any trace of bacterial invasion.

Irina was lucky. Her precious Niko would not have to endure two weeks or more of hospitalization with an IV imbedded in his arm, receiving intravenous antibiotics and possibly steroids, at risk for the neurological problems that can follow meningitis, such as hearing loss, vision impairment, seizure disorder, and learning disabilities. Instead, Niko was safe and could return home with her that night, perhaps without even disturbing the sleep of his two siblings.

73

Irina's gratitude overflowed with tears. As for me, I silently gave thanks to the medical technology that let me give her such good news.

* * * * * * *

The dance of tenderness and technology is not peculiar to the hospital's intensive care units or emergency room. It ebbs and flows all around you in the hospital wherever you go, imbedded in the sights and sounds and smells that impinge upon your senses and in all the activities surrounding you. Together these two partners create a world ominously unfamiliar to its visitors and temporary residents, though to the staff who roam the halls of that world by day and by night, its sensations are so very familiar that they nearly escape attention.

This world is shaped by bright fluorescent lights, well-buffed linoleum floors, and directories on the walls indicating the location of departments with such abstruse nomenclature as cardiology, hematology-oncology, otolaryngology, obstetrics and gynecology, gastroenterology, urology, and others equally difficult for the ordinary person to decipher. It contains a labyrinth of reception desks, nurses' stations, waiting rooms and endless corridors, and it is littered with objects rarely found anywhere else: stretchers and IV poles, body lifts and mechanized beds with adjustable side rails, machines with flickering buttons and screens whose workings only a select few understand, human bodies hooked up to various kinds of monitoring devices and to lengths of clear plastic tubing extending from bags of soundlessly dripping fluids.

A ceaseless hum of activity drones in the background: the confident conversing of white-coated staff; the bustle of nurses and aides with their carts and trays; the hushed voices of families; the muffled sounds of human illness—coughing, moaning, an occasional retching; the murmur of equipment monitoring heart rate and blood pressure with a monologue of beeps and buzzes. From certain rooms comes the soft puffing and clicking of the bellows of respirators, doing the breathing for patients too ill to breathe on their own. Occasionally the sound of a running faucet or the sucking swoosh of a flushing toilet punctuates the other background noises as patients tend to their bodily functions. A hodgepodge of odors abounds— the medicinal ones of cleansers, sanitizing solutions, astringents and such, to which one's olfactory nerves become less sensitive over time—as well as more obstinate odors: the odors of human illness, excrement, and putrefaction.

Languages of every kind are spoken in the hallways and waiting rooms, for people from around the world flock to New York City for many different reasons. Spanish, Polish, Iranian, Turkish, Cambodian, Bulgarian, Hebrew, Russian, Chinese with its many dialects, and dozens more can be heard in the hospital at one time or another. As conflict, oppression, and poverty wax and wane around the world, the hospital's human diversity sways in one direction after another, often taxing the ability of the hospital's translators to keep up.

Evidence of earnest attempts to make the medical environment more hospitable can be found, of course. Cheerful pictures line the corridors and waiting rooms: alpine meadows strewn with wildflowers, well-tended English gardens, colorful sidewalk cafés in Paris—far different scenes from those immediately surrounding the viewer. Whether they are a comforting distraction or only serve to underscore the ominous presence of other concerns is hard to say, but the attempt is well intentioned and may very well provide some visitors with a fleeting sense of relief.

This unique world dedicated to patient care has evolved swiftly over the past several decades, as scientific investigations and inventions have expanded our capacity for intervening in illness and injury. Technology has increasingly come to occupy center stage in the practice of medicine, and most doctors today could not imagine practicing without it. The power it gives you to understand your patients' problems and accomplish good on their behalf is extraordinary. The ability of technology to analyze the body's chemistry and physiology has progressed so far that the biological processes operating invisibly at cellular and subcellular levels can now be understood and measured, amplifying physicians' diagnostic powers a millionfold. Detailed pictures of patients' innermost anatomy and histology can be obtained quickly and painlessly from outside the body by machines with capacities infinitely greater than Roentgen's x-ray instrument that first showed us shadowy pictures of our bones just a few generations ago. CAT scanners employing computed axial tomography, PET scanners using positron emission tomography, MRI scanners utilizing magnetic resonance imaging, and many other equally magnificent contraptions have become indispensable allies. Doctors now turn to them for answers when confronted with unclarity. They have your back, so to speak, and that is an empowering feeling.

Besides providing information, technology's innovations have also led to an unprecedented ability to jump in and undo the threatening grip of illness or injury and bring serious medical situations under control. A plethora of drugs have been engineered to support the human body's vital systems. As a doctor, you have at your fingertips medications that alter the body's chemistry in beneficial ways, that modulate the functioning of ailing organs like the heart or pancreas or thyroid gland, that help fight off invasion by all manner of malicious microbes and parasites, that boost the immune system and battle the spread of cancer. You also have at your beck and call technology that can take over the work of temporarily impaired organs, as ventilators do for the lungs, or that can step in permanently for hopelessly diseased organs, as dialysis machines do in kidney failure. Life-enhancing surgical techniques continue to grow in their sophistication and precision, too, from complex reconstructive surgery to the revolutionary frontiers of organ transplantation and bioengineered body parts. The possibilities seem almost endless.

Still, there is another side to this rosy picture. Medical technology has a deceptive lure to it, a temptation for its users to become overly enthusiastic about its accomplishments. While it cannot be denied that modern medicine has given us enormous gifts, enabling us to understand things that mystified our forbears and alleviating an untold amount of suffering in the world, it does not mean technology's achievements are flawless or without risk. They do not relieve physicians of the need to give careful consideration to the potential harm of the actions they take versus the anticipated benefits. Unfortunately, the desire to be helpful by intervening, so often generated by technology, can easily overshadow such consideration, and prudence is a lesson that we medical professionals are sometimes slow to learn.

I witnessed a time, early in my career, when the temptation to intervene, plus the arrogance that can go along with it, grew alarmingly strong, and technology seemed on the verge of pushing tenderness out of the picture altogether. This happened in the realm of obstetrics, which shares a vested interest in the birth process with pediatrics. Obstetricians as well as pediatricians know that mother or child, or even both, can die if all does not go well, as it is no small thing for two bodies that have lived as one for many months to separate.

In fact, tremendous forces must be set in motion in order to expel the infant from the comfort of the womb, and the process is a grueling one. Powerful maternal muscles create rhythmic waves of contraction that force the baby down the impossibly narrow birth canal inch by inch. The youngster's head usually leads the way, stretching apart tight maternal tissues and pushing past rock-hard bone, bearing the brunt of the work. The amount of pressure the infant's head is subjected to is so great that the young bones of its skull are squeezed hard against each other and even overlap, only regaining their normal position weeks afterward. Collections of blood often form in the infant's scalp from the battering, and the flow of oxygen to the child's bloodstream can easily become compromised as the umbilical cord is twisted and squeezed. The formidable process can continue for hours upon hours, testing the limits of endurance for both mother and child. It is enough to make an observer exclaim, "Good heavens! Why has nature made it so hard for us to enter this world?"

As medical technology advanced, the obstetrical profession increasingly called upon it for help during the rigors of labor and delivery, and the result was encouraging to all concerned. Doppler machines were designed that enabled obstetricians to monitor the fetal heartbeat, the language of the baby's body that says whether all is well or not. Special electrodes were fashioned that obstetricians could reach in and implant in the scalp of the descending fetus, giving vital information about the child's oxygen level during the coming and going of contractions. The delivery room evolved to become a highly efficient environment, as precise and ultraclean as a surgery suite, with a stirrup-bearing examination table located at the center, and intervention equipment—oxygen, medications, and surgical instruments—all within arm's reach. In such a sophisticated setting, obstetricians felt ready to take action on mother and child's behalf in any emergency that might come along.

The stage was set for lifesaving intervention, but the question of when and how much to intervene proved to be a gnarly one. For there is a shadow side to our interventions. The ability technology gives you to manipulate the workings of a person's physical systems can lead you to believe that you have more power than you really do. You may disregard the innate intelligence of the body as a highly evolved living system, and worse yet you may nearly forget the presence of the person who lives within that physical body, the one whose life has shaped it and given it a human story. You may think you know enough to take over for it.

Obstetrics fell into this trap. Technology's role in the birthing process grew too great. It became domineering and oppressive, nearly stripping away the soulfulness from human entrance into life. What began as an intention to assist and protect mother and unborn child gradually swelled out of proportion, until the technological perspective claimed an exclusive right to regulate birth. Jealously exerting that right, technological medicine declared that husbands and friends of the pregnant woman—her natural, age-old sources of support—were distracting to the necessary professional focus and would henceforth be excluded from the birthing chamber. Children were disallowed as well, considered not only possible sources of infection but also too fragile to witness the alarming sight of their mothers' extreme exertion, not to mention her bodily fluids and private parts.

Thus, an event once shared with those closest to a woman became a thing controlled by professionals—something that happened behind closed doors, with even the woman's own participation reduced to a bare minimum. Her arms and legs were strapped tightly down, and she was put to sleep with powerful sedatives, while intravenous hormones were used to hasten or delay the course of labor as deemed fit. Hand-sized, specially shaped forceps were designed to reach into a woman's birth canal and, taking a recalcitrant baby's head tightly in their metal grip, drag the infant out, presumably sparing it the last threatening part of its trip, while leaving large purple bruises on its scalp and face, and sometimes even damaging the facial nerves.

Similarly, cesarean sections, originally an extreme necessity applied only in life-endangering situations, became more and more popular for increasingly less significant reasons, until one out of three women in our country was giving birth to their babies in an operating room. The idea of avoiding the pain of childbirth and being able to set the date of their delivery appealed to them, and obstetricians found it all too easy to pick up a scalpel and cut a hole through the tightly stretched abdominal wall of a sleeping woman and then pluck her fetus

79

out. The opportunity created by medical technology to take control was too great to resist.

This was the norm in the first decade of my career, and it disturbed me deeply to be part of it. Thankfully, however, the balance that tipped too far in one direction has been moving back toward a better point of equilibrium. Women and their families have begun reclaiming childbirth as a highly personal and intimate part of human life, leaving hi-tech management for the protection of the truly problematic pregnancies. Natural childbirth, well prepared for with the help of knowledgeable professionals, has become increasingly popular and now takes place safely in homelike birthing centers as well as in people's own homes, while the resources for intervention remain at a respectful but accessible distance, giving testimony to a reemerging harmony between technology and tenderness.

This is not just a simple victory for gentleness and kindness. From my perspective, it is more than that. Our humanity has been at stake. Amid all the measuring and manipulating in this day and age, I believe it is important to ponder the mystery of our own existence, to retain a sense of awe about how it is that we each come to have a human life. The process that creates every one of us—the process of conception, gestation, and birth—may seem a natural, everyday occurrence, but that should not lull us into taking it for granted. If our eyes do not recognize the amazing process that it is—if we reduce being born to a mechanistic event best managed with detached professional skill, its marvel dismissed with scientific terminology—then we are robbing ourselves of a fuller appreciation of who and what we are.

If you really stop to think about it, the birth of a human being—a new and utterly unique individual suddenly popping out of the body of another individual—is quite extraordinary, like a feat of sorcery. That every one of us begins our life as a single cell too small for the human eye to see, buried in the depths of another person's anatomy, spending the early months of our existence being nourished by that other person's bloodstream in an intimate act of generosity, with that person's body serving as the threshold we must cross in order to gain entrance into the world—all seems like science fiction, almost more than the mind can comprehend. No amount of scientific understanding or technological expertise can do justice to the enormity of this truth or completely dispel the wonder of it. It is far too amazing for that.

* * * * * * *

While much can be said about the role technology plays in our lives, far too little is said, from my perspective, about the place of tenderness in human life. Yet it is part of our nature, and it, too, is quite remarkable.

Tenderness is easy to see if you choose to go into pediatrics and therefore encounter infants on a regular basis. At no other time is the innate tenderness of human beings more clearly visible than in those who have just recently crossed the threshold into life. All newborn babies have a sweetness about them that cannot be denied. Still cloaked with an aura of blessedness, they affected me deeply. Each time I beheld one, I knew I glimpsed basic human selfhood in all its innocence and purity. I knew, too, why we naturally regard newborns as cause for joyful celebration: they give us a taste of the miracle of our own existence.

The newborn nursery was my favorite place to work as an intern and resident, and even as an attending. Temporary home to healthy new arrivals, it was unlike any other place in the hospital. Tenderness abounded there, and the need for technology remained at a minimum. Bassinets, each containing a little bundled body, occupied spacious open rooms where large viewing windows lined the walls to offer visitors a look, while within the nursery's boundaries special rules and a different way of being prevailed. All personnel who entered were required to scrub their hands and put freshly laundered hospital robes over their street clothes, and conversation was naturally conducted in softer tones.

Nearly every time I arrived to do my newborn nursery rounds, I would find one of the nurses sitting with a baby in her arms, one that needed a little extra consoling, or perhaps one that could not be fed by its mother because she was not feeling well enough. As I went about my work, I would be enfolded in a steady stream of little sounds murmuring in the background: quiet snufflings and stirrings and occasionally a miniature hiccup or sneeze, such a sweet version of the loud eruptions made by adults that I could not help but smile. On the other hand, if several young ones happened to grow hungry at the same time, the noise level could escalate to a demanding chorus of crying, and then the sense of indignant urgency brought a smile to my face.

The main thing I noticed about the nursery was the settling effect it had on me as soon as I stepped through the door. It was a haven of sorts within the hospital, seemingly immune to the hectic, pressured pace and urgent matters so prevalent elsewhere. A subtle serenity resided there, one that never quite went away, even in the busiest of moments. Even the quality of the air seemed different, and perhaps it was. Perhaps the breath of the babies made it so. For baby breath is one of the sweetest things you may ever smell: pure and delightful. Or maybe the inherent tenderness that babies bring with them into life lingered in the nursery, filling it with an ephemeral feeling just barely noticed by the senses, innocent and soothing. All I can say is that I loved being there, doing the necessary work of conducting newborn examinations to determine the well-being of each little body, all the while basking in the exquisite fragrance of newly delivered life.

I loved, too, an interesting phenomenon that anyone working in a nursery can easily observe but which is not otherwise widely known or appreciated. Most of the little newcomers to the newborn nursery do not immediately fall off into an exhausted sleep as you might expect after the grueling work of being born. Instead, they linger awake for several hours in the "quiet alert state." Having been bathed, measured, and foot-printed by the nursery staff and now comfortably swaddled in soft white baby blankets, these newly arrived youngsters lie completely relaxed with eyes wide open, gazing about in every direction.

If you happen to be conducting the newborn examinations of such youngsters during this quiet alert phase, you notice that your manipulations do not upset their quietude in the least. Even while you stretch out their arms and legs to test for reflexes, or press with your fingers into their abdomen to feel for liver, kidneys, and spleen, they remain undisturbed. What is more, you have the amazing privilege of looking into their wandering eyes as you work.

Maybe it was my imagination, but I always felt wonder in those eyes as they looked all around—wonder at a world they were seeing for the very first time. Sometimes I found myself prompted to look around as if with newly opened eyes myself, just to see what things looked like from that perspective, and what I saw was indeed more fascinating than I usually noticed it to be.

In the course of examining roughly twenty thousand newborns during my career, I never tired of watching their eyes, especially in those moments when they looked directly back at me. Then the consciousness in those eyes slid right past my focused professional purposefulness and touched the core of my being as lightly as a feather. I experienced a delightful tingle at being the object of their impartial attention, even briefly. To me, meeting a newborn human's gaze was like catching sight of heaven. I wanted to bow my head in acknowledgment of receiving such a gift.

Medically, of course, the newborn physical exam is very important. It involves carefully searching the newborn's body for any signs of abnormality—anatomical, neurological, metabolic, et cetera—and giving a clean bill of health if none are found, or determining an appropriate course of action if one or more are. As a pediatrician, my ears were trained to recognize the sounds of abnormal heart rhythms, or murmurs made by blood flowing past distorted valves in the heart. My fingers could detect the outline of an abnormally shaped liver or kidney, or the telltale click of a femur slipping out of a malformed hip joint as I rotated the legs, or the too rapid or too slow response of reflexes that warned of neurological damage. I took this work seriously. As a guardian stationed at the entranceway to life, I could make a significant difference to the future of those young ones who came bearing some hidden defect, because identifying such defects right at the outset and tending to them immediately can give a child a great advantage.

Humanly, however, I wanted to do more than that. It seemed to me only right to also extend a welcome to these newborn beings, to acknowledge their accomplishment in making it through, and to encourage them and wish them well in the life that awaited them. So this is what I eventually decided to do.

I fashioned a simple prayer, an invocation if you will, and as I worked with each baby I whispered the words softly so that they would reach no other ears than the ones in front of me. The words are simple, and they varied from one time to the next, but they went more or less like this:

Hello! Welcome to this life. May you have a good life, a wonderful life. May there be many in your life who care about you, and may you have opportunities to follow your dreams. May you learn much in this life, and may love be one of your greatest teachers. May you use your life well and know happiness and gratitude. Blessings to you.

Without doing this one simple thing, this act of extending a conscious greeting and words of encouragement, the job of examining thousands upon thousands of full-term newborns, looking for rarely occurring medical problems, could easily have become dull, repetitive work, no matter how sweet these babies were or delightful their breath and eyes. To see so many so briefly, and to never see the vast majority again, might have gradually rendered these young beings indistinct and featureless, mere objects on a conveyor belt needing to be checked off as "approved" or "not approved." I certainly saw this happen with some of my colleagues. Instead, this act made the task a practice of the heart. It allowed me to fall momentarily in love with each one and to care about the unique human life that was theirs, waiting to be lived. It seemed a small thing to do, but the tenderness of it sustained me over the years, and perhaps made a tiny difference for those newborn beings too.

*   *   *   *   *   *   *

If we would pay more attention to tenderness, we might find it the natural antidote to over-infatuation with technology, keeping us in touch with our hearts and assuring that we will not become permanently lost in the mechanistic mindset of our technological inventions. Technology is capable of accomplishing many things, but without the heart to guide its use, it can become a stern, unfeeling master. In itself, it is incapable of caring, devoid of compassion. These are simply not in its nature, but must be brought to it by the human heart. You might say the job of tenderness is to tame technology so that it can serve us in the highest ways of which it is capable.

One place where I witnessed technology achieve such perfection was in Mortie's loving hands. He was our pediatric cardiologist, a bright-minded keeper of invaluable knowledge and expertise in our department. He ran the cardiology clinic where he cared for children with heart disease, and whenever any of the rest of us had concerns about our patients' hearts, we knew we could call on him for guidance. An energetic, youngish man with an ever-ready smile and spry sense of humor, he had a depth in his eyes that went beyond mere knowledge. Wearing a yarmulke perched on his head that attested to his faith while conveniently covering the thinning hair of a soon-to-be bald spot, and striding through the halls with a barely contained enthusiasm that put a spring in his step, he was always a welcome sight.

Mortie's prize piece of technology was his portable echocardiography machine. Standing approximately his own height, measuring three times his width, and rolling on four motorized wheels, it went everywhere with him in the hospital like a loyal, eager-to-please assistant. The two of them were a team, and when they arrived together on the ward to do an urgent consultation on a child with suspected cardiac complications, everyone felt immediately reassured by the perfect combination of compassion and competence the two of them brought.

Mortie approached his work with a devotion that easily infected others. He loved the human heart and was an expert on its anatomy, its physiology, and especially its bravery. He liked to call it the hardest-working organ in the body by far, and the admiration he felt for it would gleam in his eyes as he spoke. He enjoyed drawing others into his investigations and gladly interpreted for any onlookers the enigmatic images wavering on his mechanistic assistant's sonography screen. Frankly, I could never quite make out all that he saw, but then his eyes had many years of practice behind them and perhaps some special aptitude that mine did not.

I remember one day in particular when I called for Mortie's help. I was feeling quite concerned about a very sick four-month-old patient who had recently been admitted to the Pediatric Intensive Care Unit and assigned to my care. He was short of breath and failing to thrive, and his heart was beating way too fast. His chest x-ray showed his heart was larger than it should be, and my ears detected a murmur, though his rapid heart rate made it hard to discern its exact nature.

I stood close by to observe as Mortie maneuvered his handy assistant into position at the baby's side. The boy's eyes flickered briefly as Mortie carefully unsnapped his tiny white hospital shirt and applied ultrasound gel to his chest. Otherwise, the little boy lay motionless under the warming lights, breathing the oxygen we were giving him, too sick to be disturbed by the goings-on around him.

Mortie then took up his machine's transducer wand and, with its gleaming metal tip pressed gently against the baby's chest, moved it slowly round and round, carefully aiming the ultrasound waves produced by the wand so that they generated a three-dimensional image of the baby's heart on the sonography screen, showing it pumping steadily at a rate of two hundred beats per minute. It was an awesome sight.

Mortie, who had seen such a sight thousands of times before, moved quickly through the steps of his investigation, gathering information about the four chambers of that muscular organ, the state of the arteries and veins leading to and from it, and the condition of the valves regulating the flow of blood through it. This was his skill and his passion, and in his reassuring presence, I felt free to appreciate the miracle of what was happening: we were looking straight through this child's chest wall into the cavity where his infant-sized heart lay beating with heroic determination.

As I gazed at the astonishing effort his heart was making, an obvious truth I had never considered before struck me: that little heart was committed to beating like this over all the years of this young human being's lifetime. It would not rest for a single moment until his life was finished, no matter how long or short it would be. And more than that, every one of us in the room—Mortie, me, the other patients, and the nurses tending them—had within us a heart beating just as fervently on our behalf as the one in this little boy, a heart that would labor without pause until the day we died . . .

Suddenly, Mortie's voice broke into my reverie.

"There it is, right there," he cried, pointing to a barely discernable oval shadow on the screen. "That's the little guy's problem: a big ol' VSD!"

Yes, there it was, a ventricular septal defect, or a hole in the wall between the baby's ventricles, the two chambers responsible for the major pumping action of the heart, the right one having the job of directing a steady stream of blood to the lungs, and the left one of sending a powerful stream to the rest of the body. With a hole between the two ventricles, these two streams of blood were mixing unnaturally, forcing the boy's unfortunate heart to work twice as hard as it should. Eventually it would begin to fail.

"This little guy won't get far in life with that big defect in his heart," Mortie muttered, as much to his automated sidekick as to me.

He then announced that he would make plans for the boy to have cardiac catheterization and corrective cardiac surgery as soon as possible. My little patient would have his chest opened, his heart exposed, and the hole between his ventricles skillfully closed. His life would be saved, and his heart made whole.

As for me, I saw the mythic dimension to Mortie's work that day, a perspective I hungered for, too often overlooked amid the concrete concerns and habits of the everyday medical world. Peering over his shoulder had let me glimpse what he seemed to know so well, that while the instruments of science allow us to examine the human heart and even intervene on its behalf, they will never fully comprehend it—not the complexity, not the perfection, and not the courage that is its nature.

* * * * * * *

Since part of being a doctor entails dealing with situations that may at any moment fly out of control—when a heart starts to fail, or a wound to bleed, or cancer to spread, or sepsis set in—you understandably become quite fond of the technology that backs you up. Justifiably fond, the way Mortie was of his echocardiography machine. One of the true enticements of technology, one of its heady thrills, really, is the sense of confidence that it gives you in the face of these inevitable times of urgency and uncertainty. You feel genuinely graced by the ability it puts in your hands to exceed the limits of nature.

Still, one limit is undeniable, one final boundary remains unbreachable for technology, and that is death. For though death can be delayed, it cannot be held at bay indefinitely, no matter how great your professional skills or numerous your technological resources. Sooner or later there comes a time when death undoes all your efforts and has its way. Answers will not be found, and the course of things will not come under your control as you would wish. Then you discover something different from all the lessons technology can teach: knowing how to accept things as they are. Sixteen-year-old Jamal showed me this.

Jamal's face was sculpted with exquisite Middle Eastern beauty, and his eyelashes were the longest I had ever seen. I remember them well because I stared at them for a long time that last day, the day that Jamal went beyond the help that our professional expertise could offer him.

Six months earlier Jamal had been diagnosed with glioblastoma multiforme, a highly aggressive type of brain tumor. A serious and popular young man who was as good at his studies as he was at sports, Jamal had been complaining of headaches for several weeks. His parents had assumed the headaches were due to the stress of entering a competitive city high school, until he had a seizure.

When our pediatric oncologist, Dr. Samuels, told Jamal's parents as gently as he could what Jamal's CAT scan revealed, it was as if a lightning bolt struck, shattering their world. They wrung their hands and asked in bewilderment what they had done wrong that would allow such a terrible thing to happen to the son they cherished, who was such a good boy with a future full of promise. Jamal, on the other hand, remained silent and unsurprised, even while being ushered to the private room he would occupy during his stay on the ward.

Because the tumor had already spread its microscopic ten-drils widely in his brain, the proposed treatment offered no hope of cure, only comfort for the months of livable time that Jamal had left. As Dr. Samuels put it when he presented Jamal's case at our weekly staff meeting, high-grade glioblastoma is a mean son of a gun. It resists most types of treatment, and it grows back quickly after every attempt to beat it back.

Nevertheless, Dr. Samuels made arrangements for Jamal to have surgery, and the neurosurgeon carefully removed as much of the tumor as he could reach, relieving a portion of the pres-sure on Jamal's brain and, for a while, some of the pain it was causing. Jamal returned home three weeks later with a long, ugly scar emblazoned across a section of his shorn scalp.

Many months of outpatient radiation therapy and chemo-therapy followed. Together these treatments shrank the tu-mor ever so slightly more, while anticonvulsants kept Jamal's seizures under control. Nothing, however, prevented his fur-ther hair loss and muscle atrophy and dismal disappearance of appetite and optimism. Through it all, Jamal conserved his diminishing energy for the two things most important to him: hanging out in a wheelchair with his buddies at the neigh-borhood basketball court where he now watched rather than played, and talking with his three younger sisters about staying out of trouble. He knew trouble was easy to stray into in the housing projects of the Lower East Side, especially without an older brother's watchful eye.

Eventually, the ground Jamal had gained began to slip away. The grinding headaches returned, accompanied by nausea and vomiting and growing loss of memory. Then one morning, when his mother went to rouse him, Jamal did not respond. An ambulance rushed him to the hospital where a CAT scan showed that his tumor had hemorrhaged into his brain. He was in an irreversible coma.

Dr. Samuels admitted him once again to the pediatric ward, where his family began a round-the-clock vigil, with turns taken by his parents, grandparents, siblings, and cousins. For three days they watched him lie unmoving, save for the rise and fall of his chest, while the IV bag dripped its hydration silently into his veins and the cardiac monitor blinked the measure of his still-beating heart.

When his breathing began to change, we knew the end was close. The air moved through his throat with a ragged sound, and his chest rose and fell in an irregular rhythm. As the senior resident on the ward, I explained to his parents, who were keeping vigil at his bedside, the meaning of what we saw. All his family came to the hospital then, eyes full of tears. They gathered quietly in the waiting room, saying they would rather wait there together in prayer than watch Jamal's disease take him away.

I made the choice to stay beside Jamal. It seemed only right, I thought, that someone should be present as death came for him. He had done the best he could with the hand that life had dealt him, and from my perspective every moment of life he still had was worth honoring. And if these final moments held too much sorrow for his family to witness, then I would gladly do it.

The end came quietly. His tired body simply seemed to accept its fate. With no more than a whisper, it let go of the effort it had been making. I felt relieved for him.

Before walking down the hall to inform his family of his passing and invite them to pay Jamal one last visit, I turned to the task of tidying the room. Generally, doctors left this chore to the nurses, but at that moment it seemed a natural continuation of the witnessing I had felt called to do. I did not want to delegate the task to others, so proceeded to do what was necessary. I disconnected the cardiac monitor and the various IV lines from Jamal's body and removed them from the room. Then I collected the other medical supplies and apparatuses and put them out of sight. Finally, I straightened the sheets and smoothed the pillow around Jamal's head and carefully folded his graceful hands across his chest.

With this completed, I stepped back to observe the results. What I saw took me by surprise.

A change had taken place, something more than greater orderliness. Serenity had come and infused the air with such quietude that my breath caught in my throat.

Had this serenity been there all the time, hidden behind the staff's focus on medical management, waiting for us to run out of the professional tasks that occupied us before it could be noticed? Or had death just opened an invisible door and invited it to enter?

I had no answer, but however it had happened, the result was clear. This particular hospital room now lay in the province of a deep peacefulness.

Above everything else, Jamal's face claimed my attention. That young face, which only a short while ago had borne the imprint of mortal illness, was now strikingly beautiful. Every other sight in the room paled into insignificance in comparison with its beauty. Framed by the stainless white of the hospital pillow, his face rested in perfect repose. His long black eyelashes, such a delicate counterpoint to a young man's growing virility, lay gently on his cheeks below his closed eyelids.

The struggle that had filled the last months of Jamal's life was gone. Not a sign of the pain he had once endured remained. How easily it all seemed to have fallen away, all the suffering we had tried so hard to spare him, now banished by the hand of death.

From some recess in my mind, triumphant words from Handel's oratorio *Messiah* came to me: "Oh death, where is thy sting? Oh grave, where is thy victory?" *Not here*, Jamal's room was clearly saying, *not here*.

When I appeared at the door of the waiting room, Jamal's family looked up as one. His father, mother, grandparents, three sisters, and two cousins were all there. Whatever the words were that I said to them, they were superfluous. My presence was enough to convey the message that Jamal had passed away.

Their eyes dry now, they followed me back down the hall, past rooms where other patients' stories were in progress, to Jamal's room where silence waited.

As they approached the room, the group faltered for a moment, as if afraid of what they were about to see. Then, as if she were preparing to enter a sacred place, Jamal's grandmother made the sign of a cross over her chest and stepped across the threshold, drawing the others after her. When she reached the bedside, she stopped and clutched her breast.

"Oh my, he's so beautiful!" she exclaimed.

Several others murmured their agreement, and then slowly reached out to stroke Jamal's cheeks and shoulders and long, perfect fingers. And so the family stood, gathered around the bed, Jamal's sisters holding hands, his grandmother with her arm around his mother's shoulders, his father and grandfather and cousins standing side by side, sharing Jamal's final peace. I left them there absorbed in stillness and slipped away to my other work.

Later, when Jamal's parents were leaving, they saw me in the hall and stopped to speak with me. They looked exceedingly weary, but their smiles were genuine. His father expressed his thanks with heartfelt words for everything we had done for his son and especially for the time the family had spent in his room. Seeing Jamal looking so beautiful and so at peace, he said, made it easier to accept his passing.

It was his mother's words, though, that spoke to the heart of the matter.

"Yes, that's Jamal, that's our boy," she said. "He looks so beautiful because he truly is. It's not a funeral-parlor kind of made-up beauty. It's the beauty that is really his—the beauty of his soul!"

Later, I thought back to what Dr. Samuels had said early that morning when making his rounds. He had paused only a moment at the door to Jamal's room, not bothering to go in as he had every day before. He had nothing more to offer.

Instead, he grimaced and swore softly under his breath: "Damn that savage disease!" Then he turned on his heel and walked away.

That man deserved a lot of compassion, I thought. He saw this happen time and time again and never stopped trying to make it turn out differently. What he said was true. Oh, so true. He had every right to rage at cancer for destroying a young life just starting to blossom.

Yet there was another truth as well, one that Dr. Samuels had not stayed to see. From the perspective of this other truth, there was no destruction in that room at all. Instead of the ruined remains of an unfulfilled beauty, there was another, unexpected beauty being revealed there, whole and strong and radiant. Had Dr. Samuels stayed, he would have seen it shining through the rubble of his unsuccessful efforts. If he had stayed, he would have seen that long after his technology had ceased to be of service, this other, indestructible beauty was embracing sorrowing hearts and tenderly comforting them.

Four

Contradictions & Incongruity

THE PROFESSION OF MEDICINE contains contradictions that can be quite confusing. Opposing currents of thought and differing standards of behavior can toss you this way and that, making you question whether the profession is really certain about what it believes. I noticed this conundrum at the very beginning of my education as a doctor, displayed by some of the professors who were teaching me. The conflicting messages their words or behavior sent out left me feeling perplexed and mistrusting and impotent, too, but as a student I dared not speak up and ask them for an accounting of their actions.

I remember well an incident from my first year of medical school. All the students in my class were seated in the main auditorium one morning, ready for one of the bigwig professors to lecture us on lung physiology. This particular man was the chair of his department and renowned for his groundbreaking research and far-reaching knowledge. He purportedly knew everything there was to know about the human lung. His status as an important figure had been carefully drilled into us lowly students the week before by our preceptors, and we had come prepared to be impressed.

What we saw, however, was not impressive, at least not from my perspective. To my disgust, the man striding back and forth across the auditorium stage, talking in a very loud voice about the marvels of the lung, was puffing all the while on a cigarette. As soon as he had smoked the one in his hand down to the very butt, he would quickly stop right there on-stage and pull out another, light it up, and then continue his marching back and forth, hardly missing a step—all that, de-spite the fact that the hazards of cigarette smoking were rap-idly becoming known.

Surely, I thought, this can't be as absurd as it seems. Maybe he's pulling our leg, waiting for some bright young star among us to grab his or her courage and stand up to point out the obvious truth—that the emperor has no clothes and can die of lung cancer just like anyone else if he persists in chain-smok-ing. The courageous one who spoke up would thereby win the master's approval, I imagined, and gain acclaim early in his or her career. Maybe this man was actually daring us to speak up, flaunting the ridiculous in our faces as a test, trying to rouse us out of our complacency.

I looked around at my fellows, expecting to see consterna-tion in their faces too. But to my surprise, they were all hurried-ly taking notes, fully occupied with the effort of catching every important bit of information flying at them from the stage.

As I continued to observe the apparent charade, a disturb-ing detail registered. Every now and then the professor would pause mid-sentence, overtaken by a hacking cough. Thick phlegm rattled in his airways, the very ones he was lecturing about. It was a sickening sound.

Doubt about my initial optimistic assessment of the sit-uation crept in. I studied his face for further clues. What I saw was not encouraging. His features were pinched and hard. Heavy eyebrows glowered over sharp, unwelcoming eyes, and thin, tight lips stretched around a down-turned mouth. A sub-tle disdain seemed to emanate from his very being. Discomfort grew in me as I watched. Instinctively, I sank lower in my seat, hoping to become less visible.

As the next spasm of coughing began, my mind staged a revolt. It stubbornly dug in its heels, closed like a fist, and refused to allow entrance to anything more this man had to say, as if the facts that he spoke were tainted with lies.

Once the lecture was over and the student body had filed out of the auditorium, I sounded out some of my comrades, curious about their reaction. Overall, they said, they thought the lecture was great.

"That guy really knew his stuff!" one proclaimed.

"Talked for an hour with no notes!" another chimed in.

"Had a hard time keeping up with him," added a third. "The smoking? Yeah, well, you know . . . he's a big shot. What do you expect?"

"No! No! No!" my mind protested vehemently. "I expect much more than this! And you should too! Don't just swallow everything you hear! It's not okay!"

But, in fact, I said nothing. I merely walked away. I had the uncomfortable feeling that whatever I said would not be heard.

* * * * * * *

Contradictions like the one I witnessed that day continued to cross my path. At times, modern medicine seemed to be a staunch guardian of the miracle of life, ready to protect it and support it in a myriad of clever and heroic ways. At other times, I perceived institutionalized health care to falter in its sense of purpose and become halfhearted in its attention, distracted by other enticements like reputation and intellectual gratification. It showed an unfortunate tendency to indulge in extra helpings of pride and become intoxicated with admiration over its own accomplishments. At its very worst, it could demean the miracle of life it was pledged to protect, coldly disregarding its preciousness and trampling on its vulnerability.

The question of where I stood amid this confusion intensified when I progressed from the initial period of book learning into actual clinical experience. In the third year of medical school we fledgling doctors-to-be were sent to try out our wings and engage with real patients under the supervision of our seniors. My group's first clinical rotation of the year was in the Department of Medicine where, perched way down on the least significant rung of the hierarchical ladder, our role was to pay close attention and do as we were told, while staying out of the way of those who had real responsibilities.

Bedecked in my new, still-crisp, hip-length white doctor's coat, with stethoscope slung casually around my neck in careful imitation of my seniors, I learned to march obediently through the hallways as house staff rounds were made. Everyone's rank was clear: the chief resident marched at the fore, followed by senior residents and first-year residents, and then fourth-year students. We third-year students brought up the tail end of the daily parade, which followed a set routine of pausing beside bed after bed, listening to an update on each patient's condition. We diligently observed as, one after another, the patients were poked and prodded by our higher-ups' examining fingers in order to demonstrate the presence or absence of pathology.

As the days progressed, I grew increasingly unsettled. These residents and fourth-year students, even the attendings who periodically came by in their more important knee-length white coats to lead the troupe on teaching rounds, were leaving something out. They talked with conviction about their patients—the abnormalities noted on their physical exams and various test results, the complexity of their diagnoses, the certainty or uncertainty of their prognoses—and had much of importance to say. Yet I detected a certain ignorance hiding in their words. I heard it in the tone of their voices, saw it in their self-absorbed expressions. Their understanding of the disease each person had far outstripped their comprehension of the person who had the disease. They seemed fascinated by their own knowledge, preoccupied with their agility in juggling sound bites of medical information. They never once addressed the human experience of being sick, of being afraid, of being alone.

One day, early on, while my surprise over these things was still new, we paused on rounds at the bedside of an older woman diagnosed with leukemia. Her face was pale, her breathing shallow, and she did not stir, though we clustered close around her bed. I resisted the thought that with her softly curling gray hair, she looked a little like my grandmother. Instead, I stared at the dark-red blood oozing from the corners of her mouth. Did no one else notice that?

The third-year resident droned on in a dry voice: "The patient is responding poorly to chemotherapeutic regimen . . . peripheral blood loaded with malignant cells . . . platelet count critically low despite transfusions . . . do-not-resuscitate order being proposed . . ."

As the technical commentary went on, I stared at the human being lying there before us. Was she a person, or just a medical challenge? Were we writing her off just because her illness hadn't responded to our treatment?

Naively I spoke up, asking, "Isn't there *something* we can do for her?"

The resident looked at me with condescending patience.

"There's nothing we can do. She has *terminal disease*," he replied.

He enunciated the last two words carefully, as if indicating that within them lay the full logic for why there was nothing to do. She was dying, and there was nothing that could be done about *that*. Therefore, end of discussion. Next patient, please.

As the resident turned away, I held my tongue, for clearly we were speaking two different languages. What I was really asking was: even if there is nothing to do about her illness, isn't there some response we can make to her dying? Don't we want to take a moment to look on her with compassion and somehow acknowledge the final chapter of her life?

My heart ached. Was this the way her story would end, casually passed by, dismissed as unresponsive to treatment, left alone in a corner bed that, once empty, would be filled again so fast that there would be no memory of who had been there before? But we were moving on, for there were many more patients to see, and the milling white coats quickly swept me back to my position at the rear of our procession.

Rightly or wrongly, my anger at the health-care system began that day. I promised myself not to allow such human experience to go unnoticed. With righteous indignation, I vowed to be a better kind of doctor than the others that I saw. I would work harder, care more, and challenge the health-care system to do a heck of a lot better than I thought it was doing. Little did I know how complex an undertaking that would prove to be.

* * * * * * *

Critiquing the medical profession is not difficult to do, for it has an abundance of weaknesses and inconsistencies. Yet it is one thing to recognize the faults that other humans and human-made systems have, and quite another to recognize your own. Fortunately, if you pay close enough attention, the practice of medicine will help you discover the faults within yourself and, sooner or later, challenge you to do something about them.

Take moral courage, for example. You learn quite a bit about this dimension of yourself during your training. Many situations in medicine accost your sense of right and wrong and challenge you to cast yourself into the fray on the side of that in which you most believe. You learn fairly quickly how strong your moral courage is and how well it holds up under pressure, since pressure is part of the daily fare of this profession.

I can recall many times when a fierce energy flared up in me in protest over a situation that did not seem right, propelling me into action with a gratifying surge of strength and certainty. I also recall times when I failed to take a stand, when my moral courage let me down and I fell flat on my face. One of these times makes me want to bow my head in dismay at my own faintheartedness even now.

One morning, when I was a neophyte third-year student doing my monthlong rotation in the Department of Surgery, I was assigned to accompany a second-year surgery resident as he made his work rounds. I trotted obediently along behind him as he paid one rapid visit after another to patients occupying the long row of rooms along one hallway of the surgical ward. His terse responses to my questions made me well aware that he was three years my senior, a huge status differential in the world of medical training.

Finally we arrived at the room of Almondo Rodriguez, an elderly Hispanic man with advanced lung cancer. Unfortunately, the surgery resident spoke no Spanish, nor did I, and Señor Rodriguez spoke no English. As a result, the resident was unable to explain to the poor gentleman that he needed to have a large-bore needle inserted through his chest wall to extract the malignant fluid accumulating there. The resident tried in a cursory sort of way to indicate what he was about to do through hand gestures, but he was either very tired or uncaring or both, for his patience ran out quickly. I offered to run and look for an interpreter, but the offer elicited a disdainful snort. There was no time for that, the resident said, and besides, the patient had already signed the consent form and should be prepared well enough by now.

Since the ailing Señor Rodriguez did not understand that he was expected to remove his shirt for the procedure, the resident simply pulled it off him. After swabbing the gentleman's rib cage with disinfectant, the resident prepared his needle and motioned for Señor Rodriguez to sit on the side of the bed, bend forward with his head on the bedside table, and remain there without moving.

But Señor Rodriguez did not comply. Instead, he kept lifting his head up from the table and mumbling words in Spanish. Either he did not understand what was about to happen, or he understood perfectly well and was not ready for it to happen. Whichever it was, it was to no avail. The resident wanted to get this over with.

Suddenly, the resident reached out and shoved Señor Rodriguez's head down onto the table. The man's forehead struck the surface with a sharp smack and was held there.

I was shocked. I wanted to cry out in protest, in anger, in outrage. I wanted to push that burly, insensitive resident up against the wall and pummel him. I wanted to shame him and say it was a joke for him to call himself a doctor. I wanted to come to the rescue of this poor helpless man, to protect him and be his champion and undo the wrong that was being done to him.

Instead, I cringed. What power did I have to wield? I was nobody compared to the surgery resident. His knowledge and experience dwarfed me, his status within the medical hierarchy made my insignificance glaringly clear. My voice felt tiny and weak, and I could not make it work. I stood there, mute and unmoving, in the grip of an awful paralysis.

The danger I cowered from was the probability that my words would be utterly discounted, that I would be brushed aside as a nobody. And since I was working very hard to become a somebody, to have a voice that would be heard in a strictly hierarchical world, this was a threat too great for me to counter. I caved in. The best I could do was to hold Señor Rodriguez's hand apologetically as the resident's needle pierced the side of his chest.

The memory of that shameful incident haunted me for weeks. I had the opportunity to be courageous, to come to the aid of a fellow human being, and I failed miserably. The sour scent of cowardice clung to me, and I felt a stab of shame whenever I thought of Señor Rodriguez. I was thrown off balance and walked about with a limp, albeit an inward one, noticeable only to me. I had discovered a serious defect in myself. A muscle that was supposed to exert itself had failed to hold, and now a disquieting uncertainty tainted my every act.

What was that stab of shame, I wondered, and where did it come from? Was it the product of a thwarted sense of pride? Was it caused by the bruising of an idealistic self-image that accepted nothing less than perfection? Or was it the lament of a still-young moral courage that aspired to do good but knew it was falling short?

Eventually, I decided it was the latter. I saw that the very pain of falling short fueled my development of this kind of courage. It strengthened my will to act. From this perspective, I came to see my failures as an important part of my learning. They taught me how to forgive myself for moments of weakness. I learned to hold my pangs of regret with sympathy, knowing that it was always easier to look back and see how things could have been done better than figuring them out in the moment, as they were rushing headlong toward me. I vowed I would try to be more patient as this part of my humanness learned how to speak its truth.

* * * * * * *

Not all of the dissonance that challenged me in medical school came from my surroundings. I saw that it could come as well from within my own psyche, from internal forces that tugged me in conflicting directions or tied me up in knots. Fortunately, some unforeseen event usually came along that helped me see where I really wanted to go. Once such guidance came to me in quite a surprising way, literally bringing me to my knees with its power.

The incident occurred during my fourth year of medical school, when I was expected to choose an area of specialization for my subsequent years of residency training. By doing a monthlong rotation in each of many different specialties—internal medicine, surgery, obstetrics and gynecology, psychiatry, radiology, and others—I was supposed to learn which of these I felt drawn to and which I did not. This particular incident happened during my surgery rotation, not long after the bullet-removal experience, and it made me decide that my father's chosen path of surgery was not meant to be mine. The decision had nothing to do with feeling squeamish about oozing wounds or upset about the consequences of violence. I probably could have adjusted to seeing such things, given time. No, it was for a different reason entirely—and it clobbered me with its intensity.

It happened in the OR. I was scheduled to assist in cardiothoracic surgery, assigned to a team performing open-heart surgery that day. Though the job did not require any particular skill, it was a vital part of the procedure, and I simmered with excited anticipation.

Preparing for surgery was an elaborate process. First came the ritual of getting dressed in full surgical regalia. In the locker rooms labeled separately for men and for women, we each removed our everyday hospital clothes and donned the freshly laundered green scrub suits, together with the requisite caps and booties. Last of all, we tied our surgical masks in place and marched in single file to the scrub room. There we took turns standing at the big stainless-steel sinks, scrubbing every inch of our hands and forearms with hard-bristled brushes and antiseptic soap for the required number of minutes. Then, holding clean hands carefully up high in the air, each of us backed through the big swinging doors into the operating room where we were met by gowned, gloved, and masked OR nurses who held up long-sleeved, sterile OR gowns into which we slipped our arms. The nurses tied the gowns snuggly behind our backs, and then proceeded with well-practiced skill to assist each of us into sterile surgical gloves, which they stretched up tight over the ends of our sleeves and let snap smartly into place.

The ritual accomplished, we assumed our positions around the operating table.

My job in the proceedings was to hold a retractor, a beautiful stainless-steel instrument shaped like an enormous bent spoon approximately a foot and a half long, elegantly curved and exquisitely smooth. The retractor is designed to serve an important purpose: to pull the ribs and muscles out of the way when a cardiothoracic surgeon needs to go digging about inside a patient's chest cavity. Holding the instrument during such surgery requires using both hands plus a good deal of muscle power, as well as absolute steadiness and endurance. It also puts the holder less than an arm's length from everything taking place.

The view I had from that vantage point was beyond words. Exposed beneath the bright glare of the OR lights was the unceasing activity that keeps each one of us alive. The glistening, softly gurgling activity, proceeding covertly, without any conscious guidance, was more bizarre than anything I had ever imagined. Oblivious of my prying gaze, it continued with singular, all-consuming purpose as I stared.

Two lungs, resembling fleshy sea sponges and composed of millions of tiny air-filled chambers, steadily inflated and deflated like a synchronized pair of bellows in the never-ending cycle of inspiration and expiration, in-breath and out-breath. Nestled between them, the gleaming, ruddy-red four-chambered heart, its valves opening and closing with a resonant lub-dub, lub-dub rhythm, was positively aquiver with life as its muscular walls pumped volumes of blood around and around the vast network of blood vessels whose tendrils spread through every cubic millimeter of this person's body. As the chief surgeon wielded his scalpel and this sight unfolded in front of me, I clung tight to my retractor, following his every move.

Meanwhile, out of the corner of my eye, I could see the face of the man whose body we were cutting into, only inches from my elbow. He appeared to be enjoying a peaceful sleep, unperturbed by our invasion of his inner flesh-and-bone self.

But not so for me. The sight of his apparent relaxation juxtaposed with the sight of the nonstop, wet, and noisome activity going on inside his body was too much. Astonishment threatened to overwhelm me.

With irreconcilable realities clashing in my mind, my sensory system suddenly went haywire. A ringing in my ears grew steadily louder, dimming the sounds of the activities around me. As the noise approached deafening proportions, my blood seemed to drain from my upper body to my feet, my vision lost its bearings, and the room began to spin. I looked down on the surgery proceedings from a greater and greater distance, as if viewing the scene through a very long tunnel. I knew in another moment my consciousness would disconnect from my body altogether.

I managed to squeak out the words: "I think I'm going to faint . . ."

The chief surgeon immediately let out a growl of disgust.

"Grab that retractor, and get her out of here!" he ordered another assistant.

So dizzy I could no longer stand, I yielded my grip on the retractor to someone else and sank shakily to the floor. After taking a few deep breaths that helped my confused nervous system and circulatory system recalibrate, I crawled slowly on all fours toward the distant swinging doors. It was an ignominious exit after such an exalted entrance.

For my next assignment to assist in major surgery, several days later—this one, the opening of an elderly woman's abdomen to remove widespread cancer—I studiously prepared. I would not make a fool of myself a second time. I entered the OR feeling steady and strong, only to find that the same thing happened all over again.

I decided then that surgery was not my path. I needed to stay grounded.

Soon thereafter, the path I was looking for became clear. During my rotation in Pediatrics, I discovered how good I felt taking care of children and helping them heal. The simplicity and straightforwardness of these young patients offered a counterbalance to the medical profession's contradictions and incongruities that bothered me so much, and their vulnerability roused me to courage and determination on their behalf. This was what I was looking for. I decided on Pediatrics as my specialty for residency training. I chose to put my trust in the openheartedness of children. My intuition told me these young patients would safeguard my own heart by calling me back to it again and again, and this proved to be true, even more than I imagined.

*   *   *   *   *   *   *

The process of developing a voice you can count on in the complicated world of medicine intensifies as you enter residency training. Yet finding a strong voice to speak for you does not happen overnight. It takes time and determination and more than one excruciating experience of being caught completely unprepared!

Such a learning experience happened to me early in my first year of pediatric residency, where a typical duty of first-year residents is to present the case of a patient as an introduction to the weekly Grand Rounds lecture. Those lectures were a long-standing tradition of ongoing education for residents and attendings in clinical departments of every academic medical center, and attendance was always high. On this particular week, a distinguished pediatric cardiologist had been invited to give a lecture on congenital heart abnormalities, and since one of my patients on the ward at the time was a child born with a serious heart problem, the chief resident assigned the task that week to me.

Nervous about standing on the auditorium stage for the first time and addressing a large audience of people, most of whom knew far more than I did, I prepared my notes carefully, paying close attention to the established facts of the case: the child's symptoms and clinical condition, the results of his chest x-ray, EKG, echocardiogram, and cardiac catheterization. I could hear my father's voice filled with stern authority, admonishing me with one of his favorite pieces of advice: "Be careful. Do it right. There's no excuse for making a mistake." Yes, I was quite determined to do it right and avoid all mistakes.

When the appointed afternoon arrived, I felt properly prepared. After all, the only thing I had to do was read from my notes for a few short minutes, leaving the complex and challenging issues to be presented and discussed by the lecturer. At my cue, I strode to the podium, notes in hand, and presented the case, trying to sound as sure and knowledgeable as possible as I described the clinical signs and symptoms of my young patient's congenital heart disease, a malformation called idiopathic hypertrophic subaortic stenosis, or IHSS for short. Per house staff custom, I did not bother to pronounce the long and tortuous formal name during my recitation, but simply used the four initials with casual familiarity. I had learned this was the medical culture's subtle way of indicating that you were in the know.

The moment I finished my five-minute presentation, a hand shot up in the audience. I stared. Was it meant for *me*? Without waiting to be called upon, a voice shouted out, "What does IHSS stand for?"

Instantly, a fist clenched my solar plexus hard, and my mind went completely blank.

I paused and took a deep, desperate breath, hoping the correct response would miraculously appear on the tip of my tongue. I could feel my mind frantically rummaging about, looking for the answer, and after a panicky few seconds it presented what it had found.

I heard a voice in my head saying, "Super-cali-fra-gi-listic-ex-piali-docious."

What?!

Well, my poor brain had managed to get the cadence right at least, but instead of the name of a cardiac malformation, it had come up with Mary Poppins's famous magical incantation that she sang with perky aplomb while flying from rooftop to rooftop in early nineteenth-century London using an enchanted umbrella!

I stood frozen to the podium, afraid to open my mouth lest those crazy words come forth. As my brain continued to chant the rhyme insistently inside my head, someone else in the audience mercifully spoke up. Clearly enunciated for everyone in the auditorium to hear came the words my brain had been searching for: "Idio-pathic-hyper-tro-phic-sub-aortic-stenosis." True, it did sound very much like "super-cali-fragi-listic-ex-piali-docious."

"See," my brain said encouragingly, "not so far off!"

Cringing, I murmured my thanks to the unseen voice in the audience and made my way off the stage. Anger and humiliation writhed inside me like snakes. Just when I had had the opportunity to be taken seriously, to appear important, I had blown it. I could not trust myself. Some traitorous part of my being was refusing to play the game, was rebelling against the doctrine of self-importance, threatening to expose me as a fraud, as someone who did not really belong among these sharp-minded people with their positions of knowledge and influence, a poor imposter who had infiltrated their elite ranks and now was shown for what she really was: an ignoramus.

Looking back these many years later, I cannot help but feel compassion for the eager young resident I was then and amusement over how hard my mind tried to help me save face that day. Under terrible pressure, it came up with a brilliant substitute answer. I wish now that I had said it out loud when I had the chance. It would have been fun to see who understood the joke. Unfortunately, in those days I was too worried about looking foolish to allow myself to purposely *be* foolish and have a good laugh at myself. Yet the incident remains with me as a moment when life exposed the inherent silliness of my desire to be taken seriously, leaving me free to continue the search for my real voice.

*   *   *   *   *   *   *

As you progress through your training in medical school and then residency, the pressure to fit in, to measure up, and to perform according to rigorous standards grows ever stronger. The fear of appearing stupid, inadequate, or inept is hard to avoid. The culture can be a harsh one, and your idea of who you are as a person is frequently in upheaval. Games of one-upmanship play out subtly and not so subtly all around you, challenging you to prove that you know enough and are good enough.

Making rounds is a particularly harrowing experience. You can be thrown a question at any moment by the chief resident and, with all eyes turned on you, you must come up with an answer or admit to ignorance, which is not a highly valued commodity. On the other hand, if you are clever, there is a third alternative, and that is to fake it.

In fact, faking it is a tactic that many try, at one time or another, in order to survive. Fortunately, it is such a distasteful experience, not many adopt it as a regular practice.

I made a clumsy attempt to use this tactic during my first year of residency training, and it did not go well. I was caring for a young patient with idiopathic thrombocytopenia, a condition involving a particular type of very low blood count, and it was my job to draw the little girl's blood early every morning to monitor her progress.

As our team made rounds one morning and stood discussing her case in the hall before entering her room, the senior resident turned to me and asked me what her blood count was that day. My stomach lurched as I realized that, in the press of preparing for rounds, I had forgotten to check the results of her blood that I had drawn a couple of hours earlier. Before I could confess that I had neglected to perform this task, however, out of my mouth came my voice saying nonchalantly, "Oh, it's about the same as yesterday." When the resident looked at me quizzically and asked, "Yes, but how much is it exactly," I knew I was trapped. There was no way now of confessing my forgetfulness. The same voice desperately blurted out a number that was close to what I remembered yesterday's had been, and the senior resident, apparently satisfied, led us into the room to see the patient.

After we finished making rounds, the senior resident, someone I idolized for his seemingly infallible wisdom and experience, pulled me aside. Looking me squarely in the eye, he said that he had checked the patient's count himself, and it was not what I had said. Without waiting for an excuse—he knew full well there was none—he simply said he never wanted me to do such a thing again. This was a tiny mistake, he added, as I quavered beneath his gaze, but people who allowed themselves tiny mistakes often drifted into making larger ones.

I knew what he was saying was true, and I was grateful for his directness. This was something I did not want to repeat. The embarrassment of making a mistake felt far better than the cowardice of trying to cover one up.

It is a shame that medical education does not think to teach young doctors-in-training to avoid this type of human mistake, or learn from it if they happen to make it, just as they learn from their mistakes in drawing blood or doing spinal taps or other technical procedures that require building skill through practice. I never foresaw falling into a mistake like this—a mistake involving honesty and trustworthiness—never imagined how desperate one could get under the pressure to measure up to others' expectations. I feel fortunate to have made that mistake early on and been caught red-handed. It kept me from ever wanting to do it again. Sadly, for some people, faking it can become such a well-established pattern that they would no longer know they are doing it.

In the world of medicine, where you are entrusted with other people's well-being, this kind of unclarity, this type of lapse in personal integrity, is very problematic. You need to have a clear, discerning eye in order to tread your way through the many gray areas where the difference between what you know for fact and what you are making an educated guess about is vague. Every day you have to make difficult decisions about how best to be of help and answer complicated questions about your patients' health concerns: "Doctor, how likely is it that my child's lead poisoning will result in brain damage, and how effective is chelation therapy for the treatment of this problem?" "Doctor, what are the chances that my child's next asthma attack could be life-threatening, and what exactly are the risks of the high-dose steroid treatment you are recommending?" "Doctor, how dangerous is this chemotherapy medication that you're giving to my child?"

Every day you must ask yourself how certain you really are of what you are saying and doing, and this constantly tests your honesty with yourself. It can be instructive, too, when you encounter other people who are incapable of being honest with themselves. One resident in particular on our pediatric service had that problem. A pompous, argumentative sort of person, he acted certain about everything he said, even when he was completely wrong.

One night when he was on call alone, he started an IV drip on a child who was having seizures, using a medication that none of us had ever heard could be used in that manner. When the senior resident questioned him about it during rounds the next morning, he insisted he had read a medical article describing this as an appropriate protocol. He said he would prove it to us and bring in the article. He never did, and the chairman of our department fired him, making it clear to us all that such inability to distinguish fact from fiction in one's own mind should have no place in the world of medicine—nor should it in any other world.

*   *   *   *   *   *   *

One particularly complex issue in medical practice is pain, and there are many incongruities in the way that doctors deal with it. Some of my earliest lessons about pain came from my father, who was trained in the old school of pain management called pain denial. If one of us kids in the family happened to fall and get a scrape or a bruise, my father would say, "Oh, stop crying. A little pain never hurt anyone." With a more serious injury, such as a broken bone, he would say, "Don't make such a fuss about the pain. It won't kill you."

I can remember my father saying words like those to me as he stitched up a two-inch laceration in my foot when I was nine. I had stepped on a piece of glass while wading in a stream. My father immediately took me to his office where he flushed the wound with antiseptic solution, swept his finger through it to make sure no glass remained, and then put seven stitches in my foot without using any anesthetic. He said the gash was too little to bother numbing it, and numbing it would only require sticking me with additional needles. Better just to sew it up and get it over with. So I bit my lip every time the sharp, shiny tip of his surgical needle pierced my skin and each time his fingers drew the surgical thread tight and tied it in a knot, doing my best to master my pain and measure up to his expectations.

Later, when I started caring for patients of my own, I began to see that dealing with pain was not a simple matter. I had thought I would be rescuing people from pain, and yet far too often I found myself being the cause of it, although never with the attitude my father had. During my early years in pediatrics, the situation was pretty terrible, for patients and physicians alike.

Back then children were routinely subjected to what are called "invasive" procedures without regard for pain. Potent pain medications were considered too dangerous for children, and eliciting the cooperation of such young patients impractical. Thus, blood draws, IV insertions, spinal taps, and even bone marrow biopsies were simply done as rapidly as possible, without paying any attention to the pain they caused. Parents were not allowed to be present. We took their children behind the closed doors of the Procedure Room where their screams could not be heard and used physical force to subdue them. They would struggle and fight with all their might, trying their best to escape from us, to no avail. We pinned them down and tied them up and closed our ears to the sounds they made as we stabbed our sharp needles into the tender flesh of their arms and feet and scalps and spines.

Official doctrine claimed that the nervous system of infants and even of older children was too immature to fully register the pain these actions caused. It insisted that our patients' seemingly negative reaction to these procedures was largely reflex activity, and that they had little capacity for memory and would soon forget the temporary discomfort. Yet every time I stabbed, my hands could not help but feel how hard the young body I was holding strained to break free from my iron grip, nor could my ears help but hear the shrill cries being uttered, or my eyes avoid seeing the little face screwed up in an expression of intense distress. My entire nervous system shuddered in sympathy, and my own body yelled the truth at me: *This is pain, and you are causing it, and the official doctrine is a bunch of baloney!* Yet if any of us felt a momentary urge to protest or run away, crying, "No, no! I never imagined it would be like this," we learned instead to grit our teeth and just proceed, pretending not to notice afterward how sweaty and shaken we were. It was awful.

I remember one day during my year as chief resident when I was called to the hospital suite of one of our prominent pediatric oncologists, Dr. Rosenberg. He had a private patient with leukemia named Thelma in his exam room who needed a bone marrow aspiration to determine how she was responding to chemotherapy. Her father, an educated man who knew her case intimately and understood what was at stake, was willing to hold her down for the procedure, but since she was a very husky eleven-year-old, the two men had decided that extra help would be needed.

While Dr. Rosenberg stood with his back turned to us and prepared the large-bore needle he would use to puncture the bone in Thelma's hip and suction out some of her marrow, Thelma lay quietly on the examination table. She had not been told what was in store for her. Her father was leaning close to her shoulders with a falsely reassuring air, and I was positioned at her feet, both of us ready to immobilize her on the table when Dr. Rosenberg gave the signal. Only when he began to wipe her skin with antiseptic did she realize what he intended to do.

Suddenly Thelma's eyes went wide, and she sucked in her breath—but Dr. Rosenberg was ready. He gave the signal, and we threw our bodies on top of hers with our full weight just as she let out the bellow of an angry bull. In a flash Dr. Rosenberg thrust his needle down through her flesh and into her bone, pushing hard on it with both hands and grinding it through to her marrow, while her father and I, puffing and grimacing, kept her pinned to the table.

As Thelma continued to strain and roar, Dr. Rosenberg finished the job and was just pulling the needle out, when one of Thelma's legs wrenched itself free from my grip. Her foot aimed straight for Dr. Rosenberg's face and struck him squarely in the nose, sending his glasses flying. A second later she pulled an arm free and began pummeling her father with her fist. I held on to her remaining leg with all my might to keep her from falling off the table in her fury, but secretly I was glad for her. I thought Thelma had every right to bellow and was giving us what we darn well deserved!

I often wondered what kind of scars we were leaving in the psyches of these infants and children from our belligerent attempts to help them and our narrow-minded insistence that we knew what was good for them. Where did they store those memories of torture and betrayal? Did a hellish experience of being held down by adults who were intentionally hurting them create a reservoir of fear and mistrust somewhere deep inside them that they carried into their later life? Or were they protected somehow from remembering such awfulness by their innocence? Was there some special dispensation that took their blamelessness into account and spared them from being scarred? I fervently hoped so.

As for us, the doctors who did these abominable things, we did not go unscathed either. You bear scars within yourself from the hurt you do to others. These ghoulish deeds lay upon my conscience like a heavy blanket of shame and remorse. No matter how I rationalized them—tried to reason that the things I did were necessary and important and helpful—still they were soul-denying acts, and I continued to hold myself accountable.

Years later, after reaching the rank of attending physician, I found a way to set things right. I made it my mission to change the way pain was addressed. I studied and learned and became an expert in the newly emerging field of pediatric pain treatment. I gave lectures, established committees, and instituted new protocols and practices aimed at preventing any more of the kind of suffering my colleagues and I had blindly caused. Working with a cadre of dedicated nurses, I introduced more effective pain medications, patient-controlled pain treatment methods, and new relaxation modalities, like guided imagery and hypnotherapy. I saw to it that my department made a firm commitment to minimizing children's pain in every way possible.

Soon thereafter, the issue of pain began to come to the fore in many arenas in my hospital, affecting adults as well as children. Emergency medicine doctors, internists, physical therapists, psychiatrists, social workers, and even surgeons stepped forward to join in. Clearly, the discontent I had been feeling was felt by many. So-called pain management was an issue bursting at the seams with the burden of old mistakes and ignorance. The time was ripe for a transformation around this issue.

Within a few years, my hospital proudly became the first in the country to establish a flagship Department of Pain Medicine and Palliative Care. I eventually joined that department and finished my hospital career there, happy to be among people who shared my concern about these matters. My troubled soul was healing.

The wonder of it all is how far the management of pain has come since then. A younger colleague of mine who works as a pediatric oncologist in a major children's hospital says it is hard for her to imagine that things were once as bad as I claim they were. With the newer medications available now and with precise methods of measuring and administering them, she is able to put her patients gently to sleep for the exact amount of time she needs in order to perform their spinal taps and bone marrow biopsies, leaving them with no memory of feeling pain whatsoever. In my colleague's hospital, the once ominous Pediatric Procedure Room is now called the Sleepy Room, and there children wake up feeling happy and refreshed after their invasive procedures, declaring, "Doctor, I had a nice sleep!" My friend says her patients cheerfully wave good-bye to her as they leave her clinic and look forward to coming back for their next visit to the Sleepy Room. As for me, I breathe a deep sigh of relief.

* * * * * * *

When I was young and still believed my father to be all-powerful, I thought his work was to go out every day, and often in the night as well, to save people's lives. My certainty about this was reinforced by the fact that no one in my family was allowed to stay on the phone for longer than five minutes in case someone in urgent need of his help might be trying to call. One day, when I was about twelve or so and feeling a swell of pride over the critical role my father obviously played, I approached him and asked, "Dad, how many people's lives have you saved?"

I expected him to say a number that would dazzle my young mind with its enormity. Instead, he smiled and answered, to my puzzlement, "None, darling." Then, possibly sensing my disappointment, he went on to explain.

"Sweetheart, I don't think of what I do as saving people's lives or not saving them. I just do the best I can to help them. Whatever happens beyond that is out of my hands. If it were up to me to save them, I would get upset every time someone died, and that would make it very hard for me to continue doing my work."

He patted my head reassuringly, adding, "No, honey, all I can do is do what I can."

I remembered his words and pondered them, but I did not really accept them. I preferred to think that saving someone's life was both possible and the right thing to do. Moreover, I decided that this would be my goal in life, just as I secretly still believed it was my father's frequent accomplishment. Only years later did I begin to see that saving lives was not so simple or straightforward as I had imagined, but a complicated matter.

The neonatal ICU made this complexity exceedingly clear. There I worked hard to hone my resuscitation skills and became adept at rushing into tense situations, determined to use every means at my disposal to revive a flickering flame of life. But the art of resuscitation was a double-edged sword, and it could cut either way. It could rescue life or it could add to the harm, and sometimes it was hard to foresee which it would be until it was too late.

Late one night, during my first year of residency training, an urgent call came from the delivery suite. A woman with a full-term pregnancy was in trouble. Her labor was going badly, and the baby's heart rate had become seriously erratic. With heart pounding, I raced at the heels of the senior resident through the hospital's nearly deserted corridors, arriving in an adrenaline rush minutes later at the brightly lit delivery suite. The two of us quickly prepared our resuscitation equipment—IV setup, intubation instruments, oxygen supply, syringes with carefully calculated amounts of life-sustaining drugs—and waited for the imminent delivery.

Standing at the ready, we watched as the baby emerged. The cause of the emergency was evident instantly: the umbilical cord had wrapped tightly not once but twice around the baby's neck, cutting off his oxygen. He was blue and limp.

Flying into action, we performed our resuscitation procedures flawlessly, suctioning and intubating the child and manually pumping oxygen into his little lungs, while injecting him with drugs to stimulate his heart and circulation. Within minutes we had him stabilized and tucked into a warm incubator, which we rushed through the corridors to the NICU.

For the rest of the night, we tended to that little boy, checking his chest x-ray to see that his lungs were being aerated well, taking blood tests to monitor the amount of oxygen in his circulation and his level of electrolytes and balance of acidity and alkalinity, making adjustments in the concentration of his intravenous fluids. Lying on his back under the warming lights, now receiving adequate oxygen, he looked rosy-cheeked and healthy. His young face was beautiful, almost angelic, and peacefulness pervaded the air around him.

Watching over him as he slept that night filled me with a feeling of pride in my profession. We had done something good. We had succeeded in saving a precious life and spared two parents the pain of losing their newborn child.

As the first light of dawn began to filter through the windows of the NICU, the boy's tiny hands began to make little movements. A short time later, his feet did the same. I was elated.

Oh good news, I thought, *he's beginning to wake up! He's going to recover!*

Yet as the minutes went by and I watched further, my elation ebbed away. Soon, it was replaced by a growing sense of dread. For the little boy's eyes failed to open, and his movements intensified into twitches and tremors of obvious abnormality.

The truth was becoming clear. What I had been seeing all night was not the benign quietness of exhausted sleep, it was the unconsciousness of a traumatized brain. Nor were the movements now occurring the stirrings of a healthy newborn flexing and stretching and waking into a normal life. These movements were seizures, evidence of severe neurological damage caused by extended oxygen deprivation.

Sorrow and guilt rained down on me then. My actions, taken with the intention of doing good, had achieved the opposite. They brought an irreparably damaged human being who was about to die back to life. I had stumbled into unforeseen territory, unwittingly extending suffering rather than alleviating it, forcing a severely limited existence upon a newborn child and a lifetime burden upon the parents of that child.

With an aching heart, I tried to understand how I had ended up here. Could I have prevented this if I had done something different, if I had known more? I had wanted to do the right thing, but I no longer knew what the right thing was. My highest goal, to save human lives, had twisted into a Gordian knot.

The complexity of medical care hit me hard that night. Many of the skills I was so eagerly learning suddenly seemed tainted with ignorance about how to use them rightly. When Hippocrates wrote his famous oath admonishing generations of physicians with the instruction, *Do no harm*, he could never have imagined the things that doctors of the modern age would do in places like the NICU: blood-exchange transfusions, artificial intravenous feeding, intubation and mechanical respiration, major surgical procedures at a few weeks of life, including correction of life-threatening heart defects, removal of dying sections of intestine, and repair of serious inborn abnormalities. Some of my little patients lay in coma or drug-induced paralysis as they endured the aggressive interventions we performed on their behalf.

For many, surviving would not be the end of their struggle. I saw this in the Neonatology Clinic where we provided follow-up care for infants sent home from the NICU. Many retained deep scars from the battles they had once fought, visible in their curtailed physical and cognitive development. Some had come away with serious disabilities: cerebral palsy, chronic breathing problems, seizures, blindness. Some needed the assistance of a wheelchair and were dependent on tanks that delivered oxygen to their damaged lungs or on gastrostomy tubes permanently implanted in their stomachs to deliver adequate nutrition. Many required specialized nursing care, physical therapy, alternative education, and more. The cost to their parents was often huge: their time, finances, stamina, and faith could all be stretched thin.

Opposing points of view plagued me. Had we gone overboard with our efforts to be of help, laying an unreasonable burden on unsuspecting children and their parents? Or was human life so precious that any burden was bearable? Did such "unfair" burdens actually summon forth strengths that people would otherwise never know they had, offsetting their suffering by deepening their capacity for caring and for gratitude? Yet even if this was true, was there a line beyond which the amount of suffering was too much, and if so, how could such a line be discerned?

I wrestled with these questions for a long time, long enough to finally see that wrestling was futile. There simply were no clear-cut answers. When I admitted that, I finally understood: ignorance was an inevitable boundary within which, as a doctor, I would always have to live. I might be able to stretch that boundary as I learned more over time, but I would never live without any boundary at all.

With that realization, the wisdom in my father's approach finally made sense. You do the best you can to be of help and accept that the rest is not up to you. I was ready to live with this.

Yet there is another piece I would add to my father's good advice: the recognition that we human beings deserve compassion in this matter. Ignorance can be a heavy burden, a form of suffering in its own right. Not knowing what the outcome of your well-intentioned actions will be is no easy thing. It is tormenting to wonder whether what you do will prove to have been wanted and needed, or the exact opposite.

Maybe the hidden gift of our ignorance, if there is one at all, is to teach us to be more forgiving of ourselves. Being imperfect seems to be an unavoidable part of being human, no matter how much we strive to make it otherwise. Besides, if we were to achieve perfection, we might become insufferable to ourselves. Instead, we have the opportunity to learn humility, surely a gentler, more dimensioned quality than mere perfection.

FIVE

Loving &
Being Loved

I BELIEVE THAT LOVE lies all around us in this world, hiding in places we easily overlook, waiting for the right moment to offer us its lessons about what it means to be human. If you work in a hospital, you see these lessons unfolding every day. Some can be intense and even harrowing; others are so subtle they may nearly escape being noticed.

During my residency training, a two-year-old AIDS patient on our ward showed me that love can speak with the most unlikely of voices. This was in the late 1970's, and the AIDS epidemic was slamming my beloved New York City with devastating force. Little was yet known about this new virus that attacked the human immune system so viciously, only that pitifully little could be done to help those unfortunate enough to be infected with it. Unfortunately, the ones who were proving to be most vulnerable to the virus tended to be those who lived in the inner city neighborhoods where life was hard enough already, burdened as it was with poor housing conditions, inadequate education, drug abuse, violence, broken family bonds, and lack of opportunity. These were the neighborhoods my hospital served and where the children I was caring for were growing up.

123

We admitted a great number of children who were sick with AIDS to my hospital back in those days, and sadly we lost many of them. I remember one two-year-old boy in particular. He touched me deeply. As was typical, he had acquired the virus from his infected mother when he was born, and despite our best efforts to help him, he was slowly slipping away from us. He lay quietly in his crib, hollow-eyed and emaciated, never smiling or even crying. He simply did not have the energy.

The little boy's mother had brought him to our emergency room one night, burning up with fever. The chest x-ray we took showed he had pneumonia, and so we promptly admitted him to the pediatric ward. His mother lingered at his side for a time, but then departed and never returned. Eventually we learned she had been admitted to another hospital shortly after leaving ours and had died there from complications of her own AIDS. The one thing she had left her son was his name. She had called him Angel.

Angel had been on our pediatric ward for three months. There was no other place that wanted him, and frankly we were happy to keep him with us. At least we knew he would be fed and kept clean and sheltered and would occasionally be held in another human being's arms when one of the staff was able to spare a moment or two. We knew he had little time left.

One night, when I was on call and kept busy on the ward into the wee hours of the night, I glimpsed a side of Angel's story I had not been aware of before. The lights had all been turned down and most of the children put to sleep in their beds, and I was going about my intern's work — reviewing orders, checking on patients' vital signs, and peeking in on the sickest ones — when something caught my ear. A faint lyrical sound was whispering down one of the dimly lit hallways. Listening closely, I detected the thin notes of a melody carried by a human voice.

I was tired and still had chores to do, but the wistful sound called to me, and so I followed it, curious to learn what its source was. It led me to Angel's room. Yet what I saw through the doorway as I approached made me pause and remain in the quiet shadows of the hallway rather than enter. For it was clear that more was taking place in Angel's room than the sad wasting of an unfulfilled life. Something more intimate was happening, something that needed not to be disturbed.

With Angel was his father. I had never seen the man before, but during discussions on our daily morning rounds, I had heard that he often came in the wee hours of the night to visit his son. He was a tough-looking person, unshaven and stamped with the harsh signs of inner city life and his own battle with the AIDS he had acquired during years of drug addiction. I wondered what factors in his life prevented him from visiting in the light of day as other parents did. Perhaps he was fully occupied with trying to survive, I thought, or maybe he just preferred the lonely hours of the night, when he was less likely to encounter the accusing stares of strangers' eyes.

The man was sitting in a chair, holding Angel on his lap and feeding him infant formula with a dropper. As I watched, he waited carefully for his son's lips to accept each drop before offering him another, all the while gazing into his child's eyes and softly crooning a melody—a hauntingly soothing sound, the notes filled with reassurance and encouragement. Angel's eyes remained fastened in turn on his father's face, as if he were drinking in life-giving nourishment from the look that he saw there.

The two of them were in such a rapt communion that I remained bound in unmoving silence outside their door. It seemed that I had been summoned not to enter, but to stand as an observer of this exquisite scene, witness to an act of meaning that lay beyond my mind's measuring.

What I had been called to witness, my heart said, was the love that was shining brightly in that little room. Nothing more than that, and nothing less. In the light of that love, the tragedy of Angel's pitiful life—of both their lives—was being lifted up and set aside. I could feel the truth of that as surely as anything my medical books had ever taught me.

The shadows in the hallway seemed to whisper, *Do you see? This is what love is. It is a force more powerful than even life-destroying disease. It can tenderly embrace whatever the world has abandoned as hopeless and transform it into something to be cherished.* As I dropped my eyes and turned to go back to work, I felt deeply grateful for having seen this side of Angel's story. And I could not help but wonder: how many of us will be sung to with that much love as we lie in our own last days of life?

* * * * * * *

My experience as a pediatrician showed me that most parents love their children. They naturally revel in their children's growth and development, captivated by every step of each offspring's journey from infancy to adulthood. So taken are most parents by witnessing how every threshold is crossed and each new territory gained that they rarely consider the possibility of it all being taken away. They are never ever prepared when something horrific happens to one of their children. Yet miraculously, most parents find courage they never dreamed they had when they face the worst kind of experience imaginable: the possibility of losing their child. Circumstances like this showed me parental love coming forward to fight with its very fiercest strength.

Annie was the youngest child of parents who had produced four boys in rapid succession before she was conceived. Frazer and Sharon had not planned on having a fifth child, but as they liked to say, Annie had had a mind of her own about that, and not surprisingly, they welcomed the arrival of their baby girl with joy. It did not take long for all six of them to agree: Annie was the frosting on their cake.

Like her brothers, Annie was towheaded, athletic, and smart, and she quickly set a goal for herself to be as good at everything as her older siblings were. Thus it came as no surprise that her greatest passion at thirteen was baseball: all four of her brothers had excelled at the game. She put posters of her favorite players on the walls of her bedroom, and she played shortstop and substitute pitcher on a local Little League team. Her team had a good record during the summer season, and her parents attended every game, witnessing her hit several home runs and cheering madly as she ran across home plate, a smile on her freckled face as bright as the sun. Her mother and father were her biggest fans.

But when summer began to give way to fall, Annie's world turned upside down. It started with intermittent headaches, which no one thought much about until she also began complaining of feeling dizzy and seeing double. Her concerned pediatrician quickly referred the family to a neurologist, whose examination found that Annie had a lopsided gait and weakness of the muscles on one side of her face.

An MRI was immediately performed, revealing a large malignant tumor growing in the middle of her brain. She was booked for surgery the next week. Annie and her parents' journey on a speeding locomotive had begun.

Events unfolded at a terrifying pace. The day before her surgery, Annie developed an excruciating headache. Within an hour she was comatose. Her tumor was bleeding into her brain. She underwent emergency surgery to remove as much of the tumor and escaped blood as possible. The trauma to her brain was so significant that she was kept heavily sedated and connected to a respirator via a tracheostomy tube for an entire month. Nutrition was administered to her body through a gastrostomy tube inserted in her stomach wall. One or the other of her parents was always at her side.

The speeding locomotive that had taken Annie and her parents captive did not pause for a moment. After regaining consciousness and being weaned from the respirator, Annie was transferred to my hospital for rehabilitation therapy and a monthlong course of radiation to her brain. As the attending pediatrician on her case, I coordinated her care during those long, grueling days. After four tough weeks, she was improved, but far from fully healed. The day she departed for home in a wheelchair, she still had paralysis of her left arm and leg, diminished strength on her entire right side, deafness in her right ear, difficulty speaking, and inability to coordinate her eyes. Frazer and Sharon were grateful she was alive at all.

Once home, Annie began a rigorous program of daily outpatient physical therapy, speech therapy, and home tutoring, and for a while she seemed to be regaining lost ground. But six weeks after her hospital discharge, a follow-up MRI showed the tumor was growing back. Her oncologist suggested trying a new chemotherapy drug that was just being tested for its effectiveness with Annie's type of brain tumor. Frazer and Sharon said yes. Yet after another six weeks, Annie's tumor had failed to respond and instead had grown dramatically. She was having increased trouble speaking and now difficulty breathing as well. With the train they were on threatening to lurch out of control, Frazer and Sharon said yes to trying a second experimental drug, and Annie returned to my hospital.

During this harrowing, breakneck ride, one thing stayed surprisingly unshaken, and that was Annie's outlook on it all. Despite one setback after another, the slender, towheaded girl maintained an amazing equanimity. In spite of growing physical limitations, she remained friendly with her doctors, cooperative with her treatments, and patient with her parents. With each turn of events, she would listen carefully, and then wait to see what her father and mother thought was right to do. She was willing to undergo any kind of treatment they suggested. She could tell they were desperate for her to live, and she did not want to disappoint them. She loved them too much.

Unfortunately, the end of their fearsome journey was approaching fast. The second drug had no effect, nor did a third, and Annie's oncologist was running out of options.

It was extremely difficult for me, as well as for the other members of our pediatric team who cared for Annie day after day, to watch her endure one unpromising treatment after another, for each one took a heavy toll on her. By now she was utterly exhausted, and her connection to life was growing thin. When I looked at her, I saw someone who was dying, someone whose disease had her fully in its grip and was pulling her inexorably toward death.

Yet Frazer and Sharon never wavered in their hope of turning the tide of illness that was steadily stealing their daughter away from them. Sometimes I wondered if they were being selfish in asking her to undergo each additional agonizing attempt to buy time. But when I returned home at night and took my own two children into my arms for one last hug before tucking them into bed, I knew beyond a shred of doubt that Frazer and Sharon were doing what they had to do. They had to fight with every drop of strength they could muster to hold on to their beloved girl.

This was the magnitude of their love for Annie: it refused to let go. If and when she would die, Fraser and Sharon could only live with themselves if they had fought to the bitter end. They would not admit defeat until death overcame every one of their uncompromising efforts and tore her from their straining arms.

Annie, in turn, continued to make an effort for her parents' sake. Although a certain light had faded from her eyes, as if she herself no longer saw hope of her life being saved, she never wavered for a moment in trying her valiant best to protect her parents' feelings. She seemed to sense the anguish that would eventually overtake them and sought to hold it at bay by letting them have their way.

Thus the love between these two parents and their child remained one seamless whole, supporting them as they continued to travel the long, terrible distance together. With respectful silence and my own measure of sorrow, I waited for the end to come, the final battle between Annie's parents and her death.

I was not surprised when Frazer and Sharon decided to take Annie out of the hospital. We clearly had no further help to offer her. When I spoke with Sharon by phone several days later to see how things were going, she said they had plans to drive Annie to New Jersey to visit a sixteen-year-old boy who had been in a coma since the age of three. They had heard that some people who visited him experienced miraculous healings. She added resolutely that every additional day with Annie was worth the struggle.

Sadly, the next news I heard was that Frazer and Sharon's final hope of saving their daughter—the hope that a miracle would somehow happen—had been dashed. Annie's tumor bled into her brain during the trip, and she died before making it back home. Their journey had come to a heart-wrenching end.

Some months after Annie's passing, I paid a visit to Frazer and Sharon at their home in a small town outside the city. They welcomed me generously and led me into their living room where the mantle over the fireplace held a row of framed family pictures, remembrances from a time when the seven members of their little clan were whole and well and unsuspecting of the troubles life was to bring. The three of us sat and talked about everyday things: how their other children were doing at school and at sports, and about Sharon's plans to find a job to keep her busy. We touched only lightly on Annie's death. When it came time to leave, the three of us lingered on their front porch, watching dry leaves drift to the ground in the waning sunlight of autumn. I was grateful to turn the last page of a long story with them in this way.

As I drove back to the city, I reflected on my visit with these two parents. Frazer and Sharon had sustained a wound that would never heal completely. They had acknowledged this, with sadness in their eyes. Yet at the same time, they appeared emptied out and simplified, with a calm about them like that left in a country landscape after the last rumbles of thunder from a raging storm die away. A deep solemnity had been carved out in them, a deeper one than most people would know how to live with.

$$* \quad * \quad * \quad * \quad * \quad * \quad *$$

The fear that arises when illness strikes a child can overwhelm the strongest parent's heart. Witnessing such vulnerability always touched me deeply. When I saw love clinging desperately to hope, the parental love in my own heart sometimes rose up and drew me into the drama to lend strength and support. This often occurred most frequently in the pediatric emergency room.

The worst and scariest things that bring people to the ER have a way of happening in the middle of the night, though why that is, I am not sure. Perhaps because night is the time when people let down their guard, or maybe because certain dangers wait until the darkness comes before they spring upon their intended prey. Or maybe bad things just seem worse when people are exhausted. At any rate, I was working in the pediatric ER, about to finish my on-call duty a few minutes before midnight, when a typical scenario began to unfold: the triage nurse rushed into the pediatric suite with a frantic young couple bearing their very sick two-year-old daughter in their arms.

As the nurse and I rapidly unwrapped the child to assess her condition, the terrified parents tumbled out their story. It was short and simple. In the morning their little girl had seemed fine, behaving like her sweet, stubborn, terrible-two's self, playing to her heart's content. But in the afternoon things began to change, and what seemed innocuous enough at first—only a little fever and some mild unhappiness—had, as day turned to night, gathered momentum and become a raging forest fire. Her little body was burning up, and a fist seemed to be tightening its grip around her throat. Now every breath she took required a desperate effort.

131

Only minutes were needed to paint the picture of epiglottitis, a life-threatening bacterial infection that targets young children in particular. It typically leaps upon them out of the blue, boiling through their bloodstream and zeroing in on the epiglottis, the little flap of soft tissue in the back of the throat that flops over our windpipe when we swallow, thereby keeping us from choking on our food or drink. Once infection gets a foothold there, it can cause that handy little flap to swell like an angry red balloon and begin to obstruct the passage of air to the lungs. In an alarmingly short time the deranged flap can block the flow of air completely and suffocate a sick child to death.

I sounded the alarm for the ENT team—the intrepid ear-nose-and-throat surgeons—and they came, white coats flapping as they ran, to scoop the child up, strap her to a stretcher and whisk her away, down the long winding hallway toward the operating suite. I hurried alongside her distraught parents in the surgeons' wake, re-explaining what the rushing surgeons had told them, in rapid-fire technical terms, that they proposed to do. They had to intubate the child as quickly as possible to get lifesaving air back into her lungs. But sliding the breathing tube past that angry red balloon was a tricky and dangerous proposition. It required both skill and the best conditions possible. They would therefore have to sedate her and put all support systems in place and the necessary resuscitation equipment at the ready, in case, as the surgeons put it, things went sour.

If their attempts at intubation failed, the surgeons' only other option was to perform a tracheotomy. They would cut a hole in the front of the child's neck and insert a breathing tube directly into her windpipe in order to bypass the obstruction to her breathing. This was an emergency procedure that would have to be done quickly, before time ran out. The surgeons were hopeful, and they were skilled, but they made it clear: they could give no promises as to their ultimate success.

In no time at all, our rushing entourage reached the set of swinging doors through which only the surgeons were allowed to go, together with their stretcher bearing its tiny figure. The girl's parents and I came to a halt before the sign that sternly declared, "SURGERY—AUTHORIZED PERSONNEL ONLY."

Still breathing hard in the sudden silence, the parents stared after their vanished daughter. They knew their child's life was in danger. She was fighting a critical battle: would she return to them or not? Right then, the outcome was unknown. The scales could tip toward healing, or they could tip the other way, cutting her life short, a young bud snipped from the bush when just beginning to blossom. Only waiting would bring the answer.

My presence was no longer needed. Having delivered the child into the hands of the ENT surgeons, my job was done. They would manage her care from this point on. There was every reason for me to go, including the fact that I had to be back on duty at 8:00 a.m. Yet something held me there. As I looked at those parents—saw them engulfed in an ocean of uncertainty, clinging to each other in order not to drown in its immensity—there was no question about whether I should go or not. I simply could not.

So we stayed there together, the three of us: two frightened parents huddled close beside each other, and a stranger choosing to keep them company. We sat on two modest couches and took turns pacing about, glancing every now and again toward the motionless swinging doors. To break the heavy weight of silence, we talked in hushed voices. They spoke about their lives with an earnestness that was almost heartbreaking: how they had each moved from Puerto Rico with their families when they were teenagers to the same New York City neighborhood and had been attracted to each other from the first time they met; how he was working at two jobs in construction and she was doing housecleaning to supplement their income, while studying to become a nurses' aide during the hours their daughter was in day care.

They asked quietly about my family in return: what my husband did for work and what our plans were for bringing children into the world, curious about the fact that we had not yet done that. Life seemed simple for them. Having a family and providing for that family was of foremost importance. Their clarity about this humbled me.

My own contribution to the mood of our little circle was not confident reassurance, as much as I might have liked it to be. I had no firm foreknowledge of the outcome to offer this father and mother, and I did not feel right about propping them up with unfounded expectations that might in the end prove to be no gift at all. By now I knew that even doctors sometimes have to stand empty-handed before an uncertain future. The most important contribution I could make was to hope fervently that this little family would not have to suffer pain and heartbreak, to wish as hard as I could that healing would prevail and that their love would remain intact. My contribution, simply human, and powerful in its own way, was to care.

The truth was, I had seen children die—children whose beauty would have blessed the world, whom even the angels might have wept to see go—and I knew that such a thing was all too possible. I had learned that even the breaking of their parents' hearts was not enough to hold children here if their time to leave had come. So because I knew two hearts might well break that night, I stayed. And for several long hours, three people held vigil together in a small waiting room buried in the bowels of a mammoth hospital, holding on to one delicate thread of life, praying it would hold.

That long night finally ended as dawn was breaking. One of the ENT surgeons came bearing good news: the couple's little girl was safe and sound. They could come see her for themselves, lying with a tracheostomy tube neatly inserted in her neck, breathing comfortably at last.

The two parents' tears flowed unabashedly as the surgeon escorted them to the recovery room. There they rushed to their daughter's bed and clasped her small hands in theirs, simultaneously heaping thanks on the surgeons who were assuring them she would be well again. They explained it would be a day or two before she could be extubated, and she would have to remain in the hospital at least a week while potent intravenous antibiotics cleared the infection from her body, but she would be fine. The joy of the little girl's parents was beyond all bounds, and joy overflowed in me as well, just in witnessing theirs.

* * * * * * *

One of the calamities that can befall us human beings in the sometimes tricky business of producing our offspring is giving birth to a child with congenital defects. Such defects are created when nature "goes wrong"—that is, when an error occurs during replication of the fetal chromosomes, those marvelous molecular ribbons that contain the genetic blueprint for the developing infant's body. Depending on the degree of error, a child with chromosomal abnormalities may have minor anatomical differences from normal children or extensive abnormalities that are incompatible with life. When parents encounter the more severe abnormalities in their offspring, their capacity to love may be challenged in complex and unforeseen ways.

Take the trisomy 13 or 16 or 18 conditions, for example, where nature erroneously makes an extra copy of an entire chromosome. These babies have abnormalities in their heads, faces, and limbs, and in their internal organs as well, accompanied by moderate to extreme mental incapacity. Their life span is almost always very short, for their miscontructed bodies do not have the capacity to sustain life as other bodies do.

For parents, the birth of a baby such as this was alarming in times past, before we discovered the realm of molecular genetics and came to understand what can happen when nature accidentally alters our finely tuned genetic code. People in the prescientific era imagined all sorts of unpleasant reasons why congenital defects occurred. Many parents rejected strange-appearing babies, being stricken with shame at having brought them into the world or believing that some dark, ill-intentioned force was at work in their creation. Yet even now, with our greater clarity of scientific understanding, severe chromosomal abnormalities can be challenging to confront.

Indeed, some people find it difficult to look for very long at a baby born with extreme congenital defects, it is so painfully wrong in its appearance and so clearly incapable of surviving. There is no denying that nature has made a terrible mistake. Even as a pediatrician, the first time you see one of these children, you too may wince and want to look away if you are not prepared. And you may occasionally encounter, as I did, parents so deeply disturbed by the sight that they refuse to acknowledge the little being as their offspring.

Giving birth to a baby with multiple deformities, especially one that is not expected to live, has always struck me as one of the most soul-wrenching experiences a parent can have. Yet what I have found truly remarkable is how many parents muster the strength to meet such a challenge. As a pediatrician, you encounter these parents, too, parents who, with encouragement and support, or of their own natural accord, open their arms and their hearts to these little beings, no matter how injured or different they may appear. And having found the capacity to love such unusual children, they also grieve their passing, no matter how much it is expected or explained, and continue to cherish their memory, grateful for every minute they had together. When you see this happen, you know that you are witnessing one of the farthest reaches of the human capacity for love.

There is one such child I remember in particular. Her name was Annabelle. She was born with anencephaly, a condition caused by failure of the embryonic nervous system to develop properly, giving her only a rudimentary brain stem. She had none of the higher human brain and thus no ability to smile or think or even cry. Though the rest of her body was relatively normal, the upper half of her head from eyebrows on up was missing, leaving the top of her skull completely open and her brain exposed, covered only by a thin membrane. Anyone who looked at her could see life had given her a wound that would eventually prove to be fatal.

In fact, many babies with anencephaly die before or during birth, and the rest do not usually live more than a few days or, on rare occasions, a few weeks. When anencephaly is discovered during pregnancy, mothers are usually encouraged to have what is called a "therapeutic abortion" because the baby's condition is considered so utterly hopeless. It is considered the reasonable, even compassionate, thing to do.

However, it was not what Annabelle's mother, Jocelyn, chose to do. Jocelyn rejected this well-intentioned medical advice and said she would allow life to unfold and be whatever it was meant to be. Unwed and barely more than a girl, she lived with her aunt in the Lower East Side tenements and got by on welfare while she prepared to receive the child she felt heaven was sending her.

Before I met Jocelyn and Annabelle, I had seen only one other child with anencephaly. This other baby was born one evening years earlier, when I was doing a typical thirty-six-hour shift as a resident in the NICU. The baby's condition had been identified toward the end of its mother's pregnancy, too late for a therapeutic abortion, and the distressed parents, who could not bear to look at the child once he was born, refused all contact. I had been taught that these babies did not warrant any special intervention or life support because it would only prolong their dying. For the sake of kindness, those that survived delivery were made comfortable in a warm incubator and watched over from a distance, anticipating the merciful death that usually came within hours or days, and that is what we were doing with this little one.

What I remember most about the long night that followed is the case of hiccups the little fellow developed. All night long, he just kept hiccupping. The persistent sound of hiccups followed me everywhere I went as I did my chores, tending to the needs of the other little ones in the NICU whose hold on life was sturdier than this baby's was. It seemed to me a lonely sound, like that of a baby bird fallen from its nest, chirping for its mother. Even when I went to the on-call room across the hall to try to catch a few minutes of shut-eye before morning rounds began, the sound followed me. It came right through the walls. I remember lying on the cot imagining that this little being knew that he had my attention with the peculiar sound he was managing to make and was determined to not let me forget about him.

And I did not. A sense of that little being stayed with me even after I left the hospital that next afternoon, and when I returned to work the following morning, his hiccupping voice was the first sound I listened for. But alas—or maybe thankfully—he was gone. The little bird had flown away, back from where he had come.

I confess that I had great trouble in thinking of that little misshapen being as one of my own kind. I was prepared to care for him and be kind to him just as I would any creature, but I found it hard to see him as human. His grotesque appearance so distracted me, and my scientific perspective on his condition so occupied my thoughts, that I failed to see a deeper truth. I had to be shown how to do this, and Jocelyn and Annabelle were the ones who eventually accomplished that task.

Annabelle was a rare one among her kind. She lived far longer than anyone ever expected. She lived to be nearly one year old, an achievement thought to be impossible for an anencephalic. The last time I saw her, Jocelyn had Annabelle dressed in a frilly yellow dress and matching yellow socks, with a soft knitted cap that covered the carefully bandaged, open deformity of her head. Propped up with pillows in her stroller, with her strange, bulging eyes staring upward, she won smiles from everyone as Jocelyn paraded her through the neonatology clinic. You could feel the pronouncement life was making through the two of them: *No pity needed here, thank you very much.*

Jocelyn knew full well that Annabelle was living on borrowed time, but that did not diminish her enthusiasm over being her mother. She took round-the-clock care of Annabelle—or "pretty Anna," which she explained to people was the meaning of her daughter's name—and she knew her daughter intimately. Even though Annabelle had no discernable ability to recognize Jocelyn and never once made eye contact, to Jocelyn her every movement and every noise signified meaning and constituted relationship. Her child was dear to her, as dear as any child of any mother you could imagine. She cradled Annabelle in her arms, stroked her little hands and kissed her pudgy feet, and generally fussed over her as mothers like to do. And as she watched her little daughter, Jocelyn's face shone in a way that no observer could mistake. She was seeing Annabelle with the eyes of love, and what she saw was beautiful.

* * * * * * *

For some people, love can be a complicated matter. They may search for it all their lives, only to have it elude them. This was true for both Cleo and Ernestine, though their stories had very different endings.

I met Cleo when she entered the hospice program at my hospital and enrolled in the research project I was directing, the Project on Dying and the Inner Life, aimed at learning how people with terminal illness cope with the knowledge that death is approaching. She was in her early fifties, a heavy-set woman with permanent lines of despair etched into her face. During the two months that I paid visits to her dreary basement apartment to interview her about the experience of living with life-threatening illness, I never saw her wear anything but one set of clothes: a baggy pair of sweatpants with worn knees, a threadbare sweatshirt (certainly a size extra-extra-large since it hung way below her ample waist), and a thick, knitted scarf wound several times around her neck. I noticed that she often took advantage of the sweatshirt's voluminous size to pull the stretched-out sleeves down over her hands, as if she wanted to keep as much of herself hidden from sight as possible.

Cleo had end-stage breast cancer, which had spread some time ago to her bones and more recently to her brain. During my first visit, she talked about her great disappointment that chemotherapy had not worked for her. She knew it had saved other people, so why not her? It just gradually lost its effectiveness, she said, as if it had lost interest in helping her.

"That's it," she said with a heavy shrug of her shoulders, "I'm sitting in a boat that's taking on water fast, and I have no life preserver. All I can do is wait for the end to come."

Her words were not bitter, but more like those of someone who did not see the point of struggling anymore. Like those of someone who had ceased to care.

She had been wild in her younger days, she said, as she shared her story with me that first day. She had tried her hand at college, but somehow college had not worked for her, and she dropped out after a couple of years. She had moved from place to place after that, working at short-term jobs and ending up living in the basement apartment we were sitting in. Her real aspiration was to become a writer, but though she had dreamed a lot about it, she had never pursued the idea. She was too busy looking for a true love. She had had a succession of unhappy relationships with men, she said, when she finally fell in love with a woman.

"Marilyn was the only good thing that ever happened to me," she mused in a voice devoid of feeling.

Things seemed to go well for several years, although Cleo insisted on keeping their relationship a secret, saying she was not ready to live with "the implications." The only thing they ever argued about was when they were finally going to come out of the closet they were hiding in and let their attraction to each other be known. That was all Marilyn was asking of her—all that stood in the way of their love.

Then one day out of the blue, Marilyn said she was leaving. She told Cleo she could not live in secrecy anymore. She felt she was being untrue to herself. And anyway, she had fallen in love with someone else, a woman who was not ashamed to be seen with her. And with that, she left.

Not long afterwards, Cleo said, the first leak in her boat showed up: she found the rubbery lumps in her breasts. In fairly short order, her entire life was revolving around treatment for her cancer, and slowly the few friends she had drifted away. Now there was nothing left to do but wait for the inevitable: the gradual going under of her boat.

I found it difficult to hear this dreary story filled with loneliness. I felt myself deflating as I listened to it, as if it were sucking energy out of me. Cleo's apathy was as deadening as the stale air of her basement living quarters. She seemed to have buried the pain of her life in a graveyard of memories deep inside herself, leaving it there to murmur faintly in the flat tone of her voice and in the passive posture of her body.

With the visits of the hospice nurses, home health aides, and a psychiatric social worker, Cleo was having more company than she had had for years. Yet when I paid her my next visit and asked her how things were going, she shrugged her shoulders in the way I was getting used to seeing and replied, "I'm not asking for anyone to feel sorry for me."

Then, as if deciding more was expected of her, she added, in a disgruntled tone, "I suppose I should be trying to find a way to forgive myself."

When I asked what she might have to forgive herself for, she chewed on her lower lip for a moment and then replied,

"For a lot. For not giving myself a chance. For not helping my-self get a better education when I could have. For not letting myself do the things I wanted to do. For losing the only love I ever had."

She shook her head slowly and added, "You know, I never really got off the ground. It's like someone went and clipped my wings—and the person who did that was me."

With that, Cleo heaved a sigh and said she was too tired to talk any further. She would see me next week. Something was clearly working in her, groping for understanding, seeking a possibility of healing, but meeting significant resistance.

The following week Cleo asked me not to stay too long. She was feeling miserable, she said, and then added with a bare-ly perceptible shrug, "Maybe that's the nature of this disease. You get to feeling so bad that at some point you just stop car-ing, and then dying seems like a relief."

Over the next few days Cleo sank deeper and deeper into her misery, despite all the efforts of the hospice team to en-gage her. Her mental status deteriorated as her misery grew, and when her confusion began to interfere with her ability to care for herself, she was admitted to a chronic care hospital. The staff psychiatrist diagnosed her as having progressive de-mentia, the presumed cause being the metastatic cancer in her brain. I suspected her loss of hope played as much a role in her psychological decline as her cancer.

When I went to see her a few days later, the head nurse filled me in. Cleo had not been coherent since being admitted. All she seemed capable of saying was, "Where am I, where am I?" The psychiatrist felt this was terminal confusion: her steadily growing malignant lesion was disrupting her mental functions prior to death.

I went to Cleo's room. She lay in her hospital bed with eyes closed, covers pulled up to her chin, the side rails of the bed raised for her protection. As I approached and spoke her name softly, her eyelids flickered.

Touching her gently on the shoulder, I said, "It's Dr. Mac-Gregor. I've come to see you."

She roused and turned toward me, struggling to gain a focus, as if she were making her way upwards from a place of murky confusion. As she reached the surface, she fastened her eyes on mine.

"Where am I?" she asked immediately.

"You're in a hospital where people are taking good care of you, Cleo," I said in a slow, reassuring voice.

But she shook her head.

"No. Where am I? Where am I?" she repeated insistently, as if I had not understood her clearly.

"What do you mean, Cleo?" I asked, suddenly wondering if everyone had been misinterpreting her question. Was it possible she was really asking something different and much more important: *Where is the person I could and should have been? Where is the me I never let myself be?*

Cleo opened and closed her mouth several times, as if trying to respond. But though I held her hand and encouraged her to say whatever she could, no words came. She could only gape at me. A chasm seemed to lie between us, too wide for her to reach across.

Eventually, she lost her focus on me. She blinked her eyes and looked from side to side with a furrowed brow; then she seemed to sink slowly out of sight in front of me and become lost in a labyrinth where I could not follow. The sight was a chilling one, and I grieved for her.

Two days later, Cleo died without surfacing again. I regretted that we had not been able to do more for her. With the picture of Cleo in her oversized sweatshirt and baggy sweatpants in my mind's eye, I said an inward good-bye to her and wished her well. Then I was still for a moment and wondered: when my death approaches, will I be prepared to answer the question Cleo seemed to struggle with so much? Will I be able to say that I truly was the person I wanted to be, that I truly gave and received love as fully as I could? I fervently hoped so.

* * * * * * *

Ernestine felt completely abandoned by love. It was the first thing she told me about herself when I visited her tiny studio apartment in Brooklyn to begin interviewing her for the Project on Dying and the Inner Life. She never had *any* love in her life, she declared, none at all. Yet unlike Cleo, Ernestine was not despondent; she was annoyed and angry. She clamped her hands on her hips, stuck her chin in the air, and glared disapprovingly, as if life had broken some very basic rule in her case and should be held accountable. When love had been handed out, her attitude said, an error had been made: she had been overlooked, and that was decidedly unfair.

I liked Ernestine from the moment I met her. She was as unpretentious as they come. A tall, gray-haired woman, she wore a high-buttoned polyester dress, nylon stockings and stout, low-heeled shoes. Her small apartment was orderly and immaculate, not an easy thing to accomplish when one's entire life is contained in a single room. She had topped the tables flanking either end of her floral-patterned convertible sofa with white embroidered cloths. Her bookshelf she had adorned with a row of porcelain puppies and kittens. A bowl of individually wrapped candies sat on her coffee table, along with a newspaper and a *TV Guide* open to the current date, with several programs neatly circled in pencil. If ever the term "old maid" applied to anyone, it applied to Ernestine, and she bore it with dignity.

She served us both a cup of tea with milk and brought a plate of gingersnaps. Helping herself to two of the cookies, she proceeded to tell me her life story, starting with the present and working backwards because, as she said, "It's first about now, and then about the past that explains why now is the way it is." Her previously treated breast cancer had recurred, with metastatic spread to her bones. She had discovered a lump in her one remaining breast several months ago, knew full well what it meant, and had chosen not to tell anyone. She suspected she could have had a second mastectomy, together with radiation and chemotherapy, and possibly have fought the cancer off for a few more years, but she had chosen not to.

"I went through all that treatment nonsense once, ten years ago, and at eighty-one I'm not going to put myself through it again," she said indignantly. "I really don't care to extend my life any further. I just want to get it over with. I'm deliberately letting the cancer grow so that I can die. That's what's happening, and I don't want any fuss made about it. It's my decision, and I'm fine with it."

She folded her arms and pursed her lips firmly, as if bracing herself for any possible disagreement.

I nodded and sipped my tea, not feeling any inclination to disagree. When Ernestine realized no objection was forthcoming, she continued, spilling out the rest of her story with pugnacious vigor.

"They made me retire at sixty-five. I worked all my life as a secretary in one institution after another and finally in the mayor's office for two decades. I didn't particularly like that kind of work, but I was good at it. And then what did they do? They kicked me out! After all those years, they just told me I had to go. And it was all I had! I didn't have any particular friends, and I never married or even fell in love. I never had any love at all. Not even from my parents. My father died when I was nine, and I never felt anything from my mother except resentment. I suppose my father might have loved me in the short time I had with him before he went and died, but it doesn't count because I have no memory of it. I've always been on my own, and all this time there hasn't been a single person who cared."

She paused to catch her breath, and then looked me sternly in the eye and concluded by saying, "I've been depressed because of all this for as long as I can remember, and I've seen psychiatrists for years and years, which cost me a pretty penny. But heaven knows I had good reason to. Having a life with no love in it is a very big disappointment!"

She sat back and folded her hands in her lap with a grim air of finality.

Meanwhile, I was finding it interesting that Ernestine described herself as depressed. She did not seem to have any of the usual clinical signs of depression: low energy or passivity, lack of interest in the surrounding world, loss of appetite or inability to enjoy food, failure to care for personal needs. Perhaps the benefit of seeing a psychiatrist was more about having someone who would listen to her and give her the attention she rarely got in any other way. Maybe she liked having someone to whom she could complain. Why not, I thought. Most people appreciate complaining at one time or another, and if she could pay someone to listen to her complaints, maybe it was a good use of her money.

My periodic visits to Ernestine over the next few months were not much different from the first one. We continued to sip tea and munch on cookies while she talked about the progression of her cancer, the absence of love in her life and her disappointment at that, and her looking forward to it all being over. When the day finally came that she could no longer care for herself at home, she did not hesitate about being transferred to the hospital. As an aide guided her wheelchair to Room 411 on the hospice inpatient unit, she rode along with a little valise of personal belongings on her lap and a satisfied smile on her face.

Once settled in bed, Ernestine never left it. On the third day there, she fell into a deep sleep from which she could not be roused. On the fourth day, when I stopped by the nurses' station for an update on her condition, the head nurse said she had been completely unresponsive for the past twenty-four hours. Her condition was labeled as "terminal coma," and the staff expected her to die anytime.

I sighed and walked down the hall to Room 411, thinking I would miss Ernestine and her plucky approach to life. I found her lying propped up by the elevated head of her bed and surrounded by pillows holding her gently in place. Her head was turned to one side, her jaw was slack and her mouth open, and her breathing shallow. The bed covers had slid aside from her elderly body, and her hospital gown was askew, exposing her chest and her old mastectomy scar, a relic of the path that had brought her to this point.

I reached over the side rails and arranged her gown back over her shoulders and pulled the covers up.

"No, it won't be long," I thought, gazing down at her for what would probably be the last time. I took her hand in mine, feeling the coolness in it that marked the proximity of death, and stood for a quiet moment, musing on the mystery of life and death.

Suddenly, Ernestine's body gave a little shudder, and her head slowly turned in my direction. With my face less than two feet from hers, I saw her eyelids flutter, and then open. The eyes looking out from beneath those lids appeared glazed at first and took a few seconds to focus, as if their owner was returning from a great distance to gaze into the physical world again. When they finally cleared, they looked straight at me.

A smile spread over Ernestine's face, and then this woman who had been lying in terminal coma a moment before said, in a raspy but perfectly distinct voice, "Why, Dr. MacGregor!"

I managed to blurt out a response: "Why, Ernestine! Um . . . , how are you doing?"

With her smile growing bigger, Ernestine replied, "Wonderfully!"

She paused, looking at me with calm deliberateness. As if taking me into her confidence to share a marvelous secret, she whispered, "It's exactly what I've been wanting all this time. I just didn't know it would be this simple. Thank you for your help."

She smiled conspiratorially. Then, without waiting for a response, Ernestine returned from where she had come. Her eyes relinquished their focus on mine and turned away, her head rolled slowly back to the side, and her jaw fell slack once more. The heavy curtain of terminal coma that had miraculously lifted for one brief moment came back down.

I stared at Ernestine's face, where a remnant of her smile seemed to linger. Peacefulness emanated from her, and it settled over me as well. I gave my belated response: "I'm so glad for you, Ernestine, so very glad. Thank you for letting me know."

The next day, as I passed by the nurses' station, I asked the nurse in charge if Ernestine's condition had changed. She shook her head.

"No, not so far," she answered as she glanced up briefly from the chart she was writing in.

I nodded and walked down the hall to Ernestine's room. Approaching her bed quietly, I stood with my hands resting on the side rails, taking in her motionless form surrounded by soft white folds of sheets and blankets and puffy pillows. A good minute or more must have passed before I noticed that something was missing. With a start, I realized I heard no sound of breathing.

I bent closer. It was true. Ernestine's chest was not moving, and my stethoscope confirmed that her heart was not beating either. She was gone. She had slipped away so quietly that the ever-alert hospice nurses had not even noticed, and I nearly had not either.

"Oh, Ernestine," I thought, "you didn't want any fuss, and you got your wish."

As for Ernestine's greatest wish, her wish for love, perhaps she found it in the end as well. What else could have made her so happy in her final days, I wondered? Maybe the secret she had discovered was that, even while she had been waiting for love, love had been waiting for her. It would not surprise me at all to learn that life sometimes works that way.

SIX

$Caring$ & $Connection$

PEOPLE HAVE A REMARKABLE capacity for strengthening each other in times of need, for steadying and calming each other simply through their presence and concern. You observe this frequently in a hospital, where people are so often beset by fear and worry or overwhelmed by pain and loss. You see how people's well-being—often their very lives—depend on doctors' caring and willingness to connect. If you want to practice your profession well, you hone these basic human skills and keep them in a state of constant readiness. Yet even when you think you are prepared, the force of a particular call for connection may take you by surprise. I still feel an echo of the jolt I received one day in the delivery suite.

A repeat cesarean was scheduled for that day. The pregnant woman had run into problems during the delivery of her first child, and her obstetrician decided to play it safe and deliver this baby by cesarean section. It was an elective procedure with no anticipated problems. Standard practice required a pediatrician to be present for all C-section deliveries, and I went gladly. Watching a healthy newborn baby being brought into the world through the opened wall of its mother's belly always fascinated me.

The obstetrician, an old hand at performing cesareans, was ready. With deft strokes of his scalpel he laid open the anesthetized woman's bulging abdomen, reached in with both hands, and pulled out a wet and slippery little body, announcing triumphantly, "It's a boy!"

As I took the baby from the obstetrician's arms, intending to place him on the warm examination table, I froze. This baby's eyes were unlike any I had encountered before. They were not closed tight with the shock of leaving the warm interior of his mother's body as happens with most newborns, nor were they gazing randomly about, as happens when newborns first perceive their new environment. No, this baby's eyes were wide open, staring into mine in a most intense and deliberate way. He was seeking connection.

With a jolt, I understood why. This young one was not a normal newborn. An alarming vulnerability set him apart.

In a flash, I was scanning his body, taking in the multiple swellings and distortions in his arms and legs, recognizing them as telltale signs of fractures that had occurred during his development in the womb, evidence of a serious inborn disorder involving extreme fragility of the bones. Before I even stopped to think, the medical encyclopedia stored in my mind supplied me with the diagnostic terminology: osteogenesis imperfecta, an obscure condition whose Latin name means "the imperfect making of bones." I knew immediately that careless handling could easily cause this little boy further damage.

The infant in my arms seemed to know this too. His probing stare was clearly saying, "Please be careful as you help me!"

I laid the little fellow down gently under the warming lights and made sure his heart and lungs were working well and his general condition was stable; then I carefully transferred him to a wheeled incubator and pushed him smoothly and quickly through the halls to the NICU. There the medical system sprang swiftly into gear. Over the next few days a succession of specialists—geneticists, orthopedic surgeons, and physical therapists—evaluated him, ordered tests, and gave instructions on how to make him comfortable and safe. With skill and confidence, our team tended to the special needs of this new member of the human family, while simultaneously consoling and educating his distraught parents about his diagnosis.

The boy would have a difficult life due to his fragility. He would never run and play fearlessly as other children do, for he would be at constant risk of breaking his bones. He would have pain, and he would require physiotherapy, corrective surgery, and the use of splints and other supportive devices for his entire life. Yet there would be many people with professional expertise to care for him and help him find his way. The remarkable thing, it seemed to me, was the way he had called out for connection the moment he was born. I was glad I had been there to hear his call and respond.

* * * * * * *

The doctor-patient relationship is a special kind of human connection shaped by the need for health and healing. The old model of this relationship, the one that was prevalent when I began my career, was based on a difference in power and authority. It viewed one person in the relationship as possessing special knowledge and abilities that were essential for "fixing" the problems of the other, less capable person, who waited passively to be fixed. Over the last decade or two, however, this view has shifted significantly. We are coming to regard the doctor-patient relationship as more of a partnership shaped by the patient's need and the physician's knowledge and caring.

How well doctors and patients succeed in their shared quest for healing depends in part on the success of their human relationship, and as a doctor you spend a good deal of your time developing this connection. Every day you introduce yourself to new human beings whom you hope to be able to help. You walk into an examination room or a waiting room or a procedure room where someone is anticipating your arrival, and you begin the job of building a connection. Your intention is to reassure your patients and those who may accompany them, to let them know you are there for them.

You begin by greeting your patient by name and introducing yourself. You pull up a chair and say, "Tell me what's going on." From the way you pause and lean forward expectantly, you are saying, "I'm ready to listen." Your caring flows out of you in palpable ways: through your posture and your gestures, through your eyes and your hands, through how closely you pay attention as they tell their story, and how much you nod your head in sympathy. Your smile conveys understanding and encouragement as potently as your words, telling the person in front of you, "I see you. I hear you. I'm with you."

Doors open quickly in the face of this simple way of being. The more real it is, the more your patients invite you into the private spaces of their lives, the vulnerable places where their hopes and fears reside. Though they know little about you, if they feel you care, they entrust you with their deepest concerns. They ask you questions that they hesitate to voice with others: questions about their bodies, their sexuality, their self-worth; questions about how to cope with the difficulties of life, how to be patient, how to endure pain, and how to deal with disability or with the approach of death. Children, teenagers, and adults all willingly confide in you, simply because you are a doctor and you are genuinely interested. You create a powerful experience for these fellow human beings: the feeling of being seen and heard and cared about. This has a certain healing effect all its own, and I always loved playing a role in it.

At the same time, doctors often hear warnings about getting "over-involved," about losing objectivity and thus the ability to make balanced decisions. The assertion is often made that emotional investment in someone else's affairs can blur your vision, and certainly, in extreme situations, this is true. Unfortunately, equal consideration is seldom given to the dangers of being *under*-involved, nor do people often warn about the risk of objectivity turning into indifference. Only recently has research begun to indicate that there may be hazards in caring too little: it appears that those doctors who remain distant—those who choose not to care and those who do not know how—are more likely to become disillusioned or exhausted. Without the sustenance of human connection in their work, they burn out more easily.

As for me, I tended to disregard concerns about over-involvement. I just let myself fall in love with my patients, and frankly, I think that saved me. It not only felt good, it gave me nearly inexhaustible energy. I learned that I could be bone-tired and ready to drop, but when I opened the door to an exam room in the clinic where a family was waiting, or entered an ER cubicle to see a sick patient, or approached the bedside of yet another hospitalized child, an exciting invitation awaited me. Life was offering me the possibility of connection, and if I said yes to the invitation, my tiredness melted away. I became so engrossed in the immediate relationship that I would completely forget about the time and how much more work I still had to do.

The simple fact was, the instant I allowed myself to care, I plugged into a new outlet where I found energy to spare. I tied into an energy loop between my humanity and the humanity of my patients—a continually reinforcing, self-replenishing, positive feedback loop created by caring. It followed one straightforward law: the more I gave to it, the more I received.

* * * * * * *

Most of the sick people I have known appeared encouraged and sustained by doctors' committed attention. My own patients' mood and outlook almost always improved when I spent time with them. They became visibly stronger and more hopeful, just with caring human interaction. Yet this did not happen every time, and occasionally the feedback I got from a particular patient could be so minimal that I wondered if my caring was registering at all. This was true of Keith more than anyone else I remember.

Keith became my patient when he was seventeen, and he remained under my care until he reached his twenty-first birthday, when I referred him to the adult service, since the adolescent clinic I ran could no longer accept him. In fact, the upper age limit for our patients was eighteen, and I had stretched the limit as far as possible in my effort to assist Keith. Yet the help I provided him always seemed inadequate, accomplishing far less than I had hoped.

Keith had a condition that has no cure: sickle-cell disease. A genetically inherited disease, sickle cell emerged ages ago in Africa, India, the Middle East, and Mediterranean areas, where the genetic mutation of sickle-cell trait imparted partial resistance to the devastating effects of malaria. Unfortunately, this benefit came at an extreme cost: the mutation is a terrible curse to those who inherit the gene from both parents, not just from one. A double dose of the mutant gene radically affects the character of the person's red blood cells, causing "sickle-cell crises" in which deformed red blood cells stick to each other in microscopic clumps throughout the bloodstream. The clumps obstruct the flow of blood within the person's tissues and organs—in the kidneys, spleen, lungs, brain, eyes, and bones—depriving him or her of oxygen and causing extreme pain and, over time, serious damage. These crises can come at anytime, sometimes in response to cold weather or stress or a passing illness, and sometimes with no apparent reason at all, and the agonizing pain they inflict dominates the person's life for days or even a week or two, until the crisis passes. People often die in childhood or early adulthood from complications of this dreadfully unkind disease, and as long as they live they need enormous help to cope with it.

As it does for anyone with sickle-cell disease, pain shaped Keith's life in powerful and frightful ways. By the age of seventeen, he had been hospitalized more than sixty times for severe painful crises, and he had had many lesser crises that he suffered through without the benefit of hospital care. The recurring bouts of pain took a toll not only on his body but also on his mind and soul as well. For although he was very bright, his frequent absences from school were discouraging, and the pain made it difficult to study, causing him to fall far behind. His disease ruled his life with such a ruthless possessiveness that it also kept him from forming any enduring friendships. In the inner-city housing projects where he lived, he was an outsider, a loner. And sadly, his family, broken apart by the burdens of inner-city life, had little ability to help him with his problems.

To add to his long list of difficulties, Keith had had the unfortunate experience of being cared for in a health-care system that was, at that time, both ignorant of and resistant to effective methods of pain management. He had endured years of inadequate pain relief at the hands of doctors who were skeptical of his complaints of pain, fearful of the possibility of drug-seeking behavior, and reticent to use potent pain medications because of the overzealous concern they had about the potential for drug addiction. Keith had bounced from clinic to clinic and had rarely seen the same doctor twice. No medical personnel had ever truly come to know him, and years of seeing skeptical expressions form on the faces of doctors or nurses when he cried out with pain—of watching them turn and walk away, leaving him to suffer alone—left him viewing the world as a heartless, uncaring place.

When Keith first became my patient, he was quite a challenge, in spite of the fact that by then I was an attending physician with years of experience. He was admitted to my service from the emergency room in the middle of a full-blown sickle-cell crisis, and it was clear from the start that there was more to deal with than just his pain, which was difficult enough. He was anxious, whiny, and manipulative—an altogether unpleasant human being to deal with. Even after days of aggressive treatment with powerful intravenous pain medications, he denied feeling any better. He continued to insist that his pain score was ten on a scale of zero to ten.

To make matters worse, the residents on the ward were growing impatient with him. When I conducted daily supervisory rounds with the team and would stop in Keith's room, the residents increasingly stood at a distance with a suspicious and guarded air, while Keith hunched his shoulders in his bed and turned his head away, sulky and defensive. They were caught in a trap of mutual distrust, the roots of which lay deep in the years of Keith's failed care.

As director of the Pediatric Pain Management Program, I saw this as an opportunity to make a difference for someone who was suffering needlessly and to simultaneously educate our staff about the benefits of intelligent, caring pain relief. Surely, I thought, with good treatment and adequate attention, we could rescue Keith from a life dominated by pain. We would work to rebuild his trust. We would use the most potent pain medications available, and we would give Keith a say in his care.

I started by sitting at Keith's bedside and telling him, as the residents looked on, that I would not send him home until he informed us that he was feeling better. We would not kick him out, as he felt had been done to him so many times before. I looked him in the eye and explained that we had no way of measuring the severity of his pain—only he really knew how bad it was—and we therefore needed to rely on his judgment as to whether or not our treatment was working for him. I told him that in order for us to help him, he would have to help us, and I asked if he was willing to do that. When he gave a begrudging nod, I insisted that everyone on the team shake his hand to make the agreement official, and we did.

I kept Keith's pain medication infusing his bloodstream at a concentration that would have knocked any other person his age and size right off their feet. But Keith, whose body was very used to it, showed merely a slight drowsiness. Nearly a week passed before he finally said his pain score had dropped from ten to nine. When I asked if that was enough improvement for him to manage returning home, he scowled and shook his head, and so we continued his treatment unchanged. I hoped the residents were beginning to get the picture.

After another two days, Keith begrudgingly announced that his score was eight. When I asked if that was low enough for him to go home, he gave a disdainful shrug of his shoulders, as if to say, "Does it really make any difference?" Nevertheless, he got out of bed and immediately began to collect his belongings, asking with his back turned to the group of us whether I would be his doctor the next time he was admitted. I said that I would be if he asked for me, and the discharge nurse made a follow-up appointment for him to see me in a week.

Thus began a relationship that lasted for four years and included a great many hospitalizations. Progress happened very slowly. Keith regressed into sullen distrust frequently in the beginning and seemed to drag his heels about admitting that he was getting better, and I confess there were times when I gnashed my teeth and wondered if I was letting myself be manipulated. From the perspective of some of my colleagues, and some of the residents, too, my patient was engaging in flagrant malingering. They thought I was giving Keith too much control. The doctor should be the one to decide when a patient was ready for discharge, they said, not the patient. But I held my ground, figuring that the undoing of an entire childhood of not feeling seen or heard or cared about, but being left to suffer, was not something to rush.

Seeing Keith return again and again, wracked with pain, challenged me more than I expected. I railed against the disease he had and against the limitations of my medical knowledge that left me feeling impotent. Nevertheless, as time went by, Keith and I established a partnership of sorts that worked. We both still found it hard to wait while the drugs brought the agonizing pain under control, but we knew it could be done.

Keith did not fully abandon his whining, yet he occasionally managed a halfhearted smile. And although he never once said that his pain was less than a score of eight, we both knew that eight meant an acceptable amount of improvement. This score also seemed to communicate an important caveat, as if he were saying: *Yes, you've helped me some, but you shouldn't think that means you can stop there. I'm still vulnerable, you know, and I need someone who will continue to care about me.*

When Keith finally left our pediatric service, an unexpected sense of loss came over me. I found myself thinking of all the times I had felt irritated or impatient with him, and I regretted that I had not been unconditionally supportive. I wished I had been tougher on the residents, too, wished I had done a better job of getting them to see Keith's side of things. Moreover, I was disappointed at my skills in pain management: they were far from perfect. Why could I not have made Keith feel really well, have brought his pain score down to three or four, rather than only a pitiful eight? Why had I not been able to provide him with care that really made a difference in his life?

One morning, more than a year later, I was making rounds on the ward when one of the nurses came running up, saying there was a telephone call for me at the nurses' station. Going immediately to answer, I discovered it was Keith, calling from another hospital where he was being treated on the adult ward for a painful crisis.

When I asked him how it was going, he said, "Oh, it's okay. Not as good as being taken care of by you, of course, but it's not too bad."

I laughed at this unexpected compliment, thinking it was just a sentimental exaggeration. But Keith broke in and asserted with uncharacteristic forcefulness, "I mean it, Dr. MacGregor. You're the best doctor in the whole world! Really and truly, the absolute best!"

I thanked him and said it was good to know he felt that way. I told him, quite honestly, that I was happy he had been my patient. I had learned a lot from him and was glad we had been able to be partners in coping with his sickle-cell disease. He, in turn, talked about how he was getting on with his life, and it was gratifying to hear that he was managing fairly well.

As he was about to hang up, he paused, as if reluctant to let the connection go, and then proclaimed in a husky voice: "I'm glad you took care of me, Dr. MacGregor. I won't ever forget you, no matter where I go. Good-bye!" The earnestness of his words kept me sitting in the nurses' station for a good many minutes before the business of the day called me back.

Only much later in the day, when I had a little time to reflect on what Keith said, did I understand the wisdom in his words. In trying to deflect his compliments and tone down his seemingly overenthusiastic view of me, I nearly missed learning an important lesson.

Keith was saying that while I was despairing at how little I had done for him and wishing I could have done more, his view was quite the opposite. From his perspective, the "little" I did was enough to make a very big difference. He was saying, too, that what was important to him was not whether all of his pain was relieved or not, but whether he felt seen and heard. He was telling me that the way we become great in someone else's eyes is not by doing everything perfectly, but by caring about them. He was saying that caring is one of the greatest gifts we can give.

* * * * * * *

Another kind of connection you participate in as a doctor lies at a deeper level, a level where caring becomes almost like praying. Not that I know a great deal about praying or have done huge amounts of it, at least not overtly. But the times when I have prayed, it has seemed surprisingly familiar, akin to something that I regularly felt going on in me as I did my daily work, something that, at certain critical times with the sickest of patients, became greatly intensified. A subtle part of my being seemed to reach out to an unseen dimension of life, petitioning it on my patients' behalf, asking that it be kind to them and generous with its help. And from what I know of praying, this is often its intention too.

On the surface, of course, there are all the technical aspects of doctoring that occupy most of your attention: taking the medical history, doing the physical examination, ordering the necessary tests, arriving at a diagnosis, deciding on a course of treatment. But deeper down there lies this subjective dimension of doctoring—the *wanting* for your patients to get better, the *asking* that they may. On this level, your own humanity cares about what happens to them. You are carrying them inside of you and holding a heartfelt desire for their well-being—in fact, straining quite hard with the intensity of this desire on occasion. The sickest patients, the ones who need your fiercest caring, summon you powerfully to this level. This is, I think, why I loved caring for these patients the most. I loved the way they called me to the level of prayer.

Roman was one of these. A slender three-year-old boy, he came under my care while I was supervising the pediatric inpatient service as an attending physician. He had been admitted from the walk-in clinic because of dehydration, and for three days he had been sitting in his crib on the ward in a state of silent vigilance. He had not uttered a sound and had refused to eat or drink. Despite repeated examinations, a battery of diagnostic tests, and consultations with various specialists, we still had no idea what was wrong with him.

The child's face was drawn and pensive. He made no protest, either about being alone and away from his mother, or about being examined by strangers, nor even about having his blood drawn repeatedly and an IV kept inserted in his arm to administer needed fluids. It was as if he was conserving energy for an unseen fight that only he knew he was waging. With his large brown eyes, he watched the hospital staff intently, following our every move. He seemed to be expecting something to happen—but what?

Unhappy about our lack of progress on his case, I decided to peek in on Roman one more time before leaving the hospital that day. Perhaps he would give some indication of improving, and we would not need to continue worrying that we were missing something serious. Or perhaps this time there would be some hint as to what dark distress lurked in his little body, and we could marshal our medical expertise to fight the intruder for him and overcome it before it progressed any further and took some terrible toll. But as I stepped quietly into the doorway of Roman's room, I saw he looked no different. I felt my brow wrinkling into a disquieted frown.

In his state of hypervigilance, Roman immediately noticed my presence, and as his dark eyes turned to look toward mine, an odd thing happened. I felt a charge of energy fly across the room and pierce my mind with a stab of urgency. I understood the meaning of Roman's look as clearly as if he were speaking. It said: *Help me!*

I went to Roman's crib, picked him up and held him in my arms; then I examined him one more time, hoping for some further insight, but none came. After laying him gently down and noting with concern how little protest he made at being so quickly abandoned, I returned to the nurses' station, more disturbed than ever. Checking the order book, I saw that the CAT scan I had requested earlier was scheduled for "ASAP," and I gave instructions to the staff to page me the moment it was done. I left, mentally pleading: *Please, life, help us out here. We need some answers, and we need them soon. Show us what we have to do before it's too late!*

As evening approached, I could not get that look from Roman out of my mind. Sitting beside my husband in a sold-out concert at Carnegie Hall, I could barely keep still. Paul Simon, one of my all-time favorite musicians, was making a rare appearance in Manhattan, and I had been looking forward to this performance for weeks. Nevertheless, I kept checking my watch as the time crept by. Finally, my restlessness drove me out to the lobby where I phoned the hospital.

When I got through to the resident on call, I asked if the results of the CAT scan were available. Learning that the test had not yet been done and hearing useless excuses about why, I exploded. I heard myself shouting, "Don't tell me what the problems are! Get it done *now*, and page me with the results!"

My vehemence shocked me. I was usually patient and understanding with the overworked young docs in my department. I returned to listen to Paul Simon's melodic voice feeling tense and distracted.

An hour or so later the resident paged me with an update. The CAT scan had uncovered something bizarre and alarming. A large abscess was gnawing its way down through little Roman's chest between his esophagus and his trachea. The resident had notified the surgery team immediately. They were taking Roman to the operating room for emergency surgery at that very moment.

Several hours later, the surgeons reported their findings. The abscess had been eating through the wall of Roman's trachea. They could not explain how or why such a life-threatening infection had taken hold there, but without a doubt it would soon have broken through to his airways, filling them with so much thick pus that he would have quickly suffocated to death. The diagnosis had been made just in time.

Later that evening, after the clanging sound of danger had faded from my mind, I reflected on how precariously Roman had been balancing at the edge of life and death. I had felt it in the core of my being. Released now from the sense of urgency, I relaxed for the first time in days. I had not realized how urgently I had been calling out to life for help.

After surgery, Roman recovered quickly and uneventfully. On the day he was due to be discharged, I went to his room to discuss the medical follow-up plans with his mother. By now,

Roman was a different child: perky and playful and eating like a champ. I gave him a final examination and a little hug, gratified by his indignant squirming. Then his mother and I spoke about our mutual sense of relief that everything had turned out well.

As I moved toward the door of his room to depart, something made me glance back over my shoulder. There was Roman, looking intently at me from his mother's arms. Once again his large brown eyes met mine, and I had the sense of being seen by someone with whom I shared a deep knowing: the knowing of just how close the shadow of death had come. A moment later, the connection vanished as quickly as it had appeared. Roman turned back to his mother, who was squeezing him playfully, and I headed down the hall to tend to other patients, sending gratitude to life as I went.

*　*　*　*　*　*　*

Strong bonds tend to form between human beings when they are thrown into stressful situations together. During medical training, relationships among colleagues deepen quickly, even among people who might never have felt they had anything in common. You naturally reach out to your comrades, as you are being challenged and stretched to your limits. When you stay up all night, again and again, caring for critically ill patients, you get to know those who work alongside you very well. You may not learn a lot of personal facts about them, but you learn how strong their courage is, how deep their determination goes, how honest and good-hearted they are. You discover, too, what their rough edges are, and how long their patience will last before it gives out. You know what you can rely on them for, and you know that they know the same about you.

There is a heady thrill in battling shoulder to shoulder with colleagues against an adversary that is threatening the life of your patient. It is exhilarating to combine forces against the diabetes that has pulled a child into the darkness of diabetic coma, or the asthma attack that is forcing a youngster to struggle for every breath, or the out-of-control seizures or aggressive march of cancer threatening to rob a young person of his or her life. The goal that unites you—to save a fellow human being from harm—is a compelling one.

You cherish the bonds forged in this cauldron of mutual experience—experiences of tending to sick and hurting human beings, of suffering exhaustion and uncertainty, of being dashed down by failure and lifted up by success. You even find something precious about sharing the donuts and bad coffee and cold slices of pizza and worn-out jokes that keep you going in the long hours of being on call. The sense of camaraderie and sympathy is probably not unlike what develops among soldiers in wartime. Your closest friends outside this world will never fully appreciate this bond, and you would not trade it for anything.

Yet there are times when even bonds as strong as these are not enough to keep you afloat. Some situations are just too stressful, especially when you have had only two to three hours of sleep. You may start to doubt yourself and see more flaws than strength. You may snap at your colleagues, and worst of all, you may find your ability to care about your patients growing thin.

You arrive for an afternoon clinic, having eaten no lunch and running late, already stressed from spending the morning on the ward making rounds, seeing one seriously sick child after another, and there you find eight or nine patients already waiting to see you, their medical charts stuffed into the boxes on the doors of your three examination rooms. You keep your eyes down as you walk through the waiting area crowded with parents and children, hoping not to meet the stare of anyone who has been waiting for you so long that they have become exasperated. You wish some of them would decide it is not worth their while to wait, and leave. You try not to think about who they might be. You tell yourself they can simply reschedule. Surely it will not hurt to postpone addressing their problems for a few more days.

Or you arrive for a night shift in the pediatric ER, finding fifteen to twenty charts stacked up in the in-box and the waiting area packed with children coughing and crying and running high fevers. It is flu season, and you know that most of the children probably have a viral infection that requires no treatment other than common sense. But how many of these parents have an adequate dose of *that*, you wonder petulantly. Unfortunately, there might be one child among them who has pneumonia or meningitis. The only way to find out who is truly in need of your medical skills is to see them one by one—which will take several hours, and how many more charts will pile up during that time? Why do parents always wait until the middle of the night to decide their child is so sick they need to go to the hospital? Why did the doc on the previous shift let things get so backed up? Why can't the nurses do a better job of triaging the patients and flagging the ones who look the sickest so that you can be more efficient? Grumble, grumble, grumble!

If neither denial nor blame is successful in relieving your stress, you can always resort to magical thinking. Lying on the cot in the NICU on-call room, you try to take advantage of a momentary lull in the onslaught of problems and catch a couple of minutes of desperately needed shut-eye. You tell yourself that if you breathe very softly, no alarms will go off. If you lie perfectly still and do not move a muscle, none of the preemies will turn blue for at least half an hour. If you think positive thoughts hard enough, the woman in the delivery room whose body is threatening to expel her premature triplets will not go into active labor. If you can ward off your own ominous thoughts of disaster, all will remain calm and quiet for just long enough. But which is worse: to lie with eyes open, staring into the dark, exhausted but afraid to relax, or to let go into sleep, only to be blasted awake by the sound of your beeper, summoning you to an emergency?

The fabric of care does fray. Exhaustion is a common cause of fraying during the stress of residency training, and even when residency ends and fatigue as a source of stress lessens, other sources of stress arise. The burden of responsibility grows heavier as you climb higher on the professional ladder. As a supervising physician, you may not work through the night that often anymore, but you assume responsibility for others' actions in addition to your own, and that brings its own concerns. More is expected of you, and you expect more of yourself as well. Under such pressure, your critique of your own caring skills can become quite harsh.

You learn that caring about others is not without risk. There are some who believe that the more you offer of yourself, the more you have to lose. As they say, "the more you care, the more you despair," and there is some degree of truth in this. To enter a room where suffering patients are waiting for you, turning expectant eyes to meet you as you approach, is a challenge, a kind of balancing act. You want to offer as much encouragement as you can and fight on their behalf to make things better, but you also do not want to promise the impossible. You want to support them in their trouble and hurt, but you do not want to identify so much with their pain that you are pulled under by it. That would not be good for anyone.

Among my many memories, one stands out where the combined pressures of overwork and over-caring caused the fabric of our pediatric staff's working relationships to become alarmingly tattered. Many of us were pulled too far into one child's painful story and nearly lost our way in it. It began when a five-month-old baby was brought into the emergency room by his mother because of irritability and lack of interest in feeding. When the baby was noted to have tremors and an enlarged head, he was whisked to our Pediatric Special Care Unit for an urgent workup under my supervision as an attending.

The story given by the child's mother, Roxie, a single woman in her early thirties, was troubling. Mikey was her only child, she said. He was born very early—after only twenty-four weeks of life in her womb instead of the usual thirty-eight to forty—and he developed many of the complications of extreme prematurity, including jaundice and severe respiratory distress syndrome with episodes of interrupted breathing and turning blue. For two and a half months he was kept in the NICU of another hospital where the doctors gave him blood transfusions for his jaundice and maintained him on a ventilator while his lungs slowly matured. Roxie's contact with him was severely limited by his many medical problems and the intensive care he required.

According to Roxie, Mikey did well after being discharged, until two or three weeks ago, when he started being unusually fussy. She said she had thought he was teething. When asked if she had noticed that his head was enlarging, she said she had, but had not considered it significant. And when asked if any accidents or trauma might have happened to Mikey, she replied, with an edge to her voice, that he had once bumped his head on the sink when she was giving him a bath a month or so ago.

It did not require any great skill to see that Mikey was very ill. He was tremulous and lethargic, his eyes drifted aimlessly, and his skin was clammy and pale. His poor little head was markedly enlarged. The soft spot at the top was bulging, and the bones of his skull were spread apart. We started his workup immediately, having little doubt, by that time, about what we would find.

The CAT scan of Mikey's head revealed large pools of blood beneath the bones of his skull, and it showed that these pools were compressing his brain. I sent an urgent message to the neurosurgeons, and they came immediately—only to concur with us that before they could take him to their OR to drill through his skull and drain the pools, Mikey required an emergency transfusion to replace the large amounts of blood he had lost from his circulatory system, because his little body was in shock. When the chief resident went looking for Roxie in the waiting room where she had been asked to wait, she was gone. Instead of asking Roxie to sign the forms acknowledging her consent to having these procedures performed on her son, we had to obtain approval from the hospital administrator on night duty.

Mikey's hospital stay was a tumultuous one. For three weeks, everything that could go wrong did go wrong. For starters, after his neurosurgery, he had a cardiac arrest in the recovery room. He was resuscitated with difficulty. Back in the Special Care Unit, he lay beneath warming lights, intubated, and attached to a ventilator, a cardiac monitor, and two intravenous lines. There, one storm after another swept through his little body, including seizures, blood infections, malignant hypertension, and kidney failure. The amount of medical and nursing care he required was huge.

Meanwhile, the bleeding in Mikey's head had made us highly suspicious of child abuse: violent shaking and/or striking typically cause such bleeding. Following the standard procedure for evaluating a child suspected of being abused, x-rays of all his major bones were obtained. The results told a dismal tale. He had multiple rib fractures, both new and old. They revealed that Mikey had been squeezed or pummeled with treacherous force by someone's hands more than once, probably at the same time that he was being savagely shaken.

Mikey's case was reported to the Bureau of Child Welfare, and the police tracked Roxie down. Under their questioning, Roxie told a story of feeling trapped and frustrated and repeatedly battering her child, beginning the day she took him home from the NICU. We learned no details about Roxie or about what traumas she herself had endured in life that might have explained how she could direct such brutality toward her son, nor did we learn whether she felt remorse about the awful harm she had caused. We did know, however, that preemies who require prolonged NICU care and thus are separated from their mothers during the critical bonding period of early life are at far higher risk of being maltreated than other babies are. Mikey became a ward of the court, and Roxie was incarcerated in a high-security prison, at which point we lost contact with her.

Almost as painful as Mikey's story was the story of those assigned to care for him during his three weeks of hospitalization. Both the nurses and the residents directly responsible for his care suffered deeply, though the anguish of these two sets of caregivers was not fueled by the same concerns. From their divergent perspectives, each group saw a different side of Mikey's story, and each shouldered a different portion of his suffering. Gradually, those differences grew to be an unforgiving wedge that drove the residents and nurses painfully apart.

The residents had the job of examining Mikey regularly, drawing his blood at least twice a day to monitor his condition, and staying on top of his various test results. Their goal was to keep his body going, and to that end they wanted to do everything that could be done. They steadfastly calculated the amount of steroids needed to reduce the swelling in his brain, titrated the dosage of phenobarbital to keep his seizures under control, prevented the sodium and potassium in his blood from falling or rising to dangerous levels, adjusted the ventilator settings to maintain an adequate flow of oxygen into his lungs, took periodic cultures of his blood and urine to make sure that serious infection was not brewing, measured his urine output to monitor his kidney function, and performed many other such chores. They saw their job as tending a flame of life that, because of human frailty, had nearly been extinguished. They felt it their duty to guard the remaining spark of hope that lingered there.

On the other hand, Mikey's nurses, who were at his side continuously, had the task of keeping him as comfortable as possible and preventing any unnecessary trauma that might result from his intensive medical care. They monitored his heart rate and blood pressure, recorded his temperature and oxygen saturation, and charted his urinary output. They applied fresh dressings to the boreholes in his skull. They changed his diapers, checked his skin for pressure sores, and kept him clean. When his little body stiffened with a seizure or with the poking of a resident's sharp needle, they were the ones who stroked his trembling arms and legs and tried their best to soothe him.

My own job was to coordinate every detail of Mikey's care: everything done by the nurses, the residents, and the consultants who came to give their expert advice on his kidneys or brain or circulatory system. I was the one to ensure that it all came together into one seamless whole. And though I knew my responsibilities well enough, the hospital administrator underscored their importance as seen from his own particular perspective one day.

"You know," he said, with a sympathetic sigh, "if the child is to die, we want to be able to say it was the result of the violence he suffered, not the fault of inadequate medical care. There's a good chance this case will go to court. His mother may try to defend herself by claiming that his death was not her fault, but someone else's—namely ours. It's important to be competent in everything we do." An unpleasant additional twist to Mikey's care rested on our shoulders.

By the second week of Mikey's hospital stay, tension began to show between the nurses and the residents. The nurses asked accusingly if so many blood samples were really needed. They twitched with impatience if the residents' needles did not find a vein on the first stick, and pointed with sour looks to Mikey's increasing number of black-and-blue marks resulting from their probing. The residents, in their turn, snapped at the nurses with annoyance when an order was not carried out quickly enough or if some slight change in Mikey's condition was not reported to them promptly. Beneath the surface of their professional interactions, resentment was building.

People who were previously friends were beginning to regard each other as being on opposing sides in the battle to help their precious patient.

As supervising physician, I felt caught in a web of challenging questions. Were we getting so enmeshed in the pain of Mikey's situation that we were not seeing clearly anymore? Were the things we were doing truly in Mikey's best interest, or were we going blindly by the book, following protocols not applicable in this situation, being driven by the fear of legal issues? Were we projecting our own pain on our patient and actually thinking more about ourselves than him? Perhaps most important of all, how could he get the care he needed when his caregivers' ability to care about each other was suffering, their connections with each other breaking down?

I called a team meeting. The residents, nurses, pediatric neurologist, kidney specialist, social worker, hospital legal counsel, and ethics committee representative all attended. Every person spoke, and by the end one thing was clear: everyone believed that Mikey's life was coming to an end. No one thought otherwise. The differences centered around what to do for Mikey in the meantime. As this question arose, the wedge between the residents and the nurses came sharply into view.

Teresa, the chief resident, a soft-spoken young woman with great integrity, spoke for the residents, evenly describing their care plan and enumerating the various ways they were supporting Mikey's heart, kidneys, immune system, and nervous system. She concluded by asking in a suddenly brittle voice, "How can we do less than everything we can to help Mikey? How can we turn away from this baby who was never given a chance in life? Should we just look in the other direction and let him die?"

Marcie, our lovable head nurse, spoke up immediately, giving the nurses' very different perspective. "Mikey," she said testily, "has suffered too much already. He's had nothing but pain and struggle from the day he was born. What we're doing to him here isn't being kind to him—isn't healing him—it's *torturing* him!"

At this, Teresa leapt to her feet. "Do you think it doesn't torture *us* to care for Mikey every day, to take responsibility for his life, to have to *do* these difficult things to him?" she shouted in an impassioned voice, her shoulders shaking as she fought to hold back tears. "Do you think we have no feelings? We're not *monsters*, you know!"

In that instant, the whole dynamic shifted. When Marcie saw Teresa's torment—a highly unusual thing to witness in this serious and hardworking resident—she stepped forward in dismay and, with tenderness in her voice, apologized for having misunderstood so terribly. Suddenly, the pain that had been pushing them apart became a common ground where they could meet. As the two women threw their arms around each other in a tearful hug, the tension in the room dissolved, and murmurs of laughter mixed with sighs of relief. Clearly, no one could imagine Teresa as a monster, or Marcie either.

I suggested that, if the team agreed, we institute a "do not resuscitate" order for Mikey. After some discussion, we took a vote, and the decision was unanimous. I would indicate in Mikey's chart that it was the opinion of the entire multidisciplinary team that no heroic measures should be taken to further prolong his life. We would not neglect him—we would support him and make him comfortable—but we would not force his tired body to keep going. If Mikey had a cardiopulmonary arrest, he would not be resuscitated. The hospital administrator would obtain the necessary legal authorization.

It almost seemed as if Mikey had been waiting for this to happen: two days later his heart stopped beating. When the alarm on the cardiac monitor sounded, someone simply reached up and turned it off, and the room fell quiet. Those who happened to be there at the time went to stand beside Mikey's warmer and gaze down at his silent little form. After he was pronounced dead, the residents and the nurses together removed the various tubes and lines and catheters from Mikey's body. Then his primary care nurse washed him and swaddled him and sat with his body in her arms until the attendant from the hospital morgue came to take it away.

The next day, at morning conference, we paused to acknowledge the passing of the little boy whose pain we had all felt so personally and who had confronted us with questions that had no simple answers. He had shown us the risks inherent in caring deeply about our patients. Yet despite the hazards that pushed us to the breaking point, we made it through together.

*   *   *   *   *   *   *

When I became a parent, I discovered a new dimension of caring I had never known as a pediatrician. I suddenly found myself programmed to recognize any indication of distress in a child, even if that child was one I had no responsibility for, but was merely passing me on the street. I felt as if I had grown a new sensory organ, one making me keenly attuned to the discomfort or despair of every youngster within my range of hearing. Whimpering, moaning, sobbing, and wailing each had a new timbre and meaning, and they all set off an alarm within my parental nervous system. They flew like slivers of glass into my heart, triggering a resonating anguish I could not disregard.

Becoming a parent also made a difference in how I practiced pediatrics. The pain of my patients was more challenging to bear, the fretting of their parents easier to be patient with. The enormity of the lessons about patience that parents must learn, and the endurance they must develop humbled me. I was sometimes mortified to recall advice I had once blithely handed out to parents about problems regarding their children's feeding or sleeping or general behavior, reassuring them that such problems could easily be solved.

I learned, too, that perils lie along the path of parent-hood: the best efforts of parents to protect their children from harm can be undone in the twinkling of an eye. The emergency room provided ample evidence of how easily a momentary lapse of attention or a sudden twist of fate can sabotage parents' care—as when a youngster runs into the street without looking, or tumbles from a jungle gym, or falls down a flight of stairs or out of an open upper-story window. Accidents happen.

The burden of self-blame that parents bear over having failed to guard their children from danger is one of the heaviest burdens imaginable and one of the hardest from which to recover. Martin, a father of four, nearly broke under its weight. He had taken his family camping one weekend, and as they were packing the car to return home, neither he nor his wife Celene were aware that their youngest son, Robbie, age five, had wandered off. When they noticed his absence, they searched for him frantically, eventually finding his little body lying facedown in the nearby lake they had gone fishing in earlier that day.

With Robbie's death, life lost all its meaning and goodness for Martin. He sank like a stone in a bottomless well of grief and guilt. The image of Robbie's lifeless body lingered like a live ember in the wreckage of his heart, burning a hole in his soul. The God he had tried all his life to follow ceased to have any relevance. If God had not been able to protect Robbie— or worse, had not cared enough to—of what use was He? Exhausted by his feelings of loss, paralyzed by unceasing pain, Martin wanted to quit. For two years he thought every day of taking his own life, only to be stopped each time by the thought of the suffering that such an act would cause Celene and his other three children.

Finally, Martin joined a group for grieving families. There other parents who knew deep loss met him in his anguish and embraced him. With the special sympathy that parental hearts feel for other parents' pain, they helped Martin find the path to self-forgiveness. And though the pain did not disappear, its bite softened as he learned how to hold it more gently.

"Forgiveness," he told me later, "is the door to love. Shut it, and your heart will die of despair and loneliness. Open it, and you can bear the unbearable."

Grateful for help he had received, Martin went on to counsel other parents grieving the loss of a child. It was this, he said, that helped him return to life more than anything else. He saw how his own deep familiarity with the pain other parents felt helped them recover from their grief. And to his surprise, the God he thought had failed him so badly came back into his life. He found Him in the caring feelings he had for those parents whose pain he understood so well.

God had not abandoned him at all, Martin said, but had been by his side, not sparing him his pain, but sorrowing over Robbie's death right along with him, with the same kind of deep caring that he himself was offering to other grief-stricken parents. That, Martin said, was how caring worked.

* * * * * * *

Not all parents are like Martin, of course, and the spectrum of parenting approaches is a wide one. I saw this spectrum displayed daily in the waiting room of the pediatric clinic. Some mothers arrived there armed with assorted snacks, toys, and children's books to help their little ones pass the time and feel at ease, making the waiting more pleasant for parent as well as child. Other mothers come with nothing but a threatening tone of voice and the sheer force of their will, sometimes backed up by a hard shake or a swift slap. Their method for enduring the sometimes lengthy waiting time was to tell their offspring, "Shut up, sit down, and don't move—or else."

I was never sure what "or else" might mean, but the children obviously knew. Its implications were ominous enough to keep them pinned to their chairs, staring wordlessly at the other children playing with their toys. And though I might repeatedly pat these mute children on the head and smile encouragingly as I passed by, or offer them a toy or picture book from the waiting room's collection, trying to model another approach, my reaching out inspired little response. The offerings I made usually lay untouched in the child's lap, the patterns of behavior too deeply ingrained to be swayed by a temporary kindness.

When parents do not have a loving bond with their children, the consequences can be dire. As a pediatrician, you can find yourself having to guard children from the very people who are supposed to be their foremost protectors—their parents—who, it is sad to say, are the primary perpetrators of child abuse. You learn to maintain a high degree of suspicion when you see injured children, because bruises, burns, and broken bones are all possible evidence of a failing connection between parent and child.

Javier, a roly-poly two-year-old, was delivered to our hospital by policemen who had answered a 9-1-1 call reporting sounds of violence coming from a neighboring apartment. When the officers arrived at the apartment, they found a man armed with a knife and a woman whose face was swollen and discolored by bruises. Despite the obvious evidence, the two both quickly denied having any problems, and the officers were turning to leave, when they heard the sound of whimpering. Lying on the floor behind a couch where he had fallen when hurled against the wall, they found Javier, and he was seriously injured.

The story we eventually pieced together was that Javier's mother had recently taken the man with the knife in as her new boyfriend. He had wooed her with compliments and cocaine and had bounced Javier on his knee and called him his new son. But the boyfriend had a temper, which had increasingly shown itself, and on that particular day Javier's antics had set it off. In a fury, the man had grabbed Javier by one of his chubby arms, swung him around his head like a lasso and sent him crashing into the wall; then he pummeled Javier's mother with his fists and threatened to put an end to her screaming with his knife.

When we examined Javier, we found he had a dislocated shoulder, a fractured arm, and a ruptured spleen, all caused by the violence of his temporary stepfather. But more than that, we discovered that his little body was covered with scars: small round ones characteristic of cigarette burns, long slender ones that told of whippings with a belt or similar implement, and large splotches typical of scaldings with hot liquid, all evidence of being abused repeatedly, most probably by his mother.

Despite the harsh conditions of his first two years of life, Javier had an exuberant spirit. While we waited for his injuries to heal and for the Bureau of Child Welfare to find him a home with a foster family, Javier's big round eyes and eager smile brought him ample attention on the ward. He loved to be held, and I often carried him on my hip while making rounds, or sat with him on my lap while writing notes in my patients' charts, and other members of the staff did the same. And when anyone tickled him, which was his favorite thing of all, his bubbling laughter filled the ward with the sounds of his delight and brought a smile to the face of every listener. At moments like that, I had to wonder, what could lead a parent to unleash harm on such a child? What awful lack of being cared for in the parent's own life could be expressing itself in this way? Whatever wounds caused such a thing, they must be terrible ones.

* * * * * * *

Unfortunately, children like Javier are part of the daily fare of hospital pediatrics, and they are the lucky ones because they can be identified and rescued. Sadly, though, those who show up in the ER with physical injuries are only the tip of the iceberg. Much of the harm that children suffer goes undetected, especially the "nonviolent" kind, the kind that leaves no outer scars, only inner ones—the shaming, belittling, berating kind. For rejection can break the spirit of children as surely as brute force can break their bones. Even mere neglect can have a powerful detrimental effect. Lack of parental attention and caring can prevent children from blossoming as they should, making failure of human bonding the most common cause of "failure to thrive" in childhood, far ahead of physical disease.

I found it quite surprising, then, whenever I discovered children who made it through without any parental nurturing at all. It was like coming upon a flower stubbornly growing amid the rubble of a deserted city lot. Such discoveries filled me with awe at the determination of life to survive.

Damaria was one of these survivors. She grew up in a dangerous and depressed neighborhood of the inner city, and her story involved perpetual ill treatment and repeated abandonment. She was born prematurely to a woman whose life was held hostage by prostitution and drug addiction. She spent the first months of her life in an NICU step-down nursery where her tiny body was tormented by continuous irritability, caused by the heroin her mother had injected during pregnancy. When Damaria turned six, her mother died of a drug overdose, and at seven the maternal aunt who had become her legal guardian died as a result of violence. Her care then passed into the hands of her grandmother, a woman whose life was severely troubled by schizophrenia.

As she grew into adolescence, Damaria saw her friends drop out of school one by one, swept away by currents stronger than they were: drug use, crime, street wars, teenage pregnancy. Damaria, on the other hand, hung on. She had a hunger for knowledge that refused to be crushed, and she managed to make it to high school. Yet the forces arrayed against her remained significant, and she turned to drinking to blunt the feelings of rage and despair that sometimes overtook her.

The counselor at Damaria's school, a woman who had years of experience with the trials and tribulations of inner-city adolescents, gave Damaria her first break. The counselor cared about her students and was good at spotting the few young souls who managed to stay afloat while so many others were sinking. She knew the signs of stubborn hope hiding behind a tough exterior. She persuaded Damaria to see a friend of hers, a female physician with a passion for taking on challenging cases. Their meeting was probably the first experience Damaria ever had of feeling trust; she told me later she could not remember ever smiling before they met.

The connection made that day led to others. Damaria's newfound physician-friend introduced her to The Door, an interdisciplinary center that provided free health care, counseling, education, and creative arts to troubled inner-city teenagers—250 of them every day. I was among the group of doctors, lawyers, educators, social workers, and artists that founded The Door, and it was there that I got to know her. She quickly became part of a lively community where the barriers between those who needed help and those who provided it were kept intentionally thin. The Door was founded on the premise that caring human relationship was the best therapeutic intervention of all.

Suddenly supported by positive human connections, Damaria set out on a long road of healing. She had many wounds from which to recover and some of her own bad habits to straighten out as well, including her alcohol use and her explosive temper and combative attitude. Yet as she wrestled with these deeply rooted issues, she grew steadily more insightful and openhearted.

With more than enough staying power to get her where she wanted to go, Damaria set her sights high. She not only wanted to save herself, but she was determined to come to the rescue of others with stories like her own. She polished off her high school credits, worked her way through college, and was admitted to medical school on a full scholarship. Choosing psychiatry as her specialty, she focused on the problems of adolescents and, after completing her residency training, went into practice in the inner-city ghetto. There she brought to her teenaged patients not only a hard-earned wisdom but also the biggest heart you could ever imagine.

Among the many memories I have of Damaria as an adolescent, the one that tops the list is the way she used to sing, especially one tune in particular, which she wrote herself. As she liked to explain, the song summed up her whole life, and you could see that it spoke for others too:

Good times or *bad* times, it's *all* the same to *me,*

I'm gonna *make* it, *just* you wait and *see!*

I got *strength* in my *body* and *brains* in my *head,*

But *if* I don't take *care* of them, I'm *gonna* end up *dead!*

I'm *not* gettin' *pregnant,* or *droppin'* outta *school,*

If I went and *did* that, I'd *be* a real *fool!*

Yeah, *I'm* gonna *make* it, and *you* can make it *too!*

If we help each *other,* we'll *ALL* make it *through!*

That song fit Damaria perfectly, and it gave voice to something vital for the other young people at The Door as well. They often pleaded with her to sing it, and could she ever belt it out! It was quite a sight to see her stand before a throng of fellow inner-city teens and onlooking staff in the central gathering space of The Door and start to strut and sway and stomp her feet.

As she gathered steam and began to fling out the words, thrusting her fists in the air with the beat, she stopped being a maltreated, unwanted teenager. She grew prouder and more resolute before our eyes. A fierce, jubilant energy welled up in her and poured out over the crowd, making everyone listening feel stronger and more certain and potently bonded to one another. She sang with everything she had, and you could tell it was not just for herself that she sang, or even for the crowd of kids around her, but for all people everywhere who were struggling to find connection. She knew very well how lifesaving that was.

SEVEN

Suffering & Compassion

SUFFERING IS NEVER far away in the hospital. It reaches out to you from the eyes of children in pain, from the faces of patients alone and afraid, from the sagging shoulders of concerned relatives and the weary steps of hardworking colleagues. In the presence of this suffering, you have the chance to see how compassion arises and steps forward willingly to meet it. You may rightly marvel at this uniquely human response that moves you to offer your help to others. It is one of the lessons that life is teaching every day in the world of medicine.

Working in hospital-based pediatrics is a full-immersion experience that matures your capacity for compassion. It is the anvil where the temper of your compassion is tested and hammered out. As you tend to the ills of your patients, you begin to develop a sixth sense that plugs you into what the young beings under your care are feeling. While you conduct your physical examinations, perform your diagnostic tests, and apply the necessary therapeutic interventions, you are simultaneously tuning in to your patients' sensations of being sick or injured and feeling the impact on them of pain and fear. You are learning the nature of suffering and being strengthened in your resolve to help.

When you tend to asthmatic children, for instance, you appreciate the scariness of not being able to breathe. When you diagnose a child with diabetes, you feel the heaviness of the lifelong burden they are living with. When you notice that a particular child's developmental milestones are not proceeding as expected and you suspect the diagnosis of autism, you sense with a chill what it means for a child not to have a life like other children, but to live with disorganized behavior, emotions that go awry, and difficulty in communicating thoughts and feelings. And when you examine a child who has weight loss, pallor, and a swollen liver and spleen, you not only recognize that you have a challenging diagnosis to make, but you also have an intimate experience of the peril the child faces from life-threatening disease. You feel it in your bones.

This dimension of being a doctor entails something different from the intellectual knowledge needed to make an accurate assessment of a patient's problem or recommend the right course of treatment. The capacity to attune to patients in this manner reflects more than activity of the mind; it comes from engagement of the heart. It is the strength of the heart that holds you steady in the face of others' bewilderment and fear, and the steadfastness of the heart that enables you to be deeply moved by their suffering without going under. The heart is where compassion dwells.

When you care for adolescents, the testing you undergo gets complex. Adolescent patients challenge you with more than physical concerns. They confront you with the turmoil and torment of their private lives, an inner suffering evident to your doctor's listening heart. You find it impossible to tackle only the "presenting problem" or to limit your investigation to the "chief complaint." You need to hear the larger story of each one's life. You must understand the particular strengths and weaknesses that come into play as each of these young people attempts to cross the hazardous divide between childhood and adulthood, between innocence and a new, self-aware maturity. You want to know the whole person, not just an itemized list of the problems they have.

I discovered early in my career that when I listened with my heart to my teenaged patients' stories, what I heard not only instructed me about their health, but it also painted a picture of human suffering in intimate detail, a picture of the terror and triumph that do battle with each other in the lives of young people as they face the challenge of growing up. I heard about boyfriends who cheated on their girlfriends and about girlfriends who deceived their boyfriends; about social competition and backstabbing, and the importance of reputation and the fragility of friendship; about feeling repulsed by one's body for being too fat or too thin or just plain ugly; about the embarrassment of untimely erections or the lack of them, or of being attracted to the "wrong" sex; about the lure of buying or selling drugs and the lies inherent in using them; about the empowering feeling of carrying a concealed weapon and the risks in making use of it; about being terrified of having picked up a sexually transmitted disease, including AIDS, or having passed one on; about being molested by an uncle or a mother's boyfriend and the shame that prevented telling; about the pressure to get pregnant or to father a child when barely out of childhood oneself. I learned much about the forces that shaped suffering in the world of adolescents, and because I allowed it to, my heart grew deeper with each story I heard.

Crystal's story was neither better nor worse than most I had heard. At fifteen, she had already been pregnant twice: one pregnancy ending in a miscarriage; one in abortion. She had kept both events a secret from her parents, who she feared would have thrown her out on the street if they knew, as happened to a friend of hers. Her mother worked two jobs, waitressing and cleaning apartments; she also did the cooking and shopping for a bedridden neighbor. Her father held a part-time job in a factory, spending the rest of his time in local bars. Her oldest brother had been killed in a drive-by shooting, and her second older brother had been talking about a basketball career until he became involved with cocaine.

When I first met Crystal, I would never have suspected how much pain she had in her life. She kept it well hidden. She looked older than her fifteen years, a pretty young woman with a swagger in her step that might have been mistaken for enticement until you got to know her better and saw the pretense in it, saw the way she used it to keep her insecurity at bay. Her eyes gave her away, though. They were the color of milk chocolate—lovely and soft, and painfully vulnerable. When I looked closely, I could see the deep pools of sorrow and loneliness in them. She avoided meeting my gaze for a long time, however. Perhaps she knew how much her eyes gave away.

Crystal was brought to my hospital by ambulance three times for attempted suicide. Each time I directed my team's response to her immediate physical problems. We pumped her stomach, flushed her bloodstream with intravenous fluids, and cleansed her gut with activated charcoal; then we admitted her to our adolescent inpatient service for monitoring of her liver function and recovery from the physical symptoms of her overdose. Each time the psychiatrists evaluated her as well, keeping her under close observation until they concluded she was no longer an active threat to herself. Crystal's first admission followed a violent argument with her mother over having stayed out all night. She swallowed half of a large bottle of aspirin tablets and confessed to her mother what she had done when she began to vomit.

Crystal's mother sat at her bedside with tear-stained cheeks, twisting a handkerchief in her hands and stepping into the conference room to speak with the psychiatrist before rushing off to work. Crystal's father, a gruff man obviously uncomfortable with a member of his family being the object of so much attention, put in a short appearance, leaving before the psychiatrist could be informed that he was there. After two days, Crystal had recovered fully physically, and after forty-eight hours of further observation by the psychiatry team, the chief psychiatrist cleared her for discharge.

Crystal's second hospitalization happened after her boyfriend jilted her. It was too much, she said, to learn that he was making the same promises to her ex-best-friend that he had once made to her. The third occurred when her brother was sent to jail for dealing drugs. She explained that he was the only one who could make her feel safe; with him gone, her fear and loneliness had begun to close in on her. Each time she swallowed a larger amount of aspirin than the time before, though still not enough to threaten her life. And each time the psychiatrists declared that she was not truly suicidal but had merely made a "suicidal gesture" in the face of stressful events.

The psychiatrists always scheduled her for a follow-up appointment in the psychiatry clinic when she left the hospital, but she failed to keep a single one. I was not surprised. From my perspective, what Crystal needed far more than a psychiatrist was to be loved. Even as she tried to claim more independence in her life, she needed to know that she had a permanent place in someone's heart, a place where she would always be remembered and sheltered, no matter what.

Not unexpectedly, the residents under my supervision were growing bored with Crystal's case. "Minor" suicide attempts like Crystal's were not thought to be motivated by a real desire to die, made by someone who had abandoned all hope in living. Rather, they were viewed as a form of "acting out," a term conveniently used to explain self-destructive behavior while simultaneously dismissing it as not significant enough to warrant alarm. Since the clinical risk of death from such behavior was slight, the overworked residents began to think that caring for patients like Crystal was a waste of their valuable time.

Then Crystal was brought in for the fourth time, in coma. This time she had consumed not only two entire bottles of aspirin but also a bottle of her mother's Prozac and one of her father's heart medications, putting her at risk for lethal cardiac and neurological effects. She was in intensive care for five days before she recovered enough to speak about what had happened, and she remained on the psychiatric unit for two weeks after that. Her mother took sick leave from work to be with her, staying at her side late into the night, while her father put in short but regular appearances, relieving his discomfort by stepping outside for frequent cigarette breaks. Occasionally, the two parents sat together and held each other's hand.

Suicide was then, and still is, the third leading cause of death for adolescents in the United States, with accidents—primarily motor vehicle accidents—and homicide being the first and second causes. To me, this chilling fact pointed to a great amount of unrecognized suffering in teenagers' lives. Even more unsettling to me was the fact that many teens make one or more "unsuccessful" attempts before being "successful." In other words, teens often make pleas for help that are not taken seriously. Perhaps, I thought, if we would listen with our feelings as well as our intellect, we would hear the cries of such floundering souls who feel unseen and unheard—souls in need of attention who know no clearer way to ask for it than to threaten to end their life, to madly flail their arms before they sink beneath the waves. Undoubtedly they believe that if others can see they are drowning, someone will hurry to save them.

This seems like a risky tactic, but for Crystal, at least, it worked. Her parents felt her pain. Her mother, who had become brittle and distant under the weight of her own disappointment in life, softened, and her father paused and woke up from his self-pitying torpor. Hearts that had become closed opened again, and a real reunion happened.

The last time I saw Crystal, she was passing through the adolescent clinic, smartly dressed in high-heeled boots, shorts, and a snug sweater, making me realize I had never seen her in anything other than a hospital gown during all the months I had known her. She was on her way to a therapy group for teens to which the psychiatrists referred her. She paused for a brief chat and told me proudly that she was studying for her high school diploma, working part-time at a coffee shop, and applying to beautician school. When I asked her if there was something she had learned from the recent events in her life that she would be willing to share with me, she smiled, as if it was a question to which she had already given a good deal of thought and appreciated being asked.

"Yes," she said, suddenly a little shy but obviously determined to push through it, "I've learned a lot. I've learned that my parents—and you doctors too—really do care and really do want to help. And I see now, that no one knew how bad I was hurting—how alone and scared I was—because I couldn't tell them. And since we couldn't communicate, we all just stayed stuck in our separate worlds, not hearing each other."

She gave a wry smile and shook her head, as if appreciating the irony of the situation, causing the large, gold-loop earrings she wore to sway back and forth emphatically.

"So anyhow," she continued, "what I'm learning now is how to tell other people what's going on inside of me—how to let them know when I'm sad or confused or lonely."

I nodded appreciatively and was about to say some wise words of encouragement, when she suddenly turned the tables on me.

"And what have you learned, Dr. MacGregor?" she asked with the purest innocence in her voice. "Our therapist says that everyone is in a process of learning, no matter who they are."

"Your therapist is very wise," I said, secretly glad to be relieved of the obligation to be wise that moment myself and instead invited to be a fellow student of life. "What I learned, Crystal, is that we doctors, and parents, too, should listen harder to teenagers so they don't have to be drowning in their pain and trying to kill themselves before we realize how much they're suffering."

Crystal nodded solemnly.

187

"That's right, Dr. MacGregor," she replied, looking at me thoughtfully with her earnest, milk chocolate eyes. "Maybe more grown-ups could learn to listen with their hearts, not just with their heads." And with a smile, she turned and continued on her way to her therapy group, leaving me to hope fervently that it could be so.

*   *   *   *   *   *   *

One important thing about compassion I have observed is that it does not pass judgment on others. It gives us the capacity to care about those who struggle with challenges in their lives without blaming or condemning them for their part in creating those challenges. I discovered this characteristic of compassion when I met Rosa, who stretched me to the limit of my own, then young and untried compassion.

Rosa's eighteen-month-old daughter, Maddy, was one of my patients during my first year of residency training. The girl had been brought to our emergency room by ambulance after being resuscitated in her home in the Lower East Side tenements by the emergency medicine technicians who answered Rosa's frantic call to 9-1-1. Rosa had been giving Maddy a bath and had stepped out of the bathroom for only a few seconds, according to Rosa's recollection. When she returned, Maddy was lying submerged in the water, blue and motionless.

From the beginning, we did everything we could to allow for the possibility that Maddy might recover. We attached her to a ventilator to keep her breathing. We dripped cardiac stimulants and blood pressure boosters into her veins to keep her heart and circulatory system functioning. We infused her bloodstream with antibiotics to prevent infection and with carefully calculated electrolyte solutions to balance her metabolism. Yet in spite of all this, the hope of recovery was steadily receding. Her heart rate was irregular and her kidneys were starting to fail, and our neurologist announced that her higher brain centers had permanently lost their ability to function.

Over the course of the week that we had been laboring to give Maddy the chance to recover, Rosa had not left her side. She paced about in Maddy's room like a caged animal, jumping at the slightest sound. A sorry-looking, tight-lipped woman, she appeared intensely uncomfortable, as if she had to use all her willpower to keep from bolting out the door. She accosted every person who entered the room, demanding to know their purpose for being there and becoming profusely apologetic when the person proved to play an important role. When you approached her to ask a question or convey some information, you never knew what kind of response you were going to get. One minute she could be obsequious, the next darkly hostile and suspicious, the next full of optimistic bluster and bravado, jumping from one persona to another so abruptly it gave the impression that inwardly she had no place to anchor herself. We were not certain if this was her usual behavior, or whether it was because her psyche had been fractured into separate pieces with the shock of what had happened to Maddy. When she left for short breaks, she returned smelling of cigarette smoke and sometimes of alcohol as well.

The Bureau of Child Welfare had been contacted when Maddy was brought in because of the vagueness in Rosa's description of what had happened that evening. Why had she left the bathroom in the middle of bathing Maddy? How could she not have heard any sound of struggle in such a tiny apartment? And how could she have been gone just a few seconds if Maddy's body was already limp and blue when she returned? Was this a case of unfortunate ignorance, or was there a possibility of negligence, or even of something worse? These were questions that the BCW workers had concerns about, but no good answers had been found. They were keeping Maddy's case open.

Then, abruptly, without waiting for these mysteries to be solved, Maddy died. Her blood pressure fell and her heart stopped, and none of our resuscitation procedures made any difference. The nurses ushered Rosa out of the room as five of us tried our utmost to bring Maddy back, but she did not respond. She was gone.

When we went out to the nurses' station where Rosa was hunched in a chair, intending to break the news to her, she took one look at us, leapt to her feet, and unleashed a torrent of profanities, screaming that we had let her baby die, that we had killed her little girl. Hurling herself at us, she attacked with her fists and her feet, landing quite a few direct hits before two of the senior residents pushed her firmly into a chair and held her there as she continued to wail and howl incoherently.

It is amazing how many thoughts can flash through one's head during a few minutes of chaos. The first thoughts that came into mine were ones of angry indignation and counteraccusation: *What right did Rosa have to be angry at us? We were doctors, for heaven's sake. We had worked hard, and we had done our best. Didn't she know that it pained us to lose a beautiful little girl too? And wasn't this her own fault, after all? Hadn't she been the one to leave her toddler alone in a slippery tub?*

Yet before too long, my stream of counteraccusations died away and a different voice began to speak in my mind, one that had waited patiently for my self-justification to finish. It asked softly: *Why be angry and feel the need to defend yourself? The woman is only pouring her guilt out on you because it's more than she can bear. Your insulted pride is nothing compared to the pain that's overwhelming her. Having her daughter die is bad enough, but accepting her own failed vigilance as the cause is too much for her. What good does blaming do?*

As these latter thoughts passed through my mind, I saw the situation from the perspective of compassion. I saw that regardless of questions of fault, for Rosa, the pain of Maddy's death was real, and it hurt tremendously.

With that simple realization, my anger dissolved and my heart went out to this woman who had been dealt such a hard blow. And I understood then what gives the human heart its ability to be compassionate: it knows how extremely desperate human pain can be. In knowing that, I was not afraid to give such pain the room it needed to express itself and feel heard.

*   *   *   *   *   *   *

Señora Hernandez chose a very hectic clinic day to make an unscheduled knock on my office door. "Por favor, Doctora," she gasped breathlessly, as if she had just jogged up all five flights of stairs to reach the adolescent floor in the urgency of her mission. After catching her breath and taking a seat in the chair beside my desk, she explained that she had just come from the hospital's Surgical Intensive Care Unit where she was visiting her eldest son Hector after his near brush with death.

I knew Hector because he had visited my adolescent clinic a few times in the past for routine physical exams. He had come to New York City from Puerto Rico at age fourteen with his mother and younger brother and sister, excited by his mother's visions of the better life they were sure to find. He was a good-looking boy with a thick shock of black hair and a flashy smile, who, I recalled, never failed to fill his pockets with condom samples when he came for his appointments.

"Got to be prepared for the unexpected!" he liked to say, with a cocky tilt of his head. But life on the streets had eventually proven to be more to his liking than the demands of high school. He had dropped out three years ago, at age seventeen, and I had not seen him since. Now, his mother was telling me, he had been the victim of the kind of mind-numbing brutality that sometimes happens in the inner city.

One week ago, Señora Hernandez explained, Hector had been found in the wee hours of the night by the Manhattan Transit Authority police, lying unconscious in a pool of blood in the Canal Street subway station. He had been badly beaten, his fancy black-leather jacket emblazoned with a large fiery-red dragon had been stripped off, and the initials of a gang had been carved into the flesh of his back with a knife. The jacket was gone, and no witnesses had been found.

Hector lost so much blood as he lay sprawled on the cold cement subway platform that he was in cardiovascular shock when he arrived at our hospital by ambulance. Rushed immediately to the OR, he had fresh-frozen plasma pumped into his body to keep his circulatory system from collapsing, while the surgeons put in more than three hundred stitches to close his wounds. Having lost a good half of his body's blood, he also had to be transfused with several units of packed red blood cells, the gift of anonymous donors that so often saves people's lives when they fall in harm's way.

The reason Señora Hernandez had come was not about Hector, however. It was about Raymundo, Hector's younger brother. Raymundo, she said, was behaving strangely, and she was terribly worried about him. At age sixteen, he was normally the more reliable one of her two sons—usually a friendly, easy-going boy, she explained with a fretful shake of her head—but since the incident had happened, he had fallen into a dark, sullen mood. No matter how much she pleaded with him to tell her what he was thinking or feeling, he remained behind a stony wall of silence.

"You know, Doctora," she said finally, with a heaviness in her voice that suggested she was coming to the crux of her concerns, "in my culture names are important. They reflect a person's spirit. They tell you who a person is."

She paused and took a deep breath to steady herself, and then continued. "The name Hector means 'one who holds on,' and I believe Hector will do that. He will come through this. I know he will. But Raymundo is different. What his name means is 'the one who protects,' and I fear it's in his nature to take his brother's problems too much into his own heart. I fear he feels he must avenge his brother for the awful thing that was done to him."

She bit her lower lip uneasily. "You see," she said, bending closer and dropping her voice, as if about to disclose something confidential, "I overheard him tell his girlfriend: *They're going to pay for what they did.*"

For a long moment, Señora Hernandez gazed down at her hands clasped tightly together in her lap. Then she lifted her head and looked at me with pleading eyes, saying, "I am afraid for him, Doctora. I do not know what to do. Please, will you speak to him?"

"Of course I will," I responded with unwarranted optimism but wanting to be supportive, and we agreed she would bring him to my office as soon as she could persuade him to come.

As I walked home from work later that day, my path took me by the Union Square subway station and the subway line that led to Canal Street, where Hector's attackers had overwhelmed him. As I passed the subway entrance, a chill seemed to emanate from the long stairway leading down to that underground world lying beneath the busy city streets. The sensation jangled my nerves and made me want to stop and shout at life and demand to know why awful things like this had to happen. But life seemed only to sigh and patiently reply that such problems were of our own human making, and it was our task to learn how to resolve them. I wondered whether that would be possible for Señora Hernandez and her two sons.

When Raymundo showed up for his appointment several days later, I hardly recognized him. For one thing, he had grown. More disturbingly, the easygoing manner I remembered him having was gone.

"Raymundo," I said, smiling at him as he got to his feet from his mother's side in the waiting room, "come on in."

But my greeting fell flat, and his face remained fixed in silent stoniness as he walked toward the exam room, pulling a pretty, black-eyed teenage girl after him.

"The name's Ray," he said shortly, as he took a seat and sat the girl on his knee possessively.

An exercise in futility followed. Ray uttered only monosyllables and paid scant attention to my inquiries about his well-being or my careful suggestions about coping with traumatic life experience. A seething fury preoccupied him, holding his body rigid and barring the doors to his heart. Even when he spoke his brother's name, no other, softer emotion found room to appear. No tears arose in his eyes, no pain shook his voice, no sorrow trembled his youthful frame. His girlfriend watched his face hopefully, but he sat cloaked in a dark self-absorption that even her attentive presence seemed unable to penetrate, and his eyes never once met mine. Though I thought it a useless gesture, I concluded by encouraging Ray to return in another week and fill me in on how things were going.

The idea did not even register. Without a word, Ray rose and jammed his fists into his pockets, turned stiffly on his heel, and stalked from the room, his girlfriend trailing timidly behind.

How painful it was to see Ray go. He was far too young to have decided he had mortal enemies and a debt to collect from them. I certainly sympathized with his anger, but I also sorrowed at his bitter refusal to allow that anger to soften. Fiercely clinging to the sense of power his anger gave him, he had no idea how easily such anger could hurt him. Remorseless rage— fearless, blind hatred—is a dangerous burden to carry. It can easily poison a person's happiness and steal their life away.

For a doctor, whose chosen mission is to help other people, it is hard not to be able to reach a particular person in their pain and help them find a way to heal. With Ray, it hurt to feel so completely impotent, to not be able to make a whit of difference in his suffering. Yet compassion's message was clear. *Listen*, it said quietly, *do not force. Know that there are times when the most that can be done for someone who is caught in suffering is simply to be patient and wait, believing that the needed change will eventually come. It is an important part of assisting these suffering ones—to hold open the space for their healing to happen, trusting that healing has its own wise pace and timing.*

One week later, Ray failed to show up for his appointment, and instead, Señora Hernandez called. The good news, she said, was that Hector was improving quickly and would be discharged from the hospital soon. The bad news, she added with the sound of weariness in her voice, was that Ray's gloom continued unabated, as did her concern for him. She had decided, therefore, that as soon as Hector was able to travel, she would take her three children with her back to Puerto Rico. The four of them were more than welcome to stay with extended family there, and she felt they would all be better off. The arrangement would allow Hector to regain his strength, she explained, and would keep Raymundo safe. I said this sounded like a good plan, and with all my heart I wished her family well.

Nearly a year later, a letter postmarked from San Juan, Puerto Rico, arrived at the clinic. It was addressed in careful handwriting to *Señora Doctora MacGregor.* Written on a piece of flower-bordered stationery was a short note from Señora Hernandez. She apologized for not having written sooner, but was glad now to be able to report good news. Hector was fully recovered. Moreover, he had found a job and was thinking about getting married. And best of all, she said, since this had been her real worry, Raymundo was doing well too. He was back in school and had more girlfriends than she could count. It had taken many months, but as Hector had healed from his wounds and left the past behind, Raymundo had gradually healed from his as well. It was all that she had hoped for, and what I had hoped for too.

* * * * * * *

Isabella acquired the AIDS virus from her mother at birth, and because she had been born before the advent of antiretroviral medications, her four short years of life had been riddled with debilitating infections and too many hospitalizations to count.

But in spite of the ordeals her body had been through, her spirit was undaunted. She was like a perpetual ray of sunshine. As soon as she began to recover from whatever setback had brought her into the hospital, she would be out of bed, cheerfully trotting through the hallways of the pediatric ward in her frilly pink nightgown and pink bunny slippers. She could often be found conducting her own rounds, pushing her IV pole along with her as she peeked into one room after another to see how each of the other children on the ward were faring. If any staff doctors happened to cross her path along the way, she would stop us, and a predictable conversation would ensue.

"Dr. Maweggor," she would bubble excitedly, if I were the one to be cornered by her, "do you know there's a new boy here? His name is Timothy!"

"Yes, Isabella, I do know Timothy is here."

"Dr. Maweggor, are you going to help Timothy get better so he can go home?"

"Yes, Isabella, I'm going to do my very best to help Timothy get better so that he can go home, just like I'm doing my very best to help you get better so that you can go home too."

Indicating her approval of this plan with a sparkling smile and a vigorous nod, Isabella would then shuffle away with her slippers and her IV pole to visit the next room, or else head for the nurses' station where she would climb up on one of the chairs and assign herself the job of "helping" whichever members of the staff were there. Truly, it was hard to resist company as sweet as hers.

But the day came when Isabella developed an infection that would not respond to treatment, and her fragile immune system began to fail. A dark cloud settled over the ward as our little ray of sunshine grew sicker and sicker. Then, late one afternoon, Isabella's adoptive mother Helena, who had cared for her since shortly after birth when Isabella's own mother had died, came looking for me to say that Isabella wanted to speak with me. With a mixture of curiosity and concern, I went quickly to her room.

Isabella was sitting in a chair beside her hospital bed, a blanket around her shoulders, an oxygen mask over her nose and mouth, and a ragged stuffed rabbit in her lap. Kneeling down on the floor so that I could be at eye level with her, I took her hand in mine. Her fingers were still greasy from the French fries she had held on to tightly all afternoon. Though she had not felt up to eating them, she had not been willing to let them go because they were her favorite food of all, and her nurse had finally teased them out of her grip while she was taking a nap.

"Hi, sweetheart," I said. "Did you want to see me?"

She managed a meager smile. Then, looking at me with big eyes and a solemn expression, she said, "Dr. Maweggor, Paco didn't get better and go home."

I sighed. Paco was a boy Isabella had come to know on the ward. He was several years older than her, and he had died recently of AIDS-related problems after a long, drawn-out decline.

"Yes, Isabella, that's true," I admitted sadly. "I'm afraid that we can't help everyone get better, even though we try. Some people just get too sick."

"I know that," she said forgivingly, still looking me in the eye. "But . . . ," she continued, frowning as if puzzling out how to put what she wanted to say, "do people *stay* sick when they go to heaven?" She leaned forward expectantly to hear my reply, holding her oxygen mask in place with one hand and clutching her rabbit so that he would not fall from her lap with the other.

The question was not one I felt I had much authority to draw upon for an answer, but if life made any sense at all, I thought, the answer surely had to be no.

"I'm not an expert about that, Isabella," I said truthfully, "but I really don't think so."

"Good," she said, brightening a bit, "because it hurts when you're sick, Dr. Maweggor, and I don't want Paco to be sick *or* hurting anymore!"

She spoke with the authority of a person who knew what she was talking about. She had had a lifetime of sickness and pain. As she paused to regain her energy, I waited, watching the sides of her oxygen mask cloud slightly with each out-breath she made. After a short while, she spoke up again.

"Dr. Maweggor, I'm tired."

A lump formed in my throat, and for a second I found it difficult to speak.

"I know, sweetheart," I murmured. "I'm sorry I can't do more for you."

She shook her head.

"That's OK," she said soothingly, as if to make clear that she was not intending to complain. "But . . . what if I get *too* tired and I can't go see the other children anymore? Will you still take care of them so they won't stay sick and hurting? Do you *promise* you will?"

To make a sworn promise to a dying child is no small matter. With her big, earnest eyes, Isabella seemed to be holding not just me but life itself accountable.

"Yes, Isabella," I said to this child whose heart contained as much compassion as that of any person I had ever met, "I promise. I'll do my very best. You can count on it."

* * * * * * *

It is not unusual in the practice of pediatrics to encounter children like Isabella, children who pay attention not just to their own pain, but to that of other people as well, as if their suffering had sensitized their heart. Terrell was another one, and his compassion showed itself in the middle of an intense situation.

At sixteen, Terrell's biggest interest in life, even more than his burgeoning interest in girls, was football. This was his passion. His sturdy build and unshakably positive attitude made him perfect as a linebacker, and with Terrell on board, everyone on the team had high hopes that their upcoming season would be the best their high school had seen in years. Sadly, their hopes were dashed the day the accident happened.

It did not look any worse than most collisions that take place during football practice, but when Terrell's friend Studs, another hefty linebacker, ran into him, Terrell hit the ground with a groan that made every listener shudder. Yet the news that circulated the following day was far worse than that of a mere torn ligament and one lost season of play, as most of the fans were expecting to hear. It raised the question of Terrell's life.

It turned out that Terrell had osteosarcoma, or cancer of the bone—the sixth most common kind of cancer to attack children and youth. This discovery explained the pain he had been feeling just above his knee for months, a pain he had tried diligently to work out by doing careful warm-ups before every football practice, by massaging the aching area afterward, and then rubbing in muscle liniment very well. But the pain had lingered and gradually grown worse, even waking him up at night, and now the reason why was deadly clear. The malignancy had been chewing up the interior structure of his femur, the mightiest bone in the body, steadily destroying the central honeycomb-like formation that makes bones strong but not too dense and heavy for our muscles to move. One hard hit finally caused his weakened femur to crack right through.

In that same instant, Terrell's dreams of a football career buckled and broke as well. The oncologists and orthopedic surgeons who came to evaluate him in the hospital, and present the results of their x-rays, CAT scans, and MRIs, gave him the worst news possible. He was going to lose his leg. In order to save his life, the surgeons would have to amputate it from above his knee.

Terrell went into a state of shock. What the doctors were saying in their gruff but earnest way was at first more than his young man's mind could accept. This was too much of a shift to make overnight: to go from being a rising athletic star who gloried in the strength and agility of his body to becoming "a cripple" with a future impossible to imagine. And to be told that if he did not agree to having his leg cut off, he would die—that was a nightmare of gargantuan proportions. For days he lay in his hospital bed in a daze, while his devastated parents met with the team of doctors to iron out the plans for surgery and initiate chemotherapy to shrink the tumor before the surgeons took up their scalpels and saws and went in. As one of the consultants, called in to advise on how best to manage the pain Terrell would have following surgery, I felt a deep concern for how he was going to cope with all of this.

However, Terrell proved to be not only strong in body but strong in spirit, too, and soon he began to focus himself. Perhaps it was the surgeons who helped. They had seen other young people his age have the rug pulled out from under them in this terrible way before. They knew the power of human beings to take such blows and go on, and their knowledge of that sounded in their voices. Perhaps, too, the sight of his parents' pain helped take his mind off his own distress and get his positive attitude engaged again. He loved his parents dearly, in spite of their flaws, and it came naturally to Terrell to sense their despair and be concerned for them.

In fact, Terrell's parents had been struggling with their own private pain for quite some time. Two earnest, caring people, both with full-time careers, they failed to see eye to eye on many things, and they had been reaching the end of a rocky road of divorce when Terrell's diagnosis was made. Now they had been swept together into the eye of a monstrous storm. It was almost more than they could take.

Over those unimaginably difficult weeks, one or the other of the two stayed at Terrell's bedside round the clock, dividing the time carefully so that they would not have to cross each other's path any more than necessary. As day after day of consultation and chemotherapy and preparation for surgery went by, they grew weary to the bone. Worry appeared permanently etched on their faces; they smiled rarely and only with effort.

Then the day of surgery arrived. It was a long procedure—which Terrell's parents endured by sitting in silent coexistence in the waiting room—and it went as smoothly as could have been expected. When I paid a visit to Terrell to make certain his pain was under control after his transfer back to the ward from the recovery room, I found him looking worn but alert, the stump that remained of his once perfect athlete's leg wrapped in white bandages and elevated to the level of his heart to facilitate circulation. Both of his parents were with him, sitting on opposite sides of the room near the end of his bed, dozing. They were so exhausted that neither one of them stirred as Terrell and I spoke, and thus neither heard what their son had to say.

He was mature and forthright. He answered my questions about the intensity and character of his pain thoughtfully and listened with careful attention to my instructions about how to self-administer the potent intravenous pain medication we were providing him via the patient-controlled pump attached to a pole beside his bed. From the beginning, he had been interested in the idea that he could be in charge of his own pain treatment. He had said it gave him some reassurance that he could make it through this whole experience.

Not wanting to wear Terrell out after what his body had just been through, I tried to keep my visit brief, but before heading for the door I asked if there was anything else I could help him with.

Terrell did not stop for even a moment to think. With a quick glance toward his sleeping mother and father, he whispered in a voice that was scratchy from his larynx having been intubated during the long hours of surgery, "Yes, my mom and dad."

He gazed at me expectantly.

"You want me to help with your mom and dad?" I asked, following his lead and keeping my voice to a whisper. I wanted to be certain I understood him correctly.

Terrell closed his eyes and nodded, letting his head fall back on his pillow for a moment. When he opened his eyes again, he explained.

"Yes," he said. "They're so sad. I want them to be happy. Can you tell them they should still be friends, even if they're not married anymore?"

He cast a cautious eye in his parents' direction. "I think they could do it, if they would only try," he added in a voice remarkably free of reproach. "They just need someone to encourage them."

He gave a wan, rueful smile. "Someone other than me, I mean. Someone they'll listen to."

I promised Terrell I would do my best. As I sat at the nurses' station writing my notes in his chart, I caught sight of Terrell's father coming out the door of his son's room, so I decided to waste no time and hurried to catch him. When I asked if I could meet with him and his wife briefly in the conference room, he nodded wearily.

When the three of us had settled in chairs at one end of the long meeting table, I proceeded to tell them about the conversation Terrell and I had just had, quoting his words as closely as possible, especially the part about his belief that they could separate and still stay friends if they would only try. I added how much Terrell's sincerity had moved me, and how remarkable I thought it was that he could be so concerned about them when he had such a heavy load to carry himself. I knew I was entering territory where I might not be welcome, but I had promised Terrell, so I decided to take a chance. I asked if they would be willing to give this a try—for his sake, if not for their own.

A hollow silence followed, during which Terrell's father turned his head away, his face contracted with emotion, and his mother brushed a soundless flow of tears from her cheeks.

After several uncomfortable minutes, they looked at each other uncertainly.

"Well," his father said gravely and cleared his throat, "if it means so much to Terrell, maybe we can try."

"Yes," his mother replied stiffly, but with determination in her voice, "the least we can do is try."

So the two of them proceeded to do what they could not have found the will to do if it were not for their injured son. The concern they shared for their only child began to thaw the icy gulf between them. They began to overlap the time they spent with Terrell, and the weary smile they saw on their son's face fueled further efforts to find common ground. Each time I visited to check on the progress Terrell was making, I could see the progress they were making as well. The atmosphere between them grew more relaxed, and the habit of blaming each other for their troubles steadily faded.

And though they carefully reiterated to Terrell that they still believed the decision to end their marriage was right, they moved from an uneasy truce to a bond of determined collaboration and the early signs of friendship. Over the time that it took for Terrell to heal from his surgery and finally be ready to leave the hospital and enter a rehabilitation center, where he would learn a new way of living in his body, their growing bond proved to be a balm for an unspoken pain that had been weighing heavily on the hearts of all three. I found this change heartening to watch, and I knew that it might never have happened, if it had not been for a teenager's determination and compassion.

*   *   *   *   *   *   *

Much of the suffering I witnessed over the years seemed to lead eventually to some redeeming outcome. Some healing happened, some important lesson was learned, some change occurred that proved to be important. But not always. Some suffering made no sense to me at all.

One on-call night during my residency training, an urgent request for pediatric backup came from the obstetrics floor at about three o'clock in the morning. A pregnant woman was being admitted from the ER. She was just entering her eighth month, and she had gone into labor precipitously. Her contractions were coming fast and furiously, and the bad news was that the baby was in the double-footling breech position, meaning coming down the birth canal feetfirst. This is an approach to birth that obstetricians and midwives always try to prevent since it is much safer if the baby's head leads the way, for then the bones of his or her skull will stretch the mother's tissues and widen the path for the rest of the baby's body to easily follow. The far less common, feet-first approach this baby was taking would leave his head, the largest part of his body, to exit last, which was much more risky. Unfortunately, it was too late in this woman's case to try to maneuver the baby into a better position or to intervene with a cesarean section because by the time she had arrived at the hospital, the birth process was too far along. Pediatricians were needed on the scene in case her baby got into trouble.

Memhet, the senior pediatric resident on duty, and I, the junior resident, took off instantly for the obstetrics floor. Arriving at a dead run, we quickly scrubbed and gloved and set up our resuscitation station. The obstetrician attending the pregnant woman turned out to be a friend of ours by the name of Joel, someone we had known when he was a star OB resident a couple of years ahead of us in his training. After graduation, he had been hired on at the hospital as a staff physician and now helped supervise a busy OB clinic.

Joel was standing by the side of the delivery table where the pregnant woman was lying, her curving, drum-tight abdomen strapped round with the ultrasonic infant heart-rate monitor. He motioned for us to join him. His face was grim.

"It's not going well," he said in a taut voice. "I've got her sedated and on oxygen, and her oxygen saturation is good, but the baby's vital signs have me worried. I think there's trouble with the umbilical cord. It may be wrapped around the little guy's neck. I want to get him out as soon as possible. Be ready."

We told him we were all set to go, and he went back to bending over his patient. It was not long before a tiny foot appeared between the woman's thighs, quickly followed by a second one. As Joel pulled steadily on the two little legs, the hips followed, and then chest and arms.

Suddenly, we heard Joel exclaim in frustration, "Damn, his head isn't coming!"

With a chill, we knew that the worst had happened. Following the passage of the baby's shoulders, the woman's muscular cervix had tightened reflexively around the baby's throat, trapping his head inside the birth canal and pinching tight the umbilical cord that was wrapped around his neck, cutting off his vital supply of oxygen-rich blood. A race against time was on.

Memhet and I stood poised to spring, itching to implement the lifesaving procedures that had been drilled into our marrow. Yet we were immobilized, frozen at the threshold of action, like a couple of high-strung racehorses fretting behind the racetrack starting gate. Feeling so useless when a life was in danger was pure torture. But there was nothing to do except hold ourselves ready and watch, keeping our eyes fixed on the drama in front of us, knowing that if we should happen to look away at the moment the baby came free, precious seconds would be lost.

One agonizing minute after another ticked by. Random thoughts drifted through the void in my mind. Had I written an order for that child in Room 604 to have the chest x-ray she needed? Had the nephrologists received my request for a consult on the little boy we had admitted earlier in the evening

with blood in his urine? My scrub suit felt stiff and uncomfortable, and I noticed that the taste in my mouth was that of
someone who had not had an opportunity to brush her teeth
in the last twenty-one hours.

Next to me, Memhet shifted his weight back and forth
from one foot to the other. From the corner of my eye, I
glimpsed him stretching his neck and shoulders this way
and that, and every now and then I heard an exasperated
"Pwhooah!" as he expelled the breath he was unconsciously holding.

As for Joel, his entire attention centered on his patient
with urgent intensity. Sweat was glistening on his forehead
and running down his neck, and he strained and grunted as
he fought with the woman's cervix, which was stubbornly
refusing to let go of its stranglehold around the baby's neck.

Eventually, after what seemed like an interminable length
of time, Joel gave a long, embattled groan, causing Memhet
and me to glance fleetingly at each other. For the briefest
moment our eyes met, each acknowledging what the other
knew: the hope we had been clinging to was, by now, almost
certainly gone.

When Joel handed us the little body that he had finally wrestled free, we knew that the baby's chance of surviving this ordeal was inconceivably small. He had been severely stressed
and deprived of oxygen far too long, surely more than any
human body could endure.

Yet he could not be abandoned. We laid his limp body
gently on the warming table, and as I quickly suctioned the
mucus from his mouth and reached for our resuscitation
implements, Memhet leaned over with his stethoscope to
listen for a heartbeat. His eyes widened for an instant as he
thought he heard the sound of a small human heart clinging
to life—but whether that was true, or it was just his own refusal to relinquish hope, we would never know. For though
we executed our resuscitation procedures with determination,

there was no response. The tiny body lay unmoving, empty of life.

The three of us stood there in the now quiet delivery room for a long moment, drained of the sense of purpose that had been driving us, unable, or unwilling, to move on. Inwardly I was shuddering with sorrow for the life unlived and for the mother who would soon wake from her anesthesia-induced sleep to find her baby gone.

How could such a thing happen, my anguished mind cried. *How could a woman's body exert so much effort to create a new life, only to snatch that life away at the very last moment? Why invest all those months in the complex process of gestation, and then, just when the goal is in sight, erect an unyielding barrier, saying, "Passage denied"? How could life contain such an inexplicable, unwarranted kind of suffering?*

I wondered how Joel could bear the task of giving his patient the terrible news. Would he actually tell her the truth— that her own body had grabbed her baby by the throat and strangled him to death—or would he cover over the truth with merciful untruths and omissions? I stepped over to him and blurted out my question.

"Oh, no," he said with a pained expression on his face, "we won't tell her the full story. The gruesome details of her baby's death are best kept for us to grapple with and lament. They're not necessary for her to hear. It will be all that she can bear just to learn that her baby has died despite everything possible having been done to save him. That's what matters to her, and that's what we have to help her with."

He paused and shook his head ruefully. "Life seems cruel sometimes, and I hate that," he admitted reluctantly, "but that's just the way it is. There's nothing to do about it except meet every moment as best as you can, and never stop caring about what you do and for whom you do it. It might seem paradoxical, I know, but the more you keep your heart open and don't resist, the more you can bear whatever life brings."

With a heavy sigh, Joel pulled off his surgical gloves, patted me on the shoulder, and walked away to look for a cup of coffee.

*   *   *   *   *   *   *

Just as significant as learning to have compassion for others (though perhaps more easily overlooked) is learning to have compassion for ourselves. Some of us take a long time to recognize the importance of this lesson, and for some it may not become clear until late in life, as it did for Randolf. When he finally came to see that having compassion for himself was not just a subtle form of self-indulgence but rather something wiser and more generous than that, it was almost too late.

I met Randolf shortly after he enrolled in my hospital's hospice program. He had been diagnosed with metastatic prostate cancer two years previously, at age ninety. His doctors had recommended modifying the treatment protocol to make it less onerous in light of his advanced age, estimating that they could probably hold off the inevitable for a couple of years or so. As expected, the cancer had slowly gained ground, spreading to many sites in his bones, causing him steady pain and whittling away at his fiercely guarded independence. Since he was open to sharing his perspective on approaching the end of life with others who cared to listen, he agreed to my conducting a series of interviews with him as part of the research of the Project on Dying and the Inner Life.

Flamboyantly eccentric and one of a kind would be the best way to describe Randolf. This was how he struck me when I first encountered him, and as I came to know this gentleman better, I realized that at age ninety-two the description did only partial justice to what had apparently been vividly true in his younger years.

The first visit I paid to his home told more than many words could about the life he had lived. His apartment was on the sixteenth floor of an aging, genteel building on Fifth Avenue, with windows that looked out over the green trees and walkways of Central Park. Along one wall of the large living room, massive hardwood bookshelves reached nearly to the ceiling, their shelves crammed with well-used books. Another wall was entirely given over to framed photographs, mostly of theatrical performance scenes and actors' profiles scrawled upon with illegible signatures, as well as an assortment of faded posters announcing the opening of shows on Broadway and in London, Paris, and other fashionable locations. Two graceful but slightly frayed royal-blue couches contrasted with a big over-stuffed, leather easy chair. A grand piano stood elegantly off to one side, a crimson shawl draped casually over the pianist's bench, while an armful of yellow tulips extended their blossoms in every direction from an ample crystal vase on the coffee table.

Randolf matched his eclectic surroundings. He was a big man who had aged well, with a stout stomach that emphasized his presence in a positive way, giving the impression of comfortable authority. Bushy white eyebrows hung dramatically over his piercing blue-gray eyes, and a white, handsomely sculpted moustache together with a deep, resonant voice that contained the hint of a European accent (though he readily confessed he grew up in Brooklyn) gave him an air of aristocracy. Shakespeare seemed to color his every gesture and figure of speech in a subtle and utterly natural way, as if Randolf's own identity was saturated with the persona of that revered theatrical genius. This was not surprising because Randolf's world had been the performing arts, and he had spent a great many years on major stages around the globe.

In fact, Randolf had worked in every aspect of theater—acting, directing, teaching, writing, reviewing, and producing—and he had received countless awards. His critique of the theatrical art form was legendary, and some of the numerous books he had written about the profession were still used as standard reference texts in the leading schools of performing arts. On our first meeting he had gestured toward a shelf that was lined with the books he had authored, with a dismissive wave of his hand.

Over the months that I knew Randolf, he would often refer fondly to "the old days," a past filled with the high drama of opening night, the bustle of gala receptions, and the glamour of extravagant, all-night parties that could take place any day of the week. He had not only been a guru of the theatrical world but also a prominent figure in the gay community and an icon at the center of a vibrant social scene in which he could often be found holding court with admiring followers.

This was a life he loved, and it continued unabated for decades. He never had any desire to "settle down," he said. He saw "settling down" as losing the juiciness of life. But eventually, though, the last of the many lovers he had, a virtuoso pianist twenty years younger than him, stayed on as his life-mate. For a while, he said, he savored a new kind of happiness. But when Randolf was just about to celebrate his eightieth birthday, his beloved partner passed away, and he had been alone ever since.

Randolf's telling of his life's tale unfolded over several weeks of regular visits. Then, one day, Randolf abruptly asked if I would like to hear "the real story," a story he did not share with everyone. He seemed to enjoy the interest that showed on my face, for he gave a gracious smile and began.

Two years ago, he said, when he was ninety, he was growing weary and beginning to wonder what it would be like to die, when suddenly he was diagnosed with cancer.

So is this the way it will end, he had thought to himself, *with a whimper and not with a bang? All those grand curtain calls and endless accolades, and all that remains is a pathetic and useless old man fading meekly away into oblivion?*

All his lifelong pleasures and accomplishments became like dust in his mouth. To think he had once imagined that he had brought some light into the world. How naive and egotistical it all appeared now—superficial and meaningless. The once firm ground he had stood on all his life turned to quicksand, he said, and he sank into a dark morass of cynicism and despair. For months he languished there, bitterly refusing all visitors, convinced they were only patronizing him. Finally, he made a plan and prepared to execute it.

A few days later, the doorman for Randolf's apartment, an elderly man named Samuel who had held that position for as long as some of the residents could remember, noticed when Randolf did not appear in the lobby that morning. Randolf was one of the predictable ones, Samuel told the police later. He would come down the elevator at eight o'clock every morning except Sunday, when Randolf liked to sleep in, pick up his *New York Times* from Samuel and chat a moment; then, regardless of the weather, he would amble down the block to the corner coffee shop and read about the latest mess the world was in over breakfast. When Randolf failed to appear that morning, Samuel said he began to get "a bad feeling."

The bad feeling grew stronger and stronger, until it led Samuel to do something unusually bold. He took the elevator up the sixteen floors to Randolf's apartment and knocked on the door. When no one answered, he banged. Finally, muttering, "I don't like the smell of this—no, I don't like it at all," he took the elevator back down to the ground floor, went to the manager's office where he located the keys to Randolf's apartment, and went back up again.

Standing in the hall, he called out at the top of his voice, "I'm coming in!"

He then unlocked the door and opened it. In less than a minute, he found Randolf collapsed on the kitchen floor, the oven door open where he had been kneeling with his head inside, the apartment filled with gas fumes.

Despite Samuel's advanced age, he was no weakling. (He had been in the military for the greater part of his life, he explained later, and was not ready to be put out to pasture yet.) He grabbed Randolf by the arms and dragged his hefty body out to the hallway, and then ran back inside, opened a window so that he could breathe, and dialed 9-1-1 on Randolph's phone.

As Randolf came to the end of his story, he shrugged his stately shoulders and gave a long sigh.

"I was in the hospital for nearly a week, recovering from that little folly," he said wryly. "It's not pleasant to speak about it, but when I look back, I see it was the best thing that could have happened to me. It literally shocked me out of my gloom. In fact, it was a lot like what you doctors do when you shock a patient who's having a cardiac arrest back to life!"

He let out a mirthful belly laugh as he savored the parallel he had suddenly observed. I had to laugh along with him, for it certainly sounded like an appropriate, if slightly macabre, comparison.

"Yes," he said when he got his breath back, "I took a good look at myself then—a more impartial look, you'd say—and what I saw was quite illuminating."

He wagged a long finger in the air emphatically as he explained.

"I saw what interesting creatures we are, we human beings," he said. "We're fragile and shortsighted, and creative and heroic, all at the same time. We're the perfect theatrical subjects! We have big dreams, and we make a monumental attempt to follow them, and in the process we can't help but make mistakes and get confused and hurt—and then we turn around and berate ourselves. What good drama we create!"

"It's ironic, the mistake *I* made," he said, suddenly leaning forward and scowling, causing his bushy Elizabethan eyebrows to meet in the center of his forehead. "I used to think the goal was to become perfect. I strove for perfection in everything I did—being a flawless actor, an impeccable director, writing superlative reviews. I critiqued myself relentlessly. But do you know what I think now?"

I shook my head.

"I think," he said, as he leaned back and let his eyebrows relax over his now serene blue-gray eyes, "that our imperfections amuse the One who created us. In fact, I think He or She may just view us as one of the most interesting shows in town!"

Randolf gazed at me with satisfaction, apparently pleased at the rapt attention his oration was receiving from his audience of one.

"So there you have it," he concluded, folding his hands over his comfortably rounded belly. "Here at the end of my life, I'm learning to have a little compassion for myself. And what it's showing me is that it's not such a bad thing to be imperfect after all!"

He smiled and twirled one end of his elegant moustache, and then added, "In fact, I would say that I'm feeling quite content with everything! Yes, I would!" And that was how he continued to feel, right up to his dying day, five months later.

EIGHT

Giving & Receiving

IN HOSPITALS, GIFTS are given and received every day. That is
the nature of a hospital. It is a place where people help each
other, sometimes in major ways, as when surgery is urgently
needed or when expert nursing care is essential to recovery,
but sometimes, too, in ways so unassuming that the person on
the receiving end may be taken completely by surprise. I once
received a gift in this way, and the giver's timing could not have
been more perfect.

I was just starting the third year of medical school, finally taking the plunge for which I had been preparing over the
preceding two long years: the plunge into direct patient care. A
month of intensive work taking care of patients on the adult
medical ward was ahead of me, and I was eager to get started.
When the chief resident assigned me to Mr. Harrison's case
with instructions to gather the details of his medical and psychosocial history, I went immediately to my patient's room
with pen and paper in hand.

A retired businessman in his mid-seventies, Mr. Harrison
had been admitted early that morning with newly diagnosed
lung cancer. As I introduced myself and pulled up a chair
alongside the bed where he lay, he observed me with a kindly
look in his eyes. He was a distinguished-looking man with hair
graying at the temples, and he listened politely while I explained
to him the task that had brought me there. Because he seemed

214

unperturbed by my obvious inexperience, I relaxed, letting the discomfort I felt from not yet having a polished professional persona melt away in the warmth of his gracious smile.

My questions revealed that Mr. Harrison had traveled widely. The facts of his psychosocial history were set against a backdrop of faraway places: the choking hubbub of the streets of Hong Kong; the timeless serenity of the Mekong Delta; the ancient temple sites of Indonesia and Mesoamerica, overtaken by jungle and cantankerous tribes of monkeys. Much of what he said had little relevance for his diagnosis of lung cancer, but because I was still too low on the hierarchic totem pole to have many other pressing tasks, there was time to listen to the fascinating stories he had to tell.

When we did finally arrive at the issue of his cancer, his easy tone became more somber. He admitted it had taken him by surprise. He knew now that he should not have smoked as much as he had. He was concerned about his upcoming treatment with chemotherapy but was trying to be optimistic, since that was his oncologist's stance in the matter. His greatest desire, he confided, was to spend more time with his children and his grandchildren, who were very important to him. In passing, he mentioned that he found the cigarette smoke in the patient lounge quite bothersome, which was unfortunate, he said, because there was no other place he could sit and talk with his family when they came to visit (it being many years before no-smoking policies were instituted in New York City's hospitals).

This was a situation I could certainly help with, I thought. After all, since cigarette smoke was the cause of Mr. Harrison's cancer, we surely had the responsibility to protect him from further exposure while he was in the hospital. I went straight to the nurses' station, grabbed some sheets of paper, a magic marker, and a roll of scotch tape, and marched down the hall to the patient lounge, where I carefully made four signs saying "No Smoking Please"; then I taped one to each wall and stood back to see how they looked. I was pleased with the effect and imagined that other patients would appreciate having smoke-free air, too, just as Mr. Harrison would. In less than ten minutes, I was back at Mr. Harrison's bedside, reporting to my new friend that it was safe for him to use the lounge.

The solution worked well for one day. The following day I was informed that the dean of the medical school wanted to see me. When I entered his office, it quickly became apparent that my action was not regarded as heroism by anyone other than a single patient and myself. Everyone else's feathers had been ruffled.

Duly reprimanded, I returned to the ward to report my plan's defeat to Mr. Harrison. We had a rueful laugh over it, and the incident continued to be a source of comic relief between us until his workup was completed, his course of chemotherapy begun, and he was discharged home.

A year and a half later, in a strange twist of fate, Mr. Harrison was readmitted to the medical ward during the month of my fourth-year rotation there. His oncologist's aggressive attempts to turn his cancer back with repeated courses of chemotherapy and radiation therapy had failed, and the cancer had spread. Now his oncologist hoped to alleviate his escalating pain by evacuating the malignant fluid building up around his lungs.

All this had been hard on Mr. Harrison. I could see it. He had lost a significant amount of weight and with it his distinguished stature. Now he appeared frail and vulnerable. His hair had thinned and turned gray-white, his smile was halfhearted, his once bright eyes disconcertingly dull, and his hand shook when he grasped mine in greeting.

As for me, I had changed, too, as does every medical student between the third and fourth year. Much more was expected of me now, and that is what I wanted. I felt ready. I had taken on direct patient care without hesitation, participating in decision making regarding treatment approaches for my patients and learning to perform procedures that required skill and confidence. The stakes were higher. I liked the way responsibility felt resting on my shoulders, and I took myself much more seriously.

Such change in medical students is regarded as natural and desirable. Taking yourself more seriously is seen as a sign of intellectual and moral development—unless you happen to go overboard about it, which unfortunately is not uncommon. Having an overly developed sense of importance about one's doctorly role is a trap in which fourth-year students sometimes get caught. I had a chance to see how that trap was set for me, with my old friend's return to the ward.

Since Mr. Harrison had been assigned to the caseload of one of the interns rather than to mine, I had little opportunity to spend time with him, though I greeted him warmly as soon as I learned that he was there. It was good to see him, though it was not good to hear that his cancer had spread. He had metastases in his liver and bones, and the toll they were taking was evident.

In fact, there was no time to spend as we had before, when I would sit on the end of his bed and chat with him, listening raptly to his stories and answering his questions about my own life. And there was certainly no room for amusing adventures like the one we had had a year ago, with our attempt to single-handedly overturn hospital rules. He was too sick for any such thing as that, and I was far too busy. A year and a half ago, we had met more simply. Now, the distinction between doctor and patient stood firmly between us.

Beyond having insufficient time, there was a more complex reason why I failed to see more of Mr. Harrison that second time around. It had to do with the different image I now had of myself. A patient who recalled me too clearly as a mere third-year student might have threatened the new status I had painstakingly achieved over the past year. Impatience twitched in me as I talked with him that first day. A voice whispered inside my head, saying I had more important things to do than engage in social niceties. It was someone else's job to take care of Mr. Harrison now, not mine. I had my own patients to attend to.

Perhaps, too, there was something uncomfortable about seeing the changes in Mr. Harrison, the all-too-clear evidence that his health was waning and his time growing short. Perhaps speaking about such serious matters unnerved my newfound confidence; perhaps they challenged my eager need to be in control. I had had little experience as yet in the arena of dying.

For the next two weeks, I heard an update on Mr. Harrison every morning on rounds, and every morning I waved to him as I hurried by his open door. But time went quickly by, and before I knew it, my rotation in adult medicine was coming to an end. On my last day on the ward, I went to his room with some chagrin to say good-bye and to wish him well. He gave an appreciative smile when I walked in and pushed the button to elevate the head of his bed so that he could converse more easily. To my surprise, he said he had something to give me.

Too ill to move very much, he directed me to look in the drawer of his bedside table and open the little cardboard box that was waiting there, and I did as he instructed. Inside the box, carefully wrapped in white tissue paper, I found a gleaming scrimshaw, or carved piece of ivory—a whale's tooth, he explained—strung on a black satin cord. Etched across the smooth surface with the finest of lines was the face of a maiden with flowing hair, bordered by a wreath of morning glory.

The object lay in my palm like a piece of perfection. He told me that his daughter was an artist and made such things, and he had asked her for one to give to me. He meant it to convey his appreciation for my caring . . . even as I guiltily thought how much more caring I could have been. He said he had thought I would like it.

How could he have possibly been so right, I wondered? I thought it was one of the loveliest things I had ever seen. I thanked him profusely, though words seemed inadequate to convey enough thanks for what he had just done—for giving me a piece of his own heart.

Because, in truth, Mr. Harrison's gift to me was more than a beautifully crafted piece of jewelry: it was a lifeline tossed out into the oceanic waters of becoming a doctor, and it came not a moment too soon. For swimming in that ocean is a risky undertaking. It can exact a heavy toll on one's body and mind, and perhaps especially on one's soul. A delicate balance exists between what you are gaining and what you are losing, and keeping track of that balance is not always easy to do. Mr. Harrison's reappearance on the ward gave me the opportunity to see where that balance was in me; it let me measure my present self against an earlier self. Something was clearly growing: confidence, stamina, and ability. I could feel it. Yet something was also waning. Innocence perhaps? Openheartedness?

Maybe Mr. Harrison recognized this waning. Maybe he sensed the danger, and that was why he was so generous with me, why he reached out to touch the soulful part of me, the part that knew what beauty was, and simplicity, and human caring. Perhaps he wanted to keep me aware of that part's worth, lest it slip too far away. If so, his gift could not have said it more clearly and kindly, and I have kept it as one of my greatest treasures to this very day.

*   *   *   *   *   *   *

Sometimes we do not recognize a gift until after the giver has gone, as if the giver's absence creates a space in which we can finally perceive what we received from them. Latwan was one whose life was so fraught with difficulty that the gifts he had to bestow were not fully celebrated by those around him until later, after the obscuring struggles of everyday life had fallen away.

Latwan had to carry a heavier load than most people do, and all his life he had shouldered that load without complaint. He had sickle-cell disease, and like my patient Keith, he suffered recurring painful sickle-cell crises that claimed him when his misshapen red blood cells would suddenly start to clump together, forming tiny clots that clogged his capillaries and caused excruciating pain that lasted for days, sometimes weeks. But unlike Keith, Latwan had not become a psychological cripple from the repeated battering his body took. Although he had endured more than fifty hospitalizations by the time he was a teenager, he remained a sweet-tempered, cheerful boy.

Many of us on the pediatric staff knew Latwan well and felt moved by his courage. We lamented whenever we saw him returning, curled up on a stretcher in pain, his face drawn and his eyes closed tight as he tried to ride out the storm. We knew that even our strongest painkillers could only blunt the pain, not banish it. Then, sooner or later, we would cheer when the storm would pass and he would find his feet again and depart for home, seemingly undaunted by the knowledge that the pain would return again, and yet again.

Latwan lived with his mother in a tiny apartment on the Lower East Side, in a neighborhood burdened with drugs, violence, and poverty. The two of them found refuge from the hardship of life at a church a block from their home, where the congregation had built a strong sense of community. Latwan and his mother were close, and though she could not afford to lose her job cleaning offices in a downtown business building, she stayed at his side as much as she could whenever he was admitted to the hospital. She would bring his homework to him and sit patiently in a chair beside his bed, reading to him and transcribing his answers to assignments. Unlike many other kids we cared for with sickle-cell disease who fell far behind in school due to their frequent absences, Latwan was determined to keep up, no matter what, and with his mother's help he somehow managed.

Over the years, I saw Latwan grow from a gangly preadolescent into a poised youth approaching manhood, so good-looking I thought for sure he must have a gaggle of girls at his heels all the time. But when I inquired, as doctors do, if he had a girl-friend, he smiled shyly and indicated he had not had time for that particular pleasantry yet. Between all his school activities and the youth group he attended at church, he had too many other things on his mind.

As his senior year in high school began, Latwan confided that his greatest goal was to graduate and be accepted to college, preferably somewhere outside the city so that he could broaden his horizons. He did not know where he would get the money, but he thought it would work out somehow. The real problem, he said, was that he was not certain his mother would be happy with his leaving. He worried about her. He knew how difficult her life had been because of him and how hard she had always worked to help him, and he did not know if she could bear to let him go. It was something he would have to work on, I remember him concluding with a smile.

The last time I saw Latwan, when he came back to the hospital in crisis again, shortly before he was due to graduate, he told me with a grin that broke right through his pain, that he had achieved his goal and been accepted to his first choice of college. Not only that, he said, but he had done so well in school that he had been awarded a scholarship—an unheard-of thing in his community—which would make it possible for him to go.

"And the best thing," Latwan said with the glint of satisfaction in his eyes, "is that it's alright with my mom. She told me that she'll definitely miss me, but that's only natural, and I shouldn't worry about her. She said she'll be able to get along just fine without me, and it's okay for me to go."

He paused for a moment of thoughtful silence, and then added, "I'm really proud of her." And in spite of the sickle-cell crisis raging in his bloodstream, he looked oddly at peace, as if he were, for the moment at least, beyond the reach of worry as well as bodily pain.

Two weeks later, shortly after his graduation ceremony, Latwan died in his sleep, at home, from a stroke. It was one of the lethal blows that sickle-cell disease can sometimes deliver. His mother found him in the morning in his bed, and she cried her heart out before she finally called the hospital to let us know.

When I heard, the news stopped me in my tracks and tears coursed down my cheeks. Other members of our staff reacted similarly as I passed the news on.

Later in the day, when the initial shock of the news had passed and its reality had sunk in, thoughts of Latwan moved through my mind as I went about my work on the ward. Latwan had known better than any of us, I realized, how uncertain the future was and how suddenly disaster could strike. He would not have been surprised, I thought, that such a thing as sudden death could happen to him. He might even have sensed, on some level, that this was coming. In fact, maybe part of his great determination to put in place his plan to live away from home had come from his desire to be able to give his mother a final gift in case he was suddenly taken away: the gift of preparing her, as best he could, for his leaving, whether temporary or permanent. After all, she was the person who would be hit the hardest by his absence. It would not be surprising, it seemed to me, if this were true. It would be a very natural thing to want to do.

Several days later, I went to Latwan's funeral together with our pediatric nurse, Marcie, who had attended to Latwan during many of his stays on the ward. We stood against the back wall of the little community church, as all the seats were taken. From there we could just make out, on the top of the altar, a framed photograph of Latwan smiling broadly in his graduation cap and gown.

The minister, a stately man with silvered hair and a flowing black robe, spoke with a resonant voice that filled the hall. He was very saddened, he said, to be conducting a service for the untimely loss of yet another young man from their community. Far too many of their youth died young, he said, almost always because of violence. He was grateful that this was not true

222

for Latwan, and he celebrated Latwan for not allowing such a thing to happen to him. Yet he regretted deeply, as they all did, that Latwan was no longer with them, but had been called home by the Lord.

When the minister finished his comments, various parishioners stood up, one after another, and gave testimony to how they had known Latwan. Clearly, a great many had been touched by him in one way or another, and both Marcie and I were comforted to know how much he had been loved.

Hearing about Latwan as he had been known by the people in his community—people who had watched him grow from a toddler into a young man—I gained a larger, richer picture of the person he had been. I also saw there was a side of Latwan that these people who loved and admired him did not know, a side that I, as his doctor, did. So finally, as the service was about to conclude, I raised my hand and asked permission to speak. When the minister nodded, everyone in the church turned their attention to the back of the room where Marcie and I were standing.

Addressing the congregation in my loudest voice, I told them that the Latwan I knew was a person of great courage. I told them that he had lived from birth with a condition that could flare up at any moment and set his body on fire with burning pain—a heartless condition that would leap on him with sharp teeth and claws and pull him down into agony that could last for days and days, no matter how hard we doctors and nurses tried to help. I told them he had fought more battles with that illness than I could count and had won every one of them. He had steadfastly refused to be defeated. He would not let hardship take his dreams away from him, and he never wasted a moment feeling sorry for himself. I said all who knew him at the hospital had been inspired by his bravery and determination.

When I finished, there was complete silence. For one terrible moment, I wondered if my speaking had been intrusive or if I might have offended Latwan's community with what I said.

But then a voice shouted "Hallelujah!" and quickly one voice after another followed with the same exclamation. As every person in the church rose enthusiastically to their feet to join in the uplifting outcry, I breathed a sigh of relief.

Soon everyone was milling around, wiping tears from their cheeks and embracing each other. I went to Latwan's mother, and we gave each other a long, heartfelt hug. Then several people asked to shake my hand and express their gratitude for having deepened their knowledge of Latwan. They had always felt that he was someone special, they said. He had given them hope in life. And they found it good to hear how others saw him: it showed them they were right to hold on to such hope.

Eventually, the minister called the gathering back together for his closing remarks. In a deep voice containing both sorrow and profound patience, he declared that Latwan's life had been a gift to their community. This young man who so many knew and admired had shown it was possible to follow one's dreams and taste their fulfillment, despite the toughest of life's obstacles. Even his death, as sad as it might be, was a gift, the minister proclaimed, because in his dying Latwan had shot up into the heavens and burst open like a glorious Fourth of July firecracker, raining down sparks of goodness on all those he loved. And though he was gone from the world now, he had left a little bit of the hope-filled light from his life in the heart of every person who had known him.

* * * * * * *

Though giving and receiving may often appear to be polar opposites, they can at times flow back and forth so seamlessly that they become indistinguishable as separate acts. We once had a four-year-old patient on the pediatric ward who made this very clear. The child's name was Nestor—at least that was his given name and the name by which we doctors knew him. To his mother, however, he was *Panchito, mi amor.*

Nestor's mother, Señora Guadalupe Zapata, had brought him to my hospital from Mexico City seeking treatment for his hepatoblastoma, a rare type of childhood cancer, which the physicians in their country had declared he had little chance of surviving, given how far advanced it was. An educated woman from the upper class in Mexico, Señora Zapata had heard that in America doctors had many more resources to draw upon in the fight against cancer than the Mexican doctors did. She had heard too that in America doctors refused to give up. And since Señora Zapata was a descendant of Emiliano Zapata, the peasant who became a national hero in the early twentieth century by leading a revolution that overthrew the corrupt dictatorship then oppressing her country, she knew what it was, she said, to fight against overwhelming odds. It was in her blood.

Nestor's hepatoblastoma had been silently growing in his body over the entire four years of his life, for the seed of this type of cancer is planted long before birth, when nature makes a mistake during the formation of an unborn baby's liver. Certain liver cells develop an abnormality that they pass on to their progeny as they multiply, and their progeny pass it on to theirs as well. The number of these abnormal cells increases rapidly during the child's first few years of life, until they create a cancerous mass so large that it begins to threaten the child's existence.

Nestor's hepatoblastoma went unnoticed until his protruding abdomen finally gave away its presence. By the time the tumor was discovered by his Mexican pediatrician just before his fourth birthday, it squatted like an enormous, overfed leech on his liver, gorging itself on the blood supply meant to fuel the important metabolic work that the liver is so marvelously designed to perform. When the pediatrician showed Señora Zapata the foreboding shadow on her child's CAT scan, she finally understood what had been stealing her son's youthful exuberance away. She understood, too, that she would have to fight with every last ounce of energy she had in order to save his life.

For three long wintry weeks, dark-haired, dark-eyed Nestor was a patient on our ward, and though he was under the care of another pediatrician, something about him continually captured my attention. At first glance, the little boy looked skinny but not critically ill, aside from his abnormally prominent belly. On closer observation, though, I could see that he was more reserved than a four-year-old usually is, and I sensed a certain vulnerability about him, the source of which was hard to pinpoint. How much was a reflection of the toll his cancer was taking on him, I wondered, and how much was the result of being uprooted from his home without any warning and deposited in a place where the things that people said and did were completely foreign to him? It was difficult to say. Either way, I felt a recurring welling up of empathy as I watched him trying to stand his ground in a storm he hardly understood.

Since his second day as a patient, Nestor had been engulfed in an intensive medical investigation, orchestrated by a small army of specialists. White-coated figures representing the fields of pediatric oncology, pediatric surgery, hepatology, radiation therapy, cardiology, neurology, and genetics came to the pediatric ward to inspect this boy with his rare form of life-threatening illness. Sometimes they came singly, sometimes in pairs, and occasionally a whole squadron of them would arrive together, gathering around Nestor's bed and watching in silence as one of their number conducted an examination. Then they would stop at the nurses' station to write orders for the various tests they desired: CAT scan of the abdomen, CAT scan of the chest, MRI, bone scan, chest x-ray, EKG, echocardiogram, and numerous blood tests.

The sound of the team's voices often drifted from the conference room as they tackled critical questions. Had Nestor's cancer spread beyond his liver to other sites in his abdominal cavity—or even further beyond, to lungs, bones, or brain? Should the oncologists administer chemotherapy to shrink the tumor prior to surgery, or should the surgeons first open up his little belly and cut away as much of the malignant tissue as possible before starting the chemo? How great was the risk of tumor rupture and lethal hemorrhage? What burden would the toxic effects of chemo put on the boy's heart, kidneys, bone marrow, immune system, and developing brain? Spurred on by some combination of fascination for Nestor's unusual pathology and heroic commitment to rescuing a child from untimely death, the team worked hard to map out the best possible strategy for winning him a cure despite the odds stacked against him.

During Nestor's stay in the hospital, Señora Zapata slept on a cot beside her son every night. Each morning she bathed him and persuaded him to nibble some breakfast from the tray of hospital food delivered to his room like clockwork at 7:30 a.m. Then she would put on her coat, kiss him good-bye in the doorway of his room, and disappear down the long hallway that led to the elevators, the staccato clicking of her high heels on the linoleum floor fading into silence behind her. She left for the duration of the day to assist with the work of an American friend in order to defray the huge cost of Nestor's hospital care. The various specialists consulted with her by phone, and on occasion, when major decisions had to be made, she would take a subway from midtown back to the hospital to discuss the options with them in person.

Despite his dire diagnosis, Nestor was a plucky little fellow, and with an ever solemn expression on his face, he endured the tests he had to undergo without protest. When not being poked or prodded by consultants, or being transported by the staff to have various diagnostic studies performed, he would let the play therapist take him by the hand and lead him to the playroom. There she would keep him occupied with colorful picture books and wooden puzzles and plastic stacking toys for much of the morning, after which he would let her lead him back to his room for lunch and a nap. The few words of Spanish that the play therapist spoke seemed enough to put him at ease, though never enough to get him to smile. Smiling he saved for his mother alone.

The afternoons were another matter. Medical tests aside, Nestor had his own plan for how that time should be used, and he would not be deterred. Although his mother rarely returned from work until after five o'clock, at approximately two o'clock every day Nestor could be relied upon to push the chair from beside his bed out to the hall and position it next to the entrance to his room. There he would sit for the rest of the afternoon, staring down the hallway that led to the elevators. He would glance only briefly, if at all, at passersby, and he stubbornly refused to be coaxed back to the playroom or even into friendly conversation with Spanish-speaking staff.

My heart ached for Nestor when I saw him waiting in the hall. He appeared so small and alone, outmatched by circumstances that dwarfed his brave little soul. I assumed, along with the rest of the staff, that he spent the afternoons staring down the empty hallway because he was lonely and pining for his mother. This certainly would have made sense—if it had been true.

But it was not true, and for some time a real understanding of Nestor's actions eluded me because of a certain blindness in my seeing. I failed to perceive how straight and alert Nestor sat in his chair, and how intent and purposeful his gaze was. It did not occur to me that he might be saving his energy for something more significant than playroom games and the words of strangers, that he was in fact a sentry manning a vital post, keeping the watch light lit that would guide his mother back to him, just as a harbormaster's lamp draws a sailing vessel safely back to port. Nor would I have guessed how important this duty was, until one afternoon when something happened to show me how far short of the mark my understanding had been.

The revealing incident occurred while I was standing at the nurses' station across the hall from Nestor's lookout spot, writing clinical notes in my patients' charts. When the staccato clicking of Señora Zapata's high heels sounded ahead of her from the long winding corridor leading to the elevators, I looked up to see little Nestor stiffen to attention. As his mother rounded the corner and came into view, he quickly scrambled down from his perch and, without a word, went running on his little legs straight as an arrow to meet her.

Seeing him coming, Señora Zapata stopped and called, *"Panchito, mi amor!"*

Carefully setting down the shopping bag of Mexican treats that she never failed to bring back for her son each day, she stood like a pillar and waited for him to reach her. As he did, Nestor threw his arms around her legs and buried his face in her thigh. She reached down with one hand and rumpled his hair; then she stooped and lifted him into her arms, kissing him first on one cheek and then on the other and hugging him tight.

Nestor's face lit up with joy, and he reached out his hand to touch his mother's face. As he carefully brushed away the tears that were falling from her eyes, I finally understood the truth. Not only Nestor was vulnerable. They both were, and each was protecting and comforting the other in their own way. While his mother took on the burdens that only an adult could bear, Nestor waited faithfully all afternoon for the important moment of greeting his careworn mother and welcoming her back.

This was the culmination of Nestor's hours of patient vigil, and it was worth every minute. In that instant the grief and gladness of mother and son could tumble together unabashedly and both find comfort in the embrace they gave each other. They could not have gone on without this daily moment. It brought them vital replenishment of spirit for their hard and uncertain journey.

A week or so after I witnessed this scene, Nestor was transferred to another medical center for surgery. No evidence of spread of his cancer had been discovered on his tests, but the tumor was found to be so large and so broadly attached to his liver that it was doubtful whether enough of his own liver tissue could be salvaged. He might well require a liver transplant, and therefore it was essential for him to be at a center where the surgeons had experience with complicated liver surgery and childhood liver transplantation. Our prayers went with Nestor, and we missed him after he was gone. The ward lost some of its character without those solemn afternoon vigils.

A few months later, a letter arrived, addressed to all the pediatric inpatient staff. It was from Señora Zapata, who wrote to say that everything had worked out better than she had dared to hope. The chemotherapy Nestor was given prior to surgery had shrunk the tumor more than expected, and the surgeons had been able to remove it completely, leaving his liver with enough healthy tissue to regenerate itself, avoiding the need for a transplant. His doctors had been very pleased. They believed he was cured.

The best part of all was the photograph that Señora Zapata included. It showed her holding Nestor in her arms, and the two of them were looking into each other's eyes with the same wholeheartedness I had witnessed that one afternoon. This time, however, no shadow of worry or uncertainty clouded their embrace. This time they radiated pure happiness.

*   *   *   *   *   *   *

I have heard it said that, in the eye of the Creator, all gifts are worthy of the same degree of divine acknowledgment, for when measured against the Infinite, every mortal act of giving has equal weight and significance. Certainly the gift that Paula gave me might have seemed of little consequence by ordinary standards, but it touched me as deeply as any gift I have ever received.

Paula became a drug addict at the age of twelve and for most of the remainder of her fifty-four years lived the life of a vagrant hustler on the streets of New York City, the kind of person you would carefully give wide berth as you walked along the street. She slept in alleyways or the basements of deserted buildings, or when the bitter cold of winter set in, she took temporary refuge in one or another of the city's homeless shelters. She got high by drinking, snorting, or injecting one substance or another as often as she could. To support her habits, she perfected the art of shoplifting, along with small-time drug dealing, forgery, and other petty crimes. Caught in her ill-doing repeatedly, she spent a total of eleven years in prison, where, she said, the living conditions were not a whole lot better than they were on the street, except that the meals were more regular. The experience did nothing to deter her from her ways.

Not surprisingly, Paula picked up both AIDS and hepatitis C along the way. Together with the drugs and alcohol she used, these diseases wreaked havoc with her liver, which eventually began to fail. At age fifty-four, she slipped into liver failure coma and lay unconscious in my hospital for two weeks before a team of specialists coaxed her body back to life. When she recovered sufficiently, they informed her that her liver was damaged beyond repair. They predicted that she had, at most, a few months left to live.

Only then, with death peering over her shoulder, did a change come over Paula. She agreed to give up her streetwise ways, including all drugs and alcohol, and enter a supervised residence for homeless people with AIDS where she could live out the rest of her life.

The residence lay directly across the street from my hospital, and when Paula enrolled in our hospice program and my research project on death and dying, I began to visit her several times a week. She was eager to talk about how different life appeared since she had realized that dying lay just down the road—inexplicably interesting and inviting in ways she had never noticed before. She was quite surprised by this new twist in her affairs, she said, giving the little cackling laugh that often punctuated her remarks.

Moving to the group home and quitting drugs and alcohol was not a last-ditch effort on Paula's part to cling to life. Rather, she told me, she had agreed to making these challenging changes because she wanted to see what the life she had rejected would have been like. She was curious about how it felt to have a home, or at least her own room and a bed, with books to read and music to listen to, and meals she could fix for herself and even share with a friend or two. Most of all, she said, she wanted to get to know herself before it was too late. She had never been interested in knowing herself before. As a child she had been told repeatedly that she was worthless—that she did not amount to squat—and because she had believed what she was told, she had spent her entire life running away from herself. Suddenly, it felt important to find out who she really was behind all the hype and hostility she had used as a front for all those years.

Consequences of Paula's lifestyle showed in her appearance. Her crooked smile revealed gaps where several of her front teeth had broken off or fallen out, while the rest were stained with tar from years of heavy smoking; her forearms and lower legs showed the telltale marks where she had pierced her veins with the needles of syringes loaded with heroin; and two fingers were crooked where they had fractured and never been set.

She could easily have been viewed as a person who had wasted her life—a broken, decrepit failure of a human being—were it not for the feisty spirit at her core and the mischievous twinkle it produced in her eyes. Even while shuffling dutifully down the hall in her raggedy, faded-blue bathrobe, and floppy slippers to pick up her morning medication at the nurses' station, she maintained an unflappable dignity, and she could serve tea in her tiny bedroom with the graciousness of the Queen Mother herself. The other residents in the home felt mysteriously drawn to her, charmed by her mixture of witty sarcasm and childlike innocence. The staff, who normally maintained a professional distance with the residents, quickly warmed to her too. All the while, Paula seemed to be chuckling to herself, as if life's unpredictable twists and turns were the most amusing joke in the world.

Over three months, I made more than thirty trips across the street to visit Paula and record the tales of her fascinating, contradictory career. Then, without warning, I was diagnosed with breast cancer, bringing my visits to an abrupt halt. Overnight, I went from being a doctor to being a patient in my own hospital. I was swept up and rushed along by a current that took me swiftly through a battery of diagnostic tests, to preparations for surgery. At the very same time, unbeknownst to me, Paula slipped back into liver failure coma.

Not much later, when conservative surgery failed to expel the malignant intruder from my body, I was scheduled for more radical surgery, still unaware of Paula's tenuous hold on life.

The day after I underwent the major surgical procedure called bilateral mastectomy, I was lying in my hospital bed, wrapped in bandages, with drainage tubes sticking out from the wounds on either side of my chest. I looked and felt very worn out. A steady stream of people passed in and out of my room—hospital staff, concerned colleagues, family and friends, all coming to check up on me—when a loud knock sounded on the door.

Several pairs of eyes—mine, my husband's, and those of the team of surgeons who had come to inspect my wounds—turned to stare quizzically toward the door as it opened and a wheelchair came into view. Pushing the wheelchair was an attendant from Paula's group home, and in the wheelchair was

Paula herself, looking just as bedraggled, if not more so, than me. She was dressed in her raggedy housecoat and slippers, and bundled up in a blanket against the March weather outside, and she held a bouquet of daisies in her arms.

For a moment both she and I were speechless, each of us taken aback by how the other looked—I, lying helplessly in bed with an intravenous line running into each arm, and she, pale as a ghost, with dark circles around her still jaundiced eyes and a fragile weariness written all over her. The scene would have made a funny cartoon where the roles of doctor and patient were utterly confused, if someone could have come up with a good caption.

Apologetically, not wishing to intrude, Paula began to explain. She related briefly how her liver had stalled out once again but finally kicked back in, and how, when she got her thinking faculties back, she had heard about what had happened to me. The news had brought her up short. It was one thing for *her* to be teetering back and forth at the brink of death, she said, but she had never imagined that such a thing could happen to me, a *doctor*. Doctors were part of the bulwark of society—not like her sort, for whom life regularly ran amuck.

If she had had the energy, and if I could have taken a deep breath without triggering a searing stab of pain, we probably would have had a hearty laugh. As it was, we settled for giving each other a rueful smile, and then, as she pushed herself closer and the surgeons stepped back, she added that she had made an interesting discovery, one she thought that I, as a medical researcher, might like to know about.

"Dr. MacGregor, all those years I lived on the street," she said in a low voice, "I *used* people. I used them in whatever way I could, so I could get what I wanted. I never cared a whit what happened to them. If they could help me pull off a heist—if I could bum a cigarette from them, or score a little of their dope—then they were cool."

She gave a careless shrug. "If not, they were just in the way."

"But lately," she said, cocking her head with a half-toothless smile, "well, I've been enjoying your company. It's been amusing to tell you my story, and it's helped me pass the time. But I didn't know it would lead to this."

I was not certain what she meant, and as she paused to catch her breath, I frowned in puzzlement.

"Lead to what?" I asked.

"To this pain I'm feeling, right in here," she said, pointing with a crooked forefinger toward the center of her chest, at her heart. "It started two days ago, when I was finally better enough to register the news that something bad was happening to you. The idea of you being sick bothered me, and all I could think about was that I had to come see if you were okay. I had to yell at my counselor to get her to agree that I could come for just five minutes. And now, when I see you lying here looking so bad, something in me *really* hurts! I never knew that could happen, I never knew that caring about another person could hurt like this. It's something totally new."

She shook her head in wonderment.

I hardly knew what to say. The sight of Paula, hunched in her wheelchair, having braved the cold and the medical bureaucracy to come see me, was quite something to take in.

"Oh, Paula," I murmured, "I'm sorry it hurts, but thank you for caring! It means a lot to me."

Paula nodded her head approvingly.

"I'm glad to hear that," she said, "but don't be sorry. It's *interesting* to discover that caring about how somebody else feels can cause you pain. And what's *most* interesting is that I don't mind this kind of pain at all!"

"In fact," she whispered as she gripped the arms of her wheelchair and leaned closer conspiratorially, "it makes me feel alive in a way I never did before!"

She gave a little cackle and stretched out her hand with the bunch of daisies toward my husband, Charles, who took them from her and placed them on the windowsill where they could easily be seen.

"Those are for you, Dr. MacGregor," she said, smiling. "I hope you like them. They were my favorite when I was a kid. I called them happy flowers because that's how they made me feel, and maybe they'll give you some of that feeling too." She shook her head wryly. "Why, I feel happy just giving them to you!"

A few minutes later, after both of us had promised to see each other as soon as we were able, Paula turned her head and nodded to the aide, who was lounging against the door, and let herself be wheeled away, leaving me to gaze at the daisies on my windowsill with a warm feeling in my heart.

* * * * * * *

Being a doctor not only allows you to see how the wounds that some human beings suffer in life inspire giving in others, it also gives you the opportunity to observe how the act of giving can make those who give feel happy, as if the very acts of generosity they direct toward others are ministering to their own hearts as well. Parents of children with special needs showed me this time and again.

Initially, I expected such parents—parents whose offspring had severe limitations compared to so-called normal children—to harbor sorrowful disappointment in their hearts or smoldering resentment toward life for depriving their child of opportunity. But rarely did I see this. Instead, I saw these parents respond to the need their children had for help with more wholehearted, optimistic giving than I often found among parents with "normal" children, where it simply was not necessary. Many of these mothers and fathers glowed with the effort their child called forth from them.

Constancia, a twenty-two-year-old legal secretary, had never imagined she would have a daughter who was unusual or that her marriage would fail because of it. But when Angelita was born, she was so clearly different from other babies that Constancia's husband left and never returned. Constancia, on the other hand, did not seem to mind. As she saw it, something wonderful had happened to her. One of God's sweetest little angels had tumbled out of heaven and landed in her arms, becoming hers alone to care for.

When I met Angelita, she was two years old, and she did indeed have the countenance of an angel. She was an albino, with pale white skin and silky white hair that set her apart from other people. Her DNA carried a mutation that blocked the metabolic pathway governing the production of melanin, the pigment that gives the different races their varying shades of skin color. Without any melanin whatsoever, and with the severe visual impairment that albinism can cause, she appeared ethereal and vulnerable: a sweet, otherworldly spirit whose ice-blue eyes were not meant for seeing in the dense domain where humans normally dwell.

Though she was intelligent and perceptive, little Angelita would face challenges in her life. Her transparency-of-being would need protection, both physically and psychologically because people with albinism may be viewed as oddities and subjected to ridicule or even persecution. In some countries they are thought to be possessed by the devil and, even today, may be stoned to death, while in others they can be abducted and killed for their body parts, which are used for making magical potions. Even without such danger, they regularly attract long looks from perfect strangers.

Constancia sensed this inhospitable attitude of the world, and for all the years I knew her, she was both her daughter's caregiver and steadfast guardian. She accompanied her child everywhere and infused her with her own optimistic outlook on life. She said being Angelita's mother

was her greatest happiness, and Angelita blossomed beautifully under her care.

Violet was another mother of a child with disability whom
I grew to know well. As was the case with Constancia, she
had nothing but adoration for her son Benjamin, even though
Benjamin had the most extreme limitations caused by Down
syndrome I had ever seen. Like all children who are born with
the trisomy-21 disorder—that is, with every cell of their body
containing three strands of the twenty-first chromosome instead of the usual two—Benjamin had slanted eyes, small ears
and chin, a wide stubby neck, short arms and legs, and broad,
flat hands and feet. In his physical features, he was no different from many children with Down syndrome who are able
to attend special educational programs, participate in modified
sports, hold simple jobs, and enjoy making friends. But the
degree of cognitive disability Benjamin had was much greater
than most. At age sixteen, he could do nothing more than lie
flat on his back and wriggle his arms and legs. He could not sit
up or even roll over, and the only sounds he could make were
high-pitched squeals. His attention span was no more than a
second or two, and except when he was asleep, the expression
on his face was a steady, indiscriminate grin. I once overheard
one of the pediatric residents refer thoughtlessly to him as
"The Blob."

To Benjamin's mother, Violet, however, who had cared
diligently for him from the day he was born, he was the ap-
ple of her eye. She lavished him with attention, painstakingly
feeding him, bathing him, rolling him from one side to the
other, and exercising his floppy limbs, all the while chattering
to him about this and that. Whenever he was admitted to the
hospital, as he occasionally was for minor problems such as
having his feeding tube replaced or being treated for a urinary
tract infection, Violet would never leave his side. She would
sit close beside him on the bed and beam at every member of
our staff who came to their room, as if delighted that others

might want to join her in what she regarded as the joy of caring for her son.

The joy that characterized Violet's relationship with Benjamin was something I also encountered with certain parents of anencephalic children, those babies whose severe malformations of the head and brain rarely allow them to survive more than a few days or weeks. Like Jocelyn, mother of Annabelle, some parents of anencephalic infants find happiness in caring for their fatally exceptional newborns. Some even go out of their way to share their experience with others, creating websites to tell the stories of the gifts of love that were so briefly given and received before their malformed babies passed away. They describe how deeply moving it was to cradle their son or daughter in their arms for a precious time and to let that soul know that he or she was cherished despite having terrible handicaps. Photographs posted on the websites portray mothers, fathers, and siblings, proudly holding these unique beings who depart so soon. Most remarkably, there is joy shining on every family member's face.

I feel enormous gratitude for these courageous parents and families who participate in life in ways the rest of us could barely conceive of doing. I wonder, too, if perhaps the purpose some souls have in coming into existence so briefly might be exactly that: to invite engagement from individuals who would otherwise never have known their hearts were capable of giving themselves so generously.

* * * * * * *

The gifts that Don and Sandi gave and received in parenting their genetically different child filled their lives for decades. Yet as often happens with parents that give birth to children who differ from the norm, they were completely unprepared at the start. The day their first child was born, they were expecting it to be the best day of their lives. But when Bobby exited the birth canal and they heard their obstetrician give an involuntary gasp, they knew immediately that something was seriously wrong.

Bobby looked different, that could not be denied. Not shockingly so, but in enough small ways that everyone who saw him knew he did not fall into the category of "normal." He had the typical heart-melting sweetness of the newly born, but his facial features—his eyes and nose and mouth and chin— somehow did not fit the usual mold. His hands and feet were all a little odd, especially his thumbs, which were very strangely shaped, and his overall body proportions were not what one's eyes were accustomed to seeing. From the perspective of the medical profession, Bobby was an unknown entity, and his well-being was therefore in question. Information was needed. He was transported to the NICU where he could be closely monitored and where a cohort of consultants could be called upon to evaluate him.

The specialists who came to inspect Bobby in his NICU incubator approached the task of making a diagnosis with unfaltering intellectual rigor, viewing the objective as a matter of finding the correct category to which he could be assigned. They searched diligently for where he belonged, ordering batteries of tests to investigate the various possibilities, while Bobby obligingly provided them with many issues on which to focus, as his body was certainly acting very unsettled. He had an alarming amount of vomiting, inexplicable episodes of fever, poor weight gain, oozing eyes, and seizures. Yet the blood tests, spinal taps, x-rays, EKGs, cultures, echos, scopes, and scans to which he was subjected could find no specific diagnosis to explain his symptoms or his odd appearance.

Whenever another specialist presented his or her opinion, Don and Sandi felt their connection with Bobby slipping one step further away, obscured by the list of problems that continued to mystify the specialists. Physical deformities, eye abnormalities, gastrointestinal malfunction, neurological deficits, mental retardation, failure to thrive, cardiac complications, and seizure disorder—all jostled for position on the daunting list. Moreover, as part of their consultation, the well-meaning experts seemed to think it their duty to forecast Bobby's future for his unsuspecting parents. One highly educated geneticist in particular felt obliged to prepare them for the worst, stating with the full authority of her professional degree that Bobby's life was at the beginning of an inevitable downward spiral.

As the days stretched on, the message Don and Sandi heard repeatedly, whether implied or stated outright, was that they should lower their expectations and accept the fact that their child's life would be one of profound limitation and abnormality. He might never walk or talk or know himself as a person. The best thing to do would be to place him in an institution where others who were better suited for the job than they were could take care of him.

As the pediatrician assigned to Bobby's case, I chose to take a more positive view; by that time many parents and their seemingly flawed children had taught me that being different was not necessarily a terrible thing. They had shown me, too, that parents' hearts have enough room in them for every so-called imperfection there is in this world. Because of these parents I had known, I felt that Bobby's mother and father needed the support of at least one voice of open-ended possibility in order to trust what their own hearts were saying. They needed confirmation that this was not some cruel mistake, a horrible disaster with irreversible consequences that had befallen them and their child, setting them on a pitifully narrow road that stretched ahead laden only with burden. They had to believe there was more to be discovered than that.

From my point of view, Bobby might have had his differences, but he was as cute and cuddly in his own way as any baby I had ever seen. I could sense in him a unique human being whose future was no more or less uncertain than any other newborn baby's is, a beautiful being who needed to be loved as much as every child does—in fact, maybe more than most, given the amount of pessimism the medical profession was raining down on him.

Because Don and Sandi seemed to be growing increasingly stressed, I suggested that we meet every afternoon at four o'clock for as long as Bobby remained in the hospital in order to review the latest opinions of the specialists. I was determined to help them keep a larger picture in view.

Viewing Bobby as a mistake, as innately defective and wrong, was too narrow a perspective to use as our starting point, I said. A better starting point to have, I suggested, would be to simply acknowledge that Bobby was different from other children, that he was traveling on a path uniquely his own and that we could not yet know where it was leading him. He might well have challenges to face that other children did not, but he would have his own strengths and positive qualities too. He would be uniquely Bobby. The wisest approach, I thought, was to give Bobby the time and space to show them who he was. He had come into the world as their child, and that would be the foundation on which everything else would rest.

Don and Sandi agreed wholeheartedly. From that point on, rather than worrying, they focused all their energy on being loving, supportive parents to their little son, and as the days rolled by, Bobby's initial problems began to resolve. His vomiting ended, his seizures stopped, his fevers did not return, his eyes cleared up, and he gained weight. When the specialists still cautioned them not to have high expectations, Don and Sandi went one step further. They set aside expectations altogether and remained open and unassuming, listening to their hearts and staying with Bobby as he took every step of his journey in life. And because they listened so well, they came to know Bobby as a human being like no other. They discovered a fascinating uniqueness that might well have been missed had they allowed his difficulties to remain the primary focus.

Don and Sandi shared some of that process of discovery with me as the years went by. From the earliest moments of his life, they said, they noticed how interested Bobby was in people. As an infant he would gaze purposely into the eyes of every person he saw, as if he were saying to them, "I'm here. Are you with me?" As he grew from child to adolescent to young adult, they saw that within Bobby's unorthodox mental and physical apparatus there lived an intact and dignified human being who both knew himself and could communicate his views with perfect clarity to people who were willing to listen. From the listening they did, Don and Sandi gained insight into the workings of Bobby's mind and learned to appreciate how different his perspective on life was from theirs.

They saw early on that Bobby did not have the necessary wiring to understand all of society's norms and conventions. Bobby could not understand, for example, that laughing is considered inappropriate in certain situations and that one should learn to quash the urge to giggle at those times. Instead, he retained a fresh, unconditioned view of life. He would laugh loudly at things others would not, such as seeing a person suddenly trip while walking by, or hearing someone give a loud hiccup, or curse at an inanimate object as if it could hear. The pressures that shape many so-called normal people—pressures to be popular, to be successful, to conform to others' expectations—never registered with him, and his freedom from them made him more easygoing. He was unable to harbor a grudge or be mean-spirited, and unpleasant subtleties like prejudice and sarcasm sailed right over his head.

One social custom that was completely meaningless to Bobby was that of considering people important because of their professional role or social status. When he was introduced to somebody new, it mattered not the slightest bit to him what title that person had. What was important to Bobby was whether the person was sincere or insincere. He was highly attuned to the difference and always right in his assessment, even if his parents failed to see it clearly themselves at first. If he experienced a person as genuinely interested in meeting him, he would be engaging and charming in response. If not, he would simply cease being aware of the person. Once, when applying for enrollment in a program for people with special needs, he was interviewed by the program's administrator, a pompous, patronizing man who quizzed Bobby with questions such as who the vice president of the United States was, in an attempt to assess his mental capacity. Knowing perfectly well that he was being poked and prodded like a specimen, Bobby, in his inimitable style, turned away in the middle of the interview, closed his eyes, and started to snore.

Still, Bobby always showed exquisite sensitivity to others' genuine feelings, and he continued to demonstrate this trait as he grew to be an adult. He would often go out of his way to approach insignificant-appearing people he did not know and tell them that they were beautiful, as if he could sense when someone had a praiseworthy heart hiding behind a plain exterior and deserved to be noticed. His naive straightforwardness also enabled him to go right to the crux of complex human experience. When a lifelong friend of his, a young woman with a severe genetic disorder, died at the age of twenty-five after years of suffering, he was deeply moved. He accompanied his parents to the cemetery where, together with her family and friends, he stood in solemn attention as her casket was lowered into the grave site and earth thrown on top of it, and he listened attentively as person after person spoke their last good-byes. But the actual depth of his attentiveness was revealed in his own words, when he went to the grieving mother of his friend and told her, "Our beautiful girl isn't dead. She's alive in our hearts."

Overall, Bobby far exceeded the expectations of the specialists who saw him in the first months of his life. Those who once predicted that he would be unlikely to ever walk or talk would be quite surprised to know that he not only mastered those skills, but learned to read and write as well. Although it took him years of effort to learn to tie his shoelaces—a thing most children do by the age of five—he did not give up and finally mastered the task at age thirteen, and with the same resolve went on to learn to use a computer for simple functions. Though Bobby's disabilities were such that he would never be able to live on his own, he could nonetheless summon great determination and persistence in order to accomplish his goals.

Of all his capabilities, what most helped Bobby to get along was his strong sense of self. He had confidence in who he was and was not easily flustered. If confronted with questions for which he had no answer, he would calmly cancel them from his awareness and proceed with what he was doing as if he had not heard. Or if the question was one he did not like, he could nullify it with a single blow. Once, when a medical student ineptly tried to engage him in conversation by asking him how it felt to be handicapped, Bobby eyed her sternly and replied with absolute clarity, "I'm *not* handicapped."

At the same time, Bobby remained open to giving questions serious consideration when they were asked out of genuine interest, even though he might not have the answer. When he was five years old and riding in the backseat of the family car one day, his younger brother Alex leaned over and stared quizzically at Bobby's hands, then asked, "Bobby, why are your thumbs squiggly?"

Bobby held up his hands and stared thoughtfully at both of his thumbs for a while, as if pondering a question that did not allow for a quick answer. Finally he responded, saying, "Well, Alex, that's a hard question," and left the matter at that.

Don and Sandi remained as proud of Bobby as they later were of their other two children who arrived after him and followed a less unusual path. Though they never would have guessed it at the outset, Don and Sandi came to regard their journey with Bobby as one of the greatest gifts of their lives. The immeasurable gift they gave Bobby in return was that of supporting him in being exactly who he was.

NINE

Turning Wounds into Wisdom

ONE OF THE GREATEST lessons I learned in my career is that we doctors *help* people get better, we do not *make* them get better. Patients do not recover by being passive recipients of care doled out by highly trained professionals; they can and must participate in their own healing. My patients taught me this. They showed me that an innate capacity for healing exists in every person, waiting to be called forth and encouraged, ready to generate strength and resilience in response to illness and injury. They taught me, too, that recovery can sometimes mean more than a return to a preexisting state of health. Sometimes a beneficent reversal can happen in people's lives, allowing the wounds from which they have suffered the most to become the source of their greatest wisdom.

Migdalia's life executed such a reversal magnificently. A sixteen-year-old inner-city teenager, she lived across the street from my hospital in a group home run by the Sisters of the Good Shepherd. The four-story brick building was a refuge and long-term home for adolescent girls referred there by the Family Court and various child protection agencies. Many of the girls had been rescued from troubled or abusive families. Some had become too wild for their families to manage and had been thrown out of their homes. Others had run away from unbearable situations and were living on the streets. Each one of the girls had her own disturbing story to tell.

The nurse for the group home, a dedicated soul by the name of Mrs. McNalley, had worked there for a good twenty years, and she had a keen eye for trouble. She would bring her girls over to see me at the adolescent clinic I directed whenever she felt they had the need for medical care or just for professional assessment and reassurance, and she could be relied upon to provide the inside scoop on whatever their problems might be. She even talked me into running a clinic over at the home two afternoons a month because she knew how much some of her girls hated to cross the street and be swallowed up by the regimented busyness of the hospital. They had already endured too much experience with bureaucracy in their young lives, she said.

Just prior to the appointment she had arranged for Migdalia, the gray-haired nurse pulled me aside to relate a few details about the girl, off the record. She came from a very troubled family, Mrs. McNalley confided with a sad shake of her head, and she had a long record of rebellious, angry acting-out behavior. Before coming to the group home, she had been staying out late every night, hanging out with a delinquent crowd and drinking alcohol and smoking pot, and then she had ended up with an unplanned pregnancy, which she unexpectedly lost in her seventh month. Her dysfunctional parents, mired in their own tangle of problems, had been only too glad to be rid of her, and so the Family Court sent her to the group home, where she had been living for the past few months.

Now Migdalia was requesting an appointment for advice about birth control methods, but there was a more important reason for Mrs. McNalley to bring her to the clinic. She was concerned that Migdalia was not grieving in the way one would expect for someone who had recently suffered the loss of so much. Perhaps she was in denial, Mrs. Mc-Nalley thought, at risk for psychological problems down the road. My opinion would be very much appreciated. And even though Mrs. McNalley went on to relate further details of Migdalia's story, I was still not prepared when I heard it in full from the girl's own lips.

When I entered the examination room to meet Migdalia, she was sitting on the exam table in a tee shirt and jeans, legs dangling off the side, a solemn, brown-eyed beauty as wistful and captivating as only the youthful feminine can be. After a few moments of introduction, she began to speak, looking me steadily in the eye. She had a medical reason for coming to see me, she said, but first she wanted to tell me what had happened to her.

Six months ago, she began, she had been stepping out of the front door of her apartment building in the Lower East Side housing projects when the sound of gunshots rang out, a not infrequent occurrence in her drug-infested neighborhood. She tried to duck back inside, but it was too late. Caught in the cross fire, she was struck three times.

She unzipped her jeans and pulled up her shirt to show me. The evidence was all too clear: five round scars, each the size of a nickel. Two lay on the far right side of her waist, front and back, where one of the bullets had passed through her abdomen, taking a bite of her liver. Two other scars were located on the front and back of her left thigh, marking the passage of the second bullet through her upper leg muscles. The fifth scar lay in the middle of her abdomen where the third bullet had entered, but there was no sixth scar to mark an exit point, as this bullet had not left her body.

Without waiting for me to comment, Migdalia zipped her jeans back up and continued with her story, describing how she had been rushed by ambulance to the nearest hospital. After emergency surgery, she said, the chief surgeon had come to her bedside to check on her and to deliver news that was very hard to hear: the baby that had been growing in her womb for the past seven months was dead and gone from her body.

Her voice quavered as she spoke the last words, but she took a deep breath and continued, quickly regaining her poise.

"The third bullet hit my baby in the head. They found it stuck in his skull. The doctor said he died instantly. He also said that the bullet came this close"—she held up her thumb and forefinger with only an inch of space between them—"to hitting one of the biggest blood vessels in my body. If it had gone any further, I would have died too."

A picture flashed across my medical mind's eye: a speeding bullet striking Migdalia's abdominal aorta, causing her to bleed to death within a few short minutes. Instead, instantaneous death for her child had meant life for her. I waited wordlessly to hear where the story would go next.

After heaving a deep sigh as if to release the burden of the memories she had just recalled, Migdalia went on, her tone lighter now. She told me how she had cherished the baby that was growing in her belly. She smiled and said she had known from the beginning that it was a boy and described how he had become a true friend to her. Everywhere she went, he had gone with her, something no one had ever done before. She would talk to him, would tell him everything, and she could feel how he listened. He made her feel special. She had loved him, she said, and she had felt he loved her in return. The warmth of the bond between them sounded in her voice, and she paused, as if reluctant to let it go.

But, yes, she admitted, with her throat suddenly going tight again, she had been devastated to wake and find that he was gone, taken from her so suddenly and savagely. She had not seen how she could go on, all alone. In the weeks that followed she had teetered on the edge of an abyss of despair, and she might have been swallowed up in sorrow forever if not for one thing. One single thought became her saving grace, she confided, and she had clung to it with fierce desperation: the thought that this child, her son and dearest friend, had laid down his life for her.

"Death was coming for me," she said, staring at me steadily, despite the moisture glistening in her eyes, "and he saved me—in more ways than one."

She leaned forward, eyeing me as if to make sure that I was with her before going further, her body taut with the intensity of making her listener understand.

"You see," she said, "I used to hate my life. I thought it was ugly and mean and unfair, and it made me despise everyone and everything!"

"But that's all changed now," she declared, as she drew herself up again and straightened her shoulders. "Now my life has become something precious to me. It's become a gift that my son gave me at the cost of his own life. It's almost like he said to me, *Here, you take this gift and use it well!*"

She shook her head softly, as if in awe at the words she was speaking, and then suddenly lifted her chin.

"And I *mean* to!" she proclaimed, kicking her heels against the examination table with a burst of energy. "I didn't know before that my life was something I could use! I thought I was stuck with it the way it was!"

She rolled her eyes at the absurdity of her oversight, adding, "But now I know, and I'm ready!"

Migdalia went on to explain that the surgeons had repaired her damaged uterus and told her that with proper care and supervision she could get pregnant again someday if she wished. And that, she said, was the reason she had asked to see me. Although she had no interest in having a boyfriend anytime soon, she did not want to let any accidents happen. She wanted to make sure she would not get pregnant again until she was ready. She wanted to wait until she had done something *good* with her life, something of her own choosing, something that would make her unborn son proud of her.

251

I had been sitting perfectly still while Migdalia spoke, silenced by the enormity of her story. As she finished, Mrs. McNalley's worried words about Migdalia suddenly came to mind, now sounding pale and unimportant.

"For all your well-intentioned concern," I thought, "this time, my friend, I think you got it wrong. I don't believe Migdalia is in denial or failing to grieve her loss. I think she's holding her grief with a heart made strong by love."

From my perspective, Migdalia needed neither pity nor professional intervention. What she needed was acknowledgment. Supporting and confirming the heroism of her very human heart was the most important thing I could do for her—and the best way to do that was to give her my unwavering attention. What I received in return was the honor of sitting before an inner-city Madonna as she looked down on me from her seat on the examination table with wisdom in her eyes, describing the secret of transforming tragedy into blessing.

Many minutes later, with Migdalia's story still ringing in my ears, I asked if she was ready to turn to the business at hand. When she gave a firm nod, I proceeded with her examination and performed the necessary tests, then counseled her about different contraceptive methods and instructed her in the choice she made.

As we came to the end of the appointment time, I said, "Migdalia, I'm so glad you told me all that you did."

"I'm glad too," she said with a smile. "Some people don't understand, but I think you do." Then she walked away toward the reception desk to make her follow-up appointment with me.

I never saw Migdalia again, however. She left the group home, and if I once knew where she went, I have forgotten it now. Perhaps the Sisters found a foster-care placement for her, a real home where she could be a teenager again and start her new life. Wherever she was, I have no doubt she found her way. She had crossed a bridge she would never have to cross again. She had changed. She had discovered a source of strength and healing in herself, and that made all the difference.

*   *   *   *   *   *   *

Migdalia's wisdom blossomed quickly, but for others it may take months, or years, or even an entire lifetime for wounds to offer up the fullness of their wisdom. Some wisdom just takes longer to hammer out. And such well-tempered wisdom may steal so quietly into a person's life that the flowering it produces can only be discerned later. This happened with Taylor. He was initially held so tightly in the grip of the terrible wounds he had suffered that he showed little sign of healing for an unbearably long time. Only with hard work and inspiration from a surprising source did his wisdom finally express itself fully and shine its luminous light into the world.

At age fourteen Taylor was in love with life. He seemed to excel at everything, from schoolwork to making friends, to playing soccer, to cracking jokes. He was funny and cheerful and inventive, and he was his parents' pride and joy. And then one terrible day, he was diagnosed with an invasive brain tumor. The destructive growth, a medulloblastoma, had sent thousands of malignant tendrils deep into his brain stem, and it refused to be vanquished in spite of being aggressively pursued by an eminent neurosurgeon's knife.

The toll taken on Taylor by the surgeon's effort to save his life was huge. He had to be resuscitated twice as he lay deeply anesthetized on the operating table, and he emerged from the lengthy surgery with a severe complication known as "locked-in syndrome," meaning that his traumatized brain had basically gone into shock and lost communication with his body. He was unable to move a single one of his muscles except those of his eyes. It was in this state of near total paralysis that he underwent a grueling course of chemotherapy followed by radiation therapy, keeping him hospitalized for nine horrific months.

I became involved in Taylor's story midway through this sequence of events. He was transferred to my hospital for his course of radiation therapy and, as the attending physician in charge of the ward where he was placed, I supervised his general medical care. When he first arrived, his parents pulled me aside to say something about their son that they thought might not be clearly stated in the medical summaries from his prior hospital, but which they felt was critical for me to know.

They explained that Taylor had suffered tremendously over the preceding months. Though it had been nearly impossible for him to communicate, they had seen the suffering in his eyes and knew things were going very badly for him. The fear and confusion they sensed in him initially had progressed to painful understanding, which in turn had been replaced by a steady, anguished desperation. As he lay helpless in the paralysis that held him hostage, he watched the life he was separated from with lonely agony in his gaze.

Meeting Taylor for the first time confirmed all that his parents had told me. When I entered his room and explained that I was overseeing the care he would be receiving at our hospital and that I anticipated he would make good progress, he gave no sign of caring about what I had said. Instead, with the meager strength that was slowly returning to one arm, the beleaguered fourteen-year-old boy molded his wavering hand into the shape of a gun and pointed it finger-first toward his temple, desperately uttering with great effort two words he had struggled to master: *Kill . . . me!* It was what he had been saying daily to every person tending him. As far as he could see, he was dismally, hopelessly trapped, and he would rather die than have to endure such a fate.

His parents said it was breaking their hearts to force him to go on, but they could not see any other way, and the torment they felt was written clearly on their faces. They had tried their best to explain that although his life would never be what it had been before, they believed he could still have a life worth living. They would help him, they promised, and together they could make it work. They begged him to try. But Taylor wanted nothing more to do with life, for all he could see of it was unbearable, and he remained unresponsive to their every effort to persuade him to see things otherwise.

Even as the oncology team pursued the cancer with radiation therapy, his parents and I summoned a steady stream of specialists and visitors to Taylor's room who all doggedly tried their hand at helping him cope. Psychiatrists, psychologists, massage therapists, music therapists, nurses with skills in guided imagery and therapeutic touch, and his best friends from school did everything they could think of to draw him out of his despondency, but to no avail.

Meanwhile, a cadre of physical therapists and speech therapists worked with him daily, pushing and cajoling him through rigorous exercises, trying to help his injured brain regain the ability to summon speech again, to chew and swallow food again, to move his arms and legs in increasing increments. It was slow and painful work, and whatever progress he made he quickly used to vent his desperation in new ways. As he developed the strength to roll his body to the side, he would attempt to throw himself off the stretcher while he was being wheeled to the radiation therapy suite for his twice-daily treatments. He would become so agitated that I had to order him to be sedated so that the treatments could be given.

After three long months and the completion of his course of radiation therapy, Taylor had made some definite progress in regaining control of his body. He could sit without toppling over, move his arms and legs in limited ways, and speak in broken phrases as his brain searched through its scrambled memory banks for the proper cues. But this was far too little from his perspective, and his outlook on life remained full of despair. With a huge sense of incompleteness and concern, then, I bid good-bye to Taylor and his parents and wished them well on the next leg of their journey. Taylor was being transferred to a specialized rehabilitation hospital for children located in Massachusetts that was reputed to do excellent work. He would stay there as long as it took for further progress to be made. His parents promised to stay in touch.

Some months later, I received a call from them. Taylor had completed his treatment at the rehab hospital and was in town for a check-up with his oncologist. Would I like to see him? I jumped at the chance, and that evening I walked across the lobby of New York City's Ronald McDonald House toward three waiting figures, two of whom were familiar and one who was not. The two I recognized smiled warmly and turned to the third, who wore a patch over one eye, saying, "Taylor, here's Dr. MacGregor. Do you remember her?"

A slender boy who was sitting in a wheelchair turned to gaze at me with a lopsided smile on his partially paralyzed face and mild curiosity in his one good eye. And though I then recognized that face as the one into which I had looked nearly every day for three months, Taylor himself shook his head and said with halting, slightly garbled speech, but clearly enough to be understood, "Sorry. I know . . . that I should . . . but I'm not sure . . . that I do."

He laughed—an easy, forgiving sound—and added, "There's a lot . . . I don't remember . . . and I'm glad . . . that I don't."

And then, as simply as that, Taylor excused himself and turned to give his attention over to a couple of old school friends who were there as well, waiting eagerly for his company. As the three moved toward a pair of pinball machines across the lobby, I could see that Taylor wielded his wheelchair with familiar precision, making up for the remaining weakness in his legs. He looked happy and full of beguiling boyishness, clad as he was in blue jeans and a velveteen Rolling Stones jacket.

With the sound of the three boys' laughter rising and falling in the background, Taylor's parents and I sat and talked about what had transpired in the past several months. They said the rehab hospital had been a success, not only because the time he spent there had helped him regain a good deal of the physical functioning of his body, but more importantly because it had helped reawaken his desire to live.

The staff had been a wonderful help, they said, but it was the other patients who had the biggest impact on Taylor. In the huge physical therapy rooms, he was surrounded by kids hard at work: kids with brain damage or spinal cord injuries, trying to train their bodies to work again; kids with amputations, learning to use their prosthetic limbs; kids with steadily worsening neuromuscular disorders, such as muscular dystrophy, fighting to retain their waning abilities. Each one had inspired him, and the young ones had inspired him most of all—the little ones clinging to the balance bars or scooting around with the aid of mechanical devices. The battles they all were fighting were enormous, and the effort he saw each one making had slowly and steadily pried his wounded heart open.

His parents went on to say that Taylor not only decided he wanted to try as hard as these other kids were trying, but he also wanted to help them. So he worked on his recovery, and as he worked, he reached out to his fellow patients, encouraging them and cheering for them and giving them hope—and rekindling hope for himself in the process. The change he underwent seemed like a miracle. His parents could not have been more grateful, and hearing what had transpired, I could not have been happier for all three of them.

I was never involved in Taylor's medical care again, yet I felt a need to know the rest of his story. I called his parents for an update every few months, and what they reported continued to be remarkable. Taylor returned home from the rehab hospital so filled with passion about the needs of kids with catastrophic illness and injury that he began to recruit family and friends to help him raise money for the support of such kids: kids disabled like himself, who needed scooters and wheelchairs and rehab therapy but could not afford them. With the help of his mother he founded a nonprofit dedicated to this goal and named it We Support Kids!

As Taylor threw himself into making a difference for these disabled children and simultaneously picked up the threads of his own very changed but livable life, the memory of the months of his locked-in experience continued to recede until they were nothing more than a faint gray cloud in the back of his mind. He graduated from high school to a standing ovation from his classmates and went on to attend Columbia University, where he rode a motorized scooter to class and became well loved, all the while pouring his energy into We Support Kids! and seeing it flourish and spread, bringing help and hope to many.

For ten precious years, far more than had once seemed possible, Taylor shone his inspiring light steadily into the world. But the bitter truth was, his tumor had never been fully vanquished, only suppressed, and during these years, it rose up to challenge him again and again. With the unwavering effort that he and his parents and doctors made, the malignant growth was held at bay long enough for Taylor to fall deeply back in love with life and share that love with many others, but more than that proved impossible. At age twenty-four, the dark presence that still lurked in his brain refused to be held in abeyance any longer, and despite all attempts to make it be otherwise, it came back in full force to claim him.

His passing was mourned by many who poured out their gratitude at having known him and been touched by him. They would always remember Taylor, they said, for his wise leadership and his hugely generous heart. Most of all, they said, they would remember him for his uncommon appreciation of being alive. As he had declared to his oncologist even as his time was running out, "I love my totally messed-up life!"

*   *   *   *   *   *   *

While some people, like Taylor, work with extraordinary determination to unearth the wisdom buried in their wounds, others have their wisdom erupt from the depths of their wounds suddenly and with such intensity that their entire life can change in the twinkling of an eye. This is how it happened for James.

I met James when he enrolled in my research project. Reading through his medical record before making my first home visit to him in his Brooklyn apartment, I learned that he not only had advanced AIDS but also a criminal record involving robbery, drug dealing, and assault. When I tracked down the social worker to ask her about the advisability of being alone with James, she smiled and assured me that I would find visiting with James a completely safe and enjoyable experience. And indeed it was—so much so, in fact, that I would look forward to every visit I made over the following months.

The first time I stepped off the subway at James' stop in Brooklyn, I knew immediately why James had insisted on waiting for me on the subway platform. This part of Brooklyn was a world in which I was out of place, as evidenced by the suspicious stares that came my way as I followed him up the steps from the dank underground station and then along the busy street. But James himself was wholly unperturbed. Calmly disregarding a group of young men loudly arguing with each other outside his building when we arrived, he stepped aside to hold the door open for me as graciously as if he were ushering me into a plush lobby on Fifth Avenue rather than into the barren entryway of a tenement building.

A short man in his late forties, James had sparkling dark brown eyes and a ready smile that took over his entire face and showed off two rows of perfect gleaming-white teeth. Though clearly not in the best of health, he still had the appearance of having once been powerfully built. After climbing four flights of stairs to reach his tiny apartment, he offered me the only comfortable chair, and then perched on the edge of his carefully made bed and began to speak about his views on living with a life-threatening illness. The perspective he had on his approaching death—which he had no doubt was coming sooner rather than later—was entirely shaped, he said, by the rather unorthodox experiences of his life. His description of these experiences occupied my interviews with James for several months, but only when he had come to trust that I would not belittle what he had to say did he fill in what proved to be the most interesting part of his story.

He had started out in life as Arnold Harry Brown, James said, but during his youth people began to say how much he reminded them of James Brown, the not very tall but masterful rock star known as the "Godfather of Soul." Since he liked the comparison, he decided to claim the name as his own: he became James Brown. In his inner-city neighborhood, it was all about image, and the image of his famous namesake strutting his stuff before crowds of screaming fans pleased him to no end.

Growing up in a rough section of Brooklyn where a disdain for life was expressed in angry graffiti and garbage thrown carelessly into the streets, he had to battle his way at every turn. Since he had always been shorter than other kids his age, he had armed himself with a major tough-guy attitude to make up for what he lacked in height. He cultivated a haughty, daredevil swagger in his step and an explosive temper to show that he was not someone to be messed with. By the time he was a teenager he was good with a knife and a gun and was fearless even when the odds were against him. He worked harder to prove himself than his other gang members did, and in so doing, grew to believe that he was invincible.

That attitude seemed to serve him well in the underworld of drugs and crime. He grew skilled in the art of burglary, and his arrogance enabled him to accomplish successful feats of breaking and entering that others would not dare to attempt. He also developed a lucrative business in the trafficking of heroin and cocaine, such that he always had a wad of $100 bills in his pocket that was one to two inches thick. He did not escape being caught red-handed, though, and was sent to prison three times, serving a total of twelve years. Incarceration never changed his ways, however, and as soon as he was let out he would immediately resume his old routines.

Eventually, though, his old ways caught up with him, especially his careless practice of shooting up with dirty needles. He contracted AIDS. And though he had not suffered the worst complications of the disease, he had witnessed it take the lives of many others he knew, and he was forced to acknowledge the power it possessed.

By the time we met, that power was growing. His AIDS was beginning to outfox the antiretroviral medications in which his doctors placed such confidence, and he was noticing certain ominous signs: a subtle waning of stamina, a gradual loss of weight, the appearance of hollows under his cheekbones, and his chronic anemia and low platelet count. Though these things did not dim the spark of his engaging personality, they were disturbing evidence that his AIDS was advancing on its deadly path.

Contemplating death was not difficult for James, not because he still harbored illusions of invincibility, he said, but because he had made peace with his belligerent life. He found it easy now to meet whatever came his way without losing his equanimity. And since he felt I had an open mind, he offered to relate a piece of his story that he generally chose to keep to himself. It was something that had happened to him ten years earlier, he confided, at the peak of his burglary career, and it had radically altered the course of his life.

James said he had known perfectly well that he was living an unlawful life. He knew it was a crime to steal, but he had rationalized it to himself, viewing robbery as nothing more than taking from those to whom life had unfairly given more than they deserved. His anger told him he was only claiming what would have been his if life were fair. He felt justified in helping himself to whatever he could, that is, until one dark and rainy night when his perspective on the matter abruptly changed.

He was out on the prowl that night, geared up to make a strike. He had his eye on a seven-story apartment building he thought he could gain easy access to via the roof of a neighboring building that was under construction. Dressed all in black, with a tight-knit cap pulled down over his ears, a knife in his pocket to pry open a likely window, and a duffle bag hanging from his belt to transport his take, he had watched the windows on the top floor of the apartment building from an alley across the street as evening came on. When no lights appeared in the windows as the night progressed, he was confident that none of the occupants were home. He was free to make his move.

In no time at all, he was closing in on his goal. He had made the leap from the roof of the neighboring building and now was standing erect on the one-foot-wide ledge that circled the uppermost floor of the apartment building, holding on to a prominent line of bricks just above his head, that served to decorate the building's facade. As he clung tightly with his hands and began inching his way forward toward the first set of windows, squinting through the rain falling steadily around him, it happened. His fingers began to slip.

What occurred next seemed to proceed in slow motion. As the rain ran along the backs of his hands and trickled down his upstretched arms inside the sleeves of his jacket, he could feel his fingers losing their hold on the lip of brick overhead.

He tried to grip harder, but to no avail. Only two fingers still touched the brick . . . and then even they lost contact, leaving only empty air. He felt gravity take hold, tilting his body backward into nothingness, and he knew without a doubt that he was going down—down seven stories in the dark of night to meet his death on the concrete below.

But it didn't happen. Instead, he felt a sudden pressure on his back, pushing against his fall, forcing him upright again. Like helpful hands, the pressure braced his back as his fingers groped to regain contact with the rim of brick. And then it was over. The pull of death was gone, and he was returned to life, left standing weak-kneed on a ledge seven stories above the ground, utterly alone in the dark of night.

As James clung to the ledge in the pitch dark and the steady rain, dazed by his deliverance from death and totally stupefied as to how it had happened, a second mysterious thing began to occur. He seemed to hear the return of the occupants of the apartment on whose ledge he was balancing. Though no lights went on, he detected the sound of two people entering and crying out in shock, as if the deed he had planned to do had been carried out and his intended victims were seeing the aftermath of his robbery. He heard a man's voice exclaim in anger and a woman's voice moan in anguish, and suddenly he was flooded with the emotions in their cries—the emotions his intended victims would have felt if his plans had succeeded. He was experiencing what it was like to be robbed, to have one's home invaded, its safety breached, its sanctity violated. It was not just about a loss of material possessions. It was a kind of rape, and he felt how much it hurt. The pain was terrible.

At this point in his story, James paused and slowly shook his head. "I have no memory of getting down to the street and making my way back home," he said, "but I do remember this: for four days and four nights, I lay right here on my bed, barely able to move. I was sick with the knowledge of what I'd been about to do—of what I'd been doing for years."

He clenched his jaw and took a deep breath before going on. "It was the hardest thing I've ever gone through, much worse than being sent to prison. Every crime I ever committed came back to me. I remembered every apartment I'd ever broken into, and I felt the pain that every single person felt when they returned and found their home trashed and their belongings gone. It was so awful, I began to think that maybe I'd died after all, and this was hell, and I was getting what I deserved. I wondered if I was going to have to feel this pain forever."

Again he paused, momentarily absorbed in the memory. When he resumed speaking, he leaned forward from his seat on the edge of his bed with fervor in his dark brown eyes. "I couldn't deny that I deserved to feel all that hurt I'd caused or that I should be made to suffer for my wrongdoing," he said. "But the strange thing was, I knew that river of pain wasn't coming to me as punishment."

He smiled wryly as he leaned back again. "You see," he said, "I wasn't being damned for what I'd done, I was being *educated*. I was being taught the impact of my actions on other human beings. And I can tell you, it wasn't a pleasant thing to learn!"

After reflecting on that thought for a moment, James continued. "My mind went round and round with questions I couldn't answer. I'd been about to die. I felt death coming to claim me, there was no doubt about it. So what had stopped it? What had saved me? And *why*? What possible difference could it make whether I lived or died? Wouldn't the world be better off without me? What about my life was worth saving? *Nothing,* as far as I could see!"

He gave a soft laugh. "Those questions were as much a torment as the pain had been. But finally the answer came to me. I was absolutely right. There *wasn't* anything about my life that was worth saving. Rather, I suddenly realized, it was what I could *still do* with my life that made it worthwhile for death to turn aside!"

That astounding thought, James said, changed everything. From that moment on, he became a different person. He was glad that he had not died before knowing what he now knew about the pain he had been bringing into the world, glad he would not have to take the unacknowledged guilt of his crimes with him to his grave. He had been given the opportunity to redeem himself, and decided to do just that. He disposed of his weapons, he severed his relationships with his fellow dope dealers and his gang, and he gave his stash of cash to his mother, an elderly lady who lived alone in a run-down, rat-infested building in one of the worst sections of Brooklyn. Even though it was dirty money, James said, he felt it would become clean in her hands since it would serve a real need. Rather than rewarding his selfishness, it could alleviate a little of the suffering in the world.

Meanwhile, James landed a job at a fast-food joint, where he learned what it was like to work for pennies and still feel grateful. He spent his free time hanging out at the local streetside basketball courts where he could watch the young males in his community exercise their testosterone, as he put it. The basketball court was a good place to see the measure of a man, he said. You could tell who was honest and who was willing to play dirty in order to score, and he could spot the kids who were most at risk for making the mistakes he had made, the ones who were hotshots and hoodlums in the making. Many of these kids were basically good at heart, he believed, but the pressure to prove yourself when you were young and poor was enormous.

James made a habit of befriending as many of those kids as possible and counseling them about the soul-stealing dangers of a life of crime. It was the least he could do, he thought, and besides, he seemed to be good at it. They tended to listen to him. They seemed to know he was speaking with the wisdom of firsthand experience, the kind of wisdom that could change a person's life. When death finally came for him, he said, he thought he would be ready. He had done his best to face his failings and make amends for them.

* * * * * * *

Now and then you may come across a person whose wounds healed so long ago that they have become nearly transparent. When you find a person like that, you see how lightly the mantle of hard-won wisdom can rest upon someone—as lightly as finest gossamer.

This was true of Hildie, though not many of those who knew her recognized the truth of what they were seeing when they looked at her. With Hildie, it was all too easy to be distracted by the toothlessness of her smile (as she frequently forgot to put her dentures in) or by the hairs blossoming on her chin even as they grew sparser on the top of her head. It did not help, either, that she often developed a glassy look in her eyes when you spoke to her, as if she were drifting off to a place more interesting than the conversation you were trying to engage her in. She had no compunction whatsoever about letting her chin drop and starting to snore right in the middle of your questions about her pain level or her bowel function. After all, she was ninety-six, and she had long ago lost interest in how polished she appeared to the perpetually busy younger folks around her.

Longevity was a strong trait in her family, according to Hildie. The first time I paid her a home visit to listen to her views on approaching the end of life, Hildie told me that every member of her family who had fled from their homeland in Hungary as the repressive Nazi regime rose to power in neighboring Germany had lived at least into their eighties. Hildie, however, had more of the longevity trait than the rest of her family, and she had outlived all of her eight siblings. As one after the other of her brothers and sisters and even her husband died and left her behind, she came to feel increasingly out of touch with life, having no one with whom to share her memories.

The younger generation, Hildie explained, had little interest in decades-old stories about the Nazis and the Holocaust, evidently happy to forget that they had among them a firsthand witness to some of the most malevolent acts ever committed. Though her family had been Christian, they had many friends who were Jewish, and they had all been deeply distressed by the rampage of persecution they saw overtaking their beloved country like an evil disease. Seeing your Jewish neighbors being rounded up and carted off in long trains of boxcars to who-knows-where, never to be heard from again, had been an awful thing and certainly not something that could ever be forgotten, no matter how dim one's memory became. Especially horrendous was the thing that happened one day near her family's town, when somehow the door of a boxcar on a train that was rumbling past came unfastened and slid open. This allowed some of the people inside to throw themselves out in desperation and, even with broken bones, to crawl across the open fields until they reached the shelter of the woods where they were found and cared for by the sympathizers in her town – except for the unfortunate ones who died beside the train tracks where they fell. She declared these were things that even a very aged mind could not forget, though the nightmarish intensity of the memory had thankfully diminished with the passing of time.

The people who had been close to her had served to anchor her in life, Hildie said, and as each one died, her world had shrunk a little further and her connection with life become more tenuous. As she drifted slowly now from one day to the next, she remembered each one of those who had been in her life with detached equanimity.

New people had come into her life, of course, but they did not fill the empty spaces. After being diagnosed with end-stage colon cancer and enrolling in hospice, she was moved from the comfortable apartment she had once shared with her husband to the ultramodern apartment of her son and daughter-in-law. She thought these younger people were probably nice enough, but they were on a different wavelength from her. They made her feel out of touch with the times she was living in, the way they were always worked up about matters completely foreign to her. They had more things to worry about than she could possibly keep track of: politicians whose names she could not remember from one moment to the next, distant countries of which she had never heard, technologies of which she had no understanding, and controversies in which she had not the slightest interest.

On the other hand, she greatly enjoyed the young Italian home health aide who came to bathe her twice a week and do her laundry. As the young lady went about her chores, she sang old Broadway tunes in a lovely voice, tunes that Hildie recognized and could hum along with. And sometimes Hildie's husband, Siegfried (or Sieggy, as she occasionally called him), would appear on the couch beside her, and they would have long, quiet conversations – until her son would come by and patiently touch her on the shoulder and remind her that Dad had died ten years ago. She did not let that fact disturb her though. She said his company was still as good as always, maybe even better.

The hospice staff assessed Hildie as having senile dementia. The term is commonly used by health-care professionals to describe people who are forgetful and who drift in and out of touch with the reality in which everyone around them is solidly anchored, people who hear and see things that no one else does and who spend a good deal of time in a world of their own. Yet there were certain facts that were perfectly clear to Hildie. She knew that the cancer had spread to multiple places in her body, and she knew her body was wearing out. Her eyesight was going, her hearing was very nearly gone, her teeth were definitely gone, and her legs refused to hold her upright anymore. She knew, too, that she would never go outside into the fresh air again: her son and his wife lived in a third floor walk-up, and it had been a struggle to get her up there in the first place. She was certainly never going down those stairs again, she said, at least not until the funeral home people came to carry her out in a big black bag. With the limitations she had seeing, hearing, chewing and walking, life had become very simple. Her main activity now was sitting by a window where the sun shone in for the better part of the day.

Once during one of the many visits I made to Hildie, I commented on always finding her sitting by that particular window. "Yes," she proclaimed with a chortle, "I like this spot. When I feel the sun shining in on me – when I feel its warmth touching me – well, it lets me know where I am. It tells me that I'm still here!" When I nodded and said that sounded like a nice way to experience being alive, she said without hesitation, "Yes, it is, dearie. Yes, it surely is! Much better than dealing with all that chemo stuff they were putting into me before!"

It made complete sense, Hildie said, to stop medical treatment and let life have its way. Why waste all that effort trying to resist the inevitable? She was tired and did not care to spend the precious little energy she had on futile nonsense. She was perfectly happy now just to sit in her favorite easy chair by the window with her prayer book in her lap and doze.

In between her dozing, she did pray, of course, Hildie said. Though her eyes could not make out the print in the prayer book anymore, her bony fingers knew the feel of its worn leather cover well, and her heart had no trouble finding words with which to speak to heaven. This was the only conversation, aside from those with Sieggy, she still felt comfortable having, and her favorite heavenly personage to converse with was Mother Mary.

Compared to the people who came and went around her, the Divine Mother was the only one who truly paid attention

to her anymore, Hildie would say, rolling her eyes. The Holy
Lady was always available to listen to the prayers she offered
over and over every day, on behalf of the world and all its
problems. Praying for the easing of others' burdens was the
least she could do while she waited for her name to be called,
she told me sternly more than once. What's more, praying enabled her to feel the Blessed Mother's presence and the deep
sympathy that emanated from Her.

I loved the fact that my work as a research physician led me
to Hildie. Spending time with her was strangely soothing. And
as I recorded her views on approaching the end of life, what
she said caused me to pause and wonder. Could it be that the
frail elderly and the dying among us – the ones we label as helpless and confused – are doing something more than pitifully
losing their capacity to function? Might they be demonstrating
a wisdom that we who rush around full of busyness are over-
looking, pointing to an important dimension of life that we
too easily forget about? What would happen, I thought, if we
all spent more time listening to these people?

* * * * * * *

Redemption is not a word we often use in everyday conversation. Perhaps we shy away from the depth of meaning it im-
plies, instinctively choosing not to use it lightly but allowing
it to retain its full import for those rare occasions when its
meaning truly fits. In Leo's case, I can think of no better word
to describe what happened.

When he was born, Leo's mother gave him the proud name
of Trahonzalee, and though he had never actually been called
by that name as far as he could remember, the unused name
had lingered in his mind, evidence of some fleeting aspiration
his mother once had but was never able to realize, oddly fore-
shadowing his own failure to spread his wings and fly. And
indeed, Leo's wings were clipped by wounds he started to

accumulate early in life, wounds which came his way so steadily that, by age seventeen, he had more than most people acquire over an entire lifetime. He was without a doubt one of the most thoroughly wounded, alienated human beings I had ever come across, and tending to his suffering challenged my skills as a doctor to the limit. At the same time, there was something so compelling about Leo that I could not help but remain fiercely determined to help him.

For the first eight years of Leo's life, no one knew that the human immunodeficiency virus lurked in his body. His mother must have thought he was just a skinny runt, if she thought about him at all, preoccupied as she was with drowning her own problems in drugs and alcohol and trading the enticements of her body for the cash she needed in order to buy herself those escapes. His abusive father had long since abandoned them both, only to be replaced by a series of other violent men. But just as Leo was entering the fourth grade at his inner city grammar school, his mother fell ill. When the doctors discovered that she was infected with the AIDS virus, they tested Leo and found that he was HIV positive, too.

When Leo's mother died from her AIDS a few months later, Leo suffered two devastating blows, and he blamed her for both of them. First, she had gone away for good, leaving him in the hands of two people he barely knew: a great-aunt and great-uncle who were as different from him as could be. Second, she bequeathed him her heaviest burden. He knew that the thing he had seen killing her was living in him too. The doctors told him her body had infected him with it when he was born. These two blows planted the seeds of a seething anger that grew stronger with each year that passed. He began hanging out on the streets and refusing to go to school or keep appointments with his doctors or counselors. By the time he turned thirteen, he was staying out all night, getting into fights and returning to his great-aunt and great-uncle's home disheveled and drunk.

When money began disappearing from the house, Leo's two elderly guardians threw up their hands in despair. This was too much. As devout Pentecostal parishioners, they had not understood the lifestyle of their wayward niece, Leo's mother, and they found it even harder to understand the behavior of their grand-nephew, much less live with it in their home. Overwhelmed and out of their league, they went to Family Court and filed a PINS petition, identifying Leo as a Person in Need of Supervision and making him a ward of the state.

The state placed Leo in foster care, and for the following three years Leo bounced from one foster family to another, exhausting the good intentions of each one before being assigned to the next one. By the time he was sixteen, a good-looking kid with an overwhelmingly negative attitude, the only option left open to him was to enter a group home for the most intractable boys in the system.

I met Leo one year later, after he had broken every rule, first at one group home and then at second. Now he was being transferred to a third one, near the large city hospital where I worked as a pediatrician and adolescent medicine specialist. Anthony, a dedicated social worker from the latest group home, escorted him to my office for a comprehensive health exam, bringing with him an armful of documents describing Leo's psychosocial history and prior medical care. He also acted as Leo's interpreter, and it was a good thing that he did, because Leo's answers to the questions I asked him about his health were muttered with such sullen indifference that they were nearly impossible to understand. As often as not, he made no attempt to reply at all, but shrugged and looked away, his handsome young face tight with disdain, leaving Anthony to fill in the blanks for me.

Leo had the biggest chip on his shoulder I had ever encountered. Yet he was perfectly transparent. Because I knew some of his history, I found it easy to see through the hostile front he hid behind, the protection he thought he needed in a harsh, untrustworthy world. Behind that front I could see a sensitive and badly hurting young person who was trying to survive in the only way he knew how. And now surviving was becoming more difficult because of his AIDS. The virus was rousing from its years of relative quiescence and starting to inflict increasing damage on his immune system—as the blood tests I began taking on a regular basis showed.

Back in the days before antiretroviral medications changed the dismal prognosis of AIDS, there was little we medical professionals could do for patients like Leo, although we certainly tried. Over the ensuing year, I saw Leo at increasingly frequent intervals in my adolescent clinic. We established a matter-of-fact relationship, getting by with a bare minimum of conversation when Anthony was not around. I did my best to stave off the infections to which his body was steadily becoming more vulnerable, and watched helplessly as other problems mounted. His gastrointestinal tract developed increasing difficulty in digesting his food, his weight fell, and chronic anemia stole his energy away. After seven months, Leo developed such intractable diarrhea that I had to admit him to our pediatric and adolescent inpatient service. It was his first hospitalization ever. I had no idea it would last an agonizingly long four months, nor did it occur to me that, once there, he might never leave.

Too many things happened over the course of those four months to recount, but the sum of it was that Leo's AIDS progressed with wanton disregard for whatever the inpatient team and I did to try to hold it back. We drew upon an extensive biomedical arsenal to wage our war against his assailant. I wrote orders for a good twenty different medications, administered from every route imaginable, aimed at boosting his blood, stimulating his appetite, relieving his pain, suppressing inflammation in his tissues, opening his airways, protecting his skin, soothing his intestinal dysfunction, balancing his blood chemistry, calming his nerves, ramping up his nutrition, and protecting him from umpteen possible types of infection. But the virus was a clever opponent and continued on its course, largely undeterred.

As intense as our focus was on Leo's medical care, however, this was only part of the story that played out over those four months of his life. Leo was a unique patient on the ward, different from the other kids who were there. The vast majority of the others came only for fleeting visits—for treatment of asthma attacks, out-of-control seizures, acute appendicitis, and other serious but manageable problems. These kids got better with treatment and returned home. He was different even from the ones who were critically ill, those with diabetic coma or bacterial meningitis or flare-up of rheumatic heart disease, who stayed longer, but in the end improved and went home too. Leo was different because he was not getting better, and there was no home waiting to receive him even if he did. The hospital was fast becoming his permanent home, and us, by default, his family.

Every member of our inpatient staff—attending physicians, residents and interns, nurses, nurses' aides, social workers, the school teacher, the music therapist—came to know this reluctant resident of the west ward well, and as we did, a peculiar thing began to happen. Every one of us began to want to do more for Leo than merely provide him with good hospital care. We all wanted to win him over. One after another, we all began searching for ways to warm Leo up and entice him out of his shell.

We tried many approaches, but because Leo was not big on personal interaction, most of them proved to be dead ends. Chatting, telling stories, cracking jokes, singing songs and playing music led nowhere. The one approach that did not fail outright was bringing him presents. When a few staff members discovered that Leo did not reject their offerings, especially if they were made wordlessly, the practice caught on quickly, and his room gradually filled with a large assortment of gifts and trinkets.

Stuffed animals capable of melting the most guarded heart lined his two windowsills: stalwart teddy bears, floppy-eared rabbits, hopeful-eyed puppies, fiery dragons, an array of grumpy trolls, and other imaginative creatures. Greeting cards, picture books and crossword puzzles littered his bedside table, while his closet held a pile of baseball caps, a catcher's mitt, and a row of tee shirts on hangers, emblazoned with the images of musicians, sports idols and movie stars. And though Leo never donned a single one of those tee shirts, nor was seen to read a book or do a crossword puzzle or even glance at any of the stuffed animals, he did not throw them away either, and so we chose to interpret his tolerance of them as a kind of begrudging acceptance of our intention to be helpful.

As the days went by, Leo undoubtedly acquired far more personal possessions than he had ever owned in all the years of his life, and these possessions, wanted or not, made his room distinctly different from every other room on the ward. It was no longer just one of many anonymous spaces identified by a three-digit number, indistinguishable from all the rest, temporarily sheltering young occupants who came and went. It became a room with a distinctive character. It became Leo's room.

As impossible as it was to know what Leo felt about those gifts, it lifted the spirits of all of us on staff to see them there. And in a funny way, their presence also helped soften the blow we felt when he would flatly refuse our attempts to engage him in conversation. For Leo did not like to talk about anything but the bare necessities, and if someone happened to forget that fact, he would make it very clear. He would lie back in his bed and pull the covers firmly over his head, refusing to say another word. Or, if the covers were not immediately within his reach, he would pull the hospital gown he was wearing up over his eyes and ears instead, holding it there until the offending person gave up and left the room.

Yet while Leo seemed intent on keeping himself barricaded behind an impenetrable wall, everyone involved in his care remained committed to finding ways to get past his defenses. Anthony, the social worker from Leo's group home, started tracking down Leo's family members, none of whom had heard from Leo for years. The first ones he found were Leo's great-aunt and great-uncle, who responded to Anthony's telephone call with an immediate request to pay Leo a visit. The elderly couple—a heavy-set man with kind eyes who walked with a cane, and his stout wife who guided him earnestly by the elbow—arrived the following day and embraced Leo with tears of joy and an outpouring of concern, ending with promises to contact other family members and to return for visits regularly. According to Anthony, Leo smiled shyly and waved as they left.

A few days later, a brother arrived for a visit and stayed a good hour. And again, when the visit was over, Leo was seen to be smiling. Encouraged, Anthony contacted a second brother, who was incarcerated in an upstate prison, and made arrangements for him to be brought to the hospital for a supervised visit. The young man arrived in handcuffs, accompanied by two police officers who removed the cuffs and stood at the entrance to Leo's room for the duration of the two-hour visit. The sounds of chatter and laughter that floated out from Leo's room caught the ear of every one of us on the ward that day and brought smiles to every face. Sadly, because of prison regulations, it was the only meeting the two brothers would have. On the other hand, that it happened at all seemed a miracle.

A few weeks later, Anthony and I talked about another way we might be able to bring some joy into Leo's life. We would submit an application on Leo's behalf to the Make a Wish Foundation, an organization dedicated to making wishes come true for seriously ill youngsters. When I told Leo about the opportunity and asked what his greatest wish would be, he hesitated a moment, as if weighing the possibility that this was a trick, then, keeping his eyes carefully averted, mumbled, "Go to Disney World." I was delighted to hear that he had such a concrete aspiration, though I was concerned about how realistic it was. Nevertheless, we submitted the application, interested to hear what the Foundation would say.

Sadly, but not surprisingly, Leo's request was turned down by the Foundation, with their regrets. They judged his condition to be too serious for them to support such a rigorous trip.

When I delivered the news to Leo, his face went hard with anger, and for the first time he didn't hold back what he was thinking. He let loose a tirade of accusations. With clenched fists, he told me he wasn't surprised, because nothing good ever happened to him. For his whole life, he had never had the things that other people got to have, things like having fun or getting a girlfriend, and now, he didn't even know if he would get to grow up to be a man. The Foundation was a joke, he said, his thin body shaking with the effort of containing his rage. How could he have been so stupid as to think he would ever get a wish fulfilled? Life stinks, he concluded bitterly as he turned away and retreated under the covers. When my suggestion that we ask the Foundation for another wish was met with stony silence, I left Leo's room filled with remorse that our attempt to bring him a little happiness had only served to fan the flames of his disappointment in life.

When I paid Leo my usual visit the next day, however, I was surprised to find that his outlook had changed. As I leaned over his bed, about to perform his daily physical exam, he held up both hands to stop me with uncharacteristic assertiveness. He had been thinking, he said gruffly, carefully avoiding my eyes, that of course it would be too difficult for him to go on a trip. Anyone could see that. And besides, he growled, he wasn't really interested in going to Disney World. There was something else he would much rather have, something more important. Could he make another wish?

When I replied that he definitely could, Leo said he wanted to describe his wish to Anthony, and then closed his eyes and lay back stiffly, indicating the conversation was finished and I was free to perform my exam. As I did, I felt a mounting excitement about Leo's new wish. Whatever it was, it had to be something really significant, I thought, to have overcome his despair of the day before.

Several days later we received a positive response from the Make a Wish Foundation, and Anthony prepared to visit nearby 14th Street, where almost anything could be purchased at a discount price. As he prepared to leave, he had a big grin on his face.

"I have a suspicion that what I'm going to buy today just might put a chink in our friend Leo's armor," he exclaimed with a wink. And since he was the one who had already worked miracles for Leo by reuniting him with his great-aunt and great-uncle and two brothers, I was inclined to believe that he knew what he was talking about.

The next morning, when I saw Anthony at the nurses' station, he was beaming.

"Look, I've got Leo's wish!" he said enthusiastically, as he reached into a shopping bag and pulled out a tissue-wrapped object. Stripping the tissue paper away, he held the object up high in the air so that all the other staff members who had gathered eagerly about could see as well.

Dangling from a thick gold-link chain gleamed a golden medallion, a good five inches in diameter, displaying the head of a roaring lion in relief and the name LEO inscribed in large raised letters across the lower portion. Truly, it was an adornment fit for a king. And, indeed, it was exactly what Leo had envisioned, given the smile that flashed briefly but broadly across his face when Anthony presented it to him shortly thereafter.

Making no comment other than a gruff, "Huh, it's okay," the obviously pleased boy carefully hung the medallion around his neck and centered it on his chest, over his heart. And from that day on, he never took it off or let another person touch it. When I would visit him on my morning rounds and approach his bed to perform his daily exam, he would hold one hand up firmly in the air to keep me from coming too close, then carefully lift the medallion to one side with the other hand. Only after this was accomplished was I free to get out my stethoscope and listen to his heart and lungs and do my usual diagnostic thumping and prodding of his body.

Clearly, the medallion was Leo's prized possession, and not just because it was a handsome piece of jewelry. It was much more than that. It was his talisman, the embodiment of the power he had never found in his life. With its flashy color and its lion roaring above his name with lips curled back in a ferocious snarl and huge fangs exposed, it announced to the world who he really was in a way he had never been able to do, showing all onlookers that he was far more than he appeared to be. It told them he was strong and noble and fierce and golden.

For a while, we were all elated by this triumph, but eventually that elation faded, for Leo was steadily losing ground. As one month had turned into two, and two into three, the AIDS virus had multiplied unchecked in his body, and his health was now declining at an accelerating pace. He had no appetite, and his stomach and intestines refused to digest whatever he could be persuaded to swallow. He ate like a bird, feeding himself one tiny fragment at a time or sipping halfheartedly on his nutritional supplement drinks. And although we gave him daily infusions of high-potency intravenous nutrition as well, his body refused to assimilate any of it.

As Leo's condition grew steadily worse and his weight continued to fall, he seemed to be wasting away before our eyes. Day after day he grew more emaciated until, as he entered his fourth month of hospitalization, his degree of malnutrition was extreme. His body appeared to be nothing more than parchment-like skin stretched tight over a collection of bones, with eyes sunken deep into their sockets, and lips, once soft and full, now drawn into a thin line across two rows of teeth. Weighing a shocking forty-eight pounds, he had become a living skeleton.

Each time I looked at Leo, I struggled to comprehend how such a body could go on, day after weary day. It hardly seemed possible. He looked like he was at the brink of death. What on earth was keeping him alive?

An answer to this question came unexpectedly, while I was making rounds one morning. As was my practice when I entered Leo's room, I greeted him and asked if there was anything he wanted to discuss with me. Not unpredictably, the question elicited only a grunt, and I began to examine his body for signs of either improvement or worsening of his condition. As I was bending over his bed, listening to his heart fluttering bravely behind his pitifully thin chest wall, I was surprised to hear the sound of Leo's voice. Pulling the stethoscope from my ears, I asked him if he could kindly repeat what he had just said.

"My mother didn't mean to give me AIDS," he muttered quietly but defiantly, as if defending her against some unspoken accusation.

"No, Leo, I'm sure she didn't," I agreed wholeheartedly and waited, hoping he would say something else about this one person he had blamed more than anyone else for his suffering. Yet even when I encouraged him, he refused to utter another word.

Still, those few words he had spoken said enough. They said that the defenses he had erected around himself were thinning. The wall of anger that had imprisoned him for so long was losing its hold on him, and the love he was starving for was beginning to find its way into his lonely heart.

Suddenly an answer to my question burst into my mind. I was seeing right in front of me what was keeping Leo alive. It was the flowering of love in his life. For someone whose life had contained so little of that defining human experience, it made sense that his need for love could create a powerful urge to survive, capable of sustaining him despite the pull of far-advanced disease. Was love really that powerful? I could see no better explanation.

As if in confirmation, a change began to come over Leo. His belligerent resistance to life started to wane, and he grew more observant. For the first time, I saw him look beyond his own unhappy, self-preoccupied world and show a flickering of interest in what was around him.

What was around him, of course, was a ward full of children—children who were not so different from him. These children knew as he did what it was to be sick and unhappy and in pain. As Leo finally began to recognize this, something happened that we never imagined would be possible: Leo took action. He asked his nurse to give one of his stuffed animals to a child in the hall he saw crying. Of course, when his nurse returned to tell him how happy he had made the child, he quickly pulled the sheet over his head. Yet the next day, he asked her to give a stuffed animal to another child he noticed going by his door, a youngster in a wheelchair. This time, his nurse knew better than to say anything about the impact of his action.

Thus began an amazing transformation. A penniless pauper all his life who had never possessed a thing of his own, Leo became a generous benefactor. Every day, he asked his nurse to identify children on the ward who were especially sick or sad and give each of them one of the stuffed animals that were so plentiful in his room, or, if the patient happened to be a teenager, then one of the tee shirts or baseball caps from the collection in his closet. He was so persistent in his instructions over the following two to three weeks that the untouched gifts in his room slowly but steadily found new owners, each of whom delighted at what they received, until finally not a single one remained. The only exception was his gold medallion. That gift he allowed himself to keep.

The change we witnessed take place in Leo over those few short weeks astounded us all. Leo, whom we had known only as a helpless victim destined to remain trapped forever by unfair circumstances, took charge of his own inner healing and accomplished more than we had with all our well-intentioned efforts. And though he did not transform entirely—he remained reclusive and sometimes still quite grumpy—he was not the same person who had come to us four months earlier. He retreated under the covers far less often, he answered in sentences—albeit short ones—when asked questions by the staff, and he spent long periods of time gazing out the door of his room at the activities on the ward.

Nor did Leo stop there. He began to assert himself and claim the right to make decisions concerning his medical care. One day he simply refused to take any more of the twenty-or-so different medications we were giving him. Shortly after that, he insisted on having all the intravenous lines removed from his body, saying they imprisoned him and he wanted to be set free.

At this point, I convened a meeting of our clinical team. Given the requests Leo was making, it seemed only right that we allow him to request a "Do Not Resuscitate" order if he wanted to, even though he was a minor and his request would not be legally binding. When our team concurred unanimously and the option was explained to Leo, he said he didn't need the time we offered him to think it over. This was something he wanted from us too: the right to decline aggressive, life-prolonging procedures should he start to die.

When I met with his great-aunt and great-uncle to ask their view on the matter as his legal guardians, they looked at each other briefly, nodded their heads, and said, "Let the boy have his way. It's high time he had the right to make his own decisions." And so, on that very day, Leo and his great-aunt and great-uncle all signed their consent on a DNR request form, and I wrote the DNR order into his chart, taking Leo one step closer to the freedom he was seeking.

A few days later, one of the nurses paged me with an urgent request. She said that Leo was behaving strangely and could I please come take a look at him. When I hurried to his room, I found him sitting up in bed, twisting the bed sheet with his hands and looking unusually agitated.

"Dr. MacGregor," he said immediately, "where's the stretcher? When are they sending it for me?"

Not being aware of any need for a stretcher, I asked, "What stretcher are you talking about, Leo?"

"The stretcher that's supposed to take me upstairs," he said impatiently. "They're waiting for me. I need to get ready!"

Puzzled, I wondered if someone could have ordered a medical procedure for Leo of which I was not aware, and I hurried out to the nurses' station to check the order sheet in his chart. Finding nothing relevant written there, I asked the nurse who paged me if she knew what this was all about. She shook her head and said that, for the past couple of hours, Leo had been asking the same question of everyone, yet no one knew of any reason for a stretcher to take him anywhere.

As the nurse and I stood looking at each other, we both suddenly nodded. The same thought had just occurred to each of us. Leo's time was drawing close, and he was feeling it.

Before leaving the hospital that day, I left careful instructions for the residents and nurses on night duty to call me if they noted the slightest change in Leo's condition. I emphasized that it didn't matter what time of the night it was or whether they were uncertain of what the change might mean. I wanted to be called so that I could come and see for myself. I wanted to be there with Leo if he was going to depart. I intended to make certain that he was as comfortable as possible in his dying, but more than that, I wanted to be witness to the final chapter of his story. To me, that was part of being his doctor—a big part.

So, when my beeper went off at midnight, I didn't waste any time. I jumped in a cab and was at the hospital within ten minutes. Yet when I tiptoed into Leo's room and stood looking down at his sleeping form, I could not detect any difference, though the nurse who called said she thought his breathing had changed. Even rousing Leo for a quick exam failed to reveal anything out of the ordinary—only his usual grumpiness at being disturbed.

Still, as I was about to leave, something made me hesitate. For one thing, I knew that Leo hated being alone at night. He sometimes overcame his dislike of talking in order to ask one person or another—a nurse, a resident, his great-aunt or great-uncle—to spend time in his room with him when night came on. It was the only request he ever made of others, and knowing how excruciatingly hard it was for Leo to ask for anything, I knew it must be very important to him not to be alone after dark.

Since it was not often that anyone was able to comply with his request, I thought, oh well, I was already there, and it was Friday night with no work the following day. It was not much to ask. Besides, I hadn't spent a night in the hospital for a long time, since night duty was not part of an attending physician's job description, and I had forgotten how soothing the muffled sounds of a ward full of sleeping children could be. On top of that, the view out Leo's window of the sleeping city and its twinkling lights was magical.

I sat in a chair near the window, where I could keep an eye on Leo without infringing on his privacy. True to character, Leo kept the covers pulled over his head to underscore the importance of that privacy, except for the few moments every so often when he would pull them down and pop his head up, checking to see if I was still there, uttering a barely audible "Hrumph" when I would ask if he wanted me to stay longer. I took the sound to mean yes, and as the hours passed, the soft murmur of Leo's breathing and the muted nighttime rumble of the great city that surrounded us allowed me to muse undisturbed on Leo's healing journey from the wounds that had so imprisoned him.

When the dark of night finally began to yield to the dawn of a new day, I sighed and stretched away my stiffness from sitting still for so long. "Well, Leo," I thought, "I guess you're not ready to go just yet," and thinking I would see him again on Monday morning, I departed for home.

But Leo didn't wait for Monday morning. He died that afternoon of a cardiac arrest.

It happened so quietly and unobtrusively that no one was aware of the fact for some time. Leo's elderly great-uncle was snoring peacefully in a chair beside Leo's bed at the time, keeping his rediscovered great-nephew company as he often did on the weekends. Having been tested by his own trials in life, the dignified bear of a man had found it easy enough to forgive his wayward niece's son. And because neither Leo nor his great-uncle were much given to exchanging words, they had settled into the comfortable habit of taking a snooze in each other's presence. Only when the nurse came by to check on Leo's vital signs did it become clear that the immense struggle of Leo's life was over. His heart had simply stopped beating, and without so much as a whisper, he had gone.

When I arrived at the hospital a short time later, having been called by the chief resident and given the news, I went to Leo's room to say a last good-bye to one of the most challenging patients I had ever had under my care, and one from whom I had learned more than words could say. Standing by his bed, looking down at the ravaged body that only a short while before had housed such a fiery spirit, the word redemption came to mind. It seemed an apt word, for there was no longer any aura of failure overshadowing Leo, nor any need for regret. He had reclaimed his life and used it well.

In case there was any doubt of that, the shining medallion lying on the center of Leo's chest, with its roaring lion and bold announcement of Leo's name, said it all. It proclaimed that Leo had the heart of a lion and the soul of a king, and that he had died triumphant. He had taken the dross of his defeated life and turned it into the purest gold.

E*pilogue*

MY PATIENTS TAUGHT ME powerful lessons about what it is like for human beings to be sick and fragile and in pain, and they showed me the courage it takes to endure such experiences. They also taught me what it is like to be cared for by others: how the skill and attentiveness of doctors, nurses, family and friends is critical to making it through and regaining good health. What they didn't teach me was how to apply those lessons to myself. Cancer had to teach me that.

One crisp, blue-skied March day, a hospital colleague strode into the examination room where I was waiting for him to tell me the results of the biopsy he had just performed on me. Moments earlier he had been bantering jovially with me; now his face was somber. Without wasting breath on a long prelude, he went straight to the facts: "I'm sorry to tell you this, Betsy, but you have something in your body that is going to kill you unless we act immediately, and even then, it's not certain you'll survive."

To be truthful, his words were not quite that stark, although the message definitely was. I had cancer, and prompt action was necessary.

But the message barely scratched the surface of my consciousness. The idea of such a thing happening was inconceivable to me, in spite of the fact that I had been working exclusively with dying patients, many of them with cancer, for the past several years. My zeal for making a difference in other people's lives and setting standards for a better way of practicing medicine occupied center stage in my mind, leaving no room for imagining something like this.

My psyche immediately threw up a wall of denial, claiming the diagnosis was not all that important. My identity as a doctor made up a huge part of the person I thought myself to be, and I was used to feeling in charge of things. Difficult problems were my daily fare; this problem could be dealt with just like all the others. No way was my professional identity going to step aside and be replaced by that of a sick person. At the initial meeting with my newly acquired oncologist, my doctor persona engaged in conversation with him from its usual rational perspective, behaving as if he and I were two colleagues sitting together in a conference room, discussing the options and outlook for a patient in another room. The fact that the patient was me was hardly acknowledged.

While my oncologist arranged for surgery and put plans in place for chemotherapy to follow, I continued my full-time schedule with stubborn single-mindedness. Doing anything other than that was unthinkable. I squeezed in the various diagnostic tests he ordered between seeing my patients, attending meetings, and giving lectures, as if having a life-threatening condition were only a minor inconvenience.

Looking back, the extent of my denial was so great I have to laugh, especially when I recall what happened two weeks after my diagnosis. I took a cab uptown to give a talk to a women's group on end-of-life issues. After being warmly welcomed by the director of the organization and seated facing a room filled to capacity, I began speaking about one of my favorite topics: the importance of palliative care for people with terminal illness.

I was well into in the lecture, and it was flowing along nicely, when my carefully prepared speech jolted to a halt in mid-sentence. The word "cancer" had just come out of my mouth.

"What was that you said?" my mind asked.

In a flash, the truth I had so staunchly denied burst through my bravado. As abruptly as if someone had just pulled a blind-fold off my eyes, I saw what had escaped me until then. Yes, I did have cancer, and, yes, I might even die. How could I possibly have been so oblivious of what was happening in my own life? I was amazed.

Not only that, how could I have been so oblivious of where I was and who I was speaking to? This was the New York City chapter of the self-help organization SHARE, and all the woman listening to me had breast cancer or ovarian cancer. I was doubly amazed.

With the remainder of my talk gone from my head, I took a deep breath and spilled out the story of my diagnosis. As the women around me received the story with knowing nods and encouraging comments, I crossed an invisible line. I left behind being a medical authority and capable caregiver and be-came instead someone who not only needed the help of others but was ready to receive that help. A new and different world opened up to me that day.

The first thing to come into view in that world was how worn down I was. After twenty-seven years of working ten- to twelve-hour shifts, five to seven days a week, I was weary to the bone. The identity I wore weighed two thousand pounds, and it had me trapped. I knew I needed to change, but I didn't know how to shed that much of myself.

That night I dreamt I was making rounds in a huge, open hall filled with sick patients lying in hospital beds. I visited one patient after another, rapidly writing orders as I went, until I came to a bed where a patient with big, dark eyes lay staring up at me, looking right past my white coat. Suddenly, I was that patient, lying in the hospital bed, dressed in a hospital gown.

The bed felt very crowded. Stacks of patient charts surround-ed me, leaving no room to stretch out my legs, which I badly wanted to do. As a nurse walked by, I called out to her, and she came to stand beside the bed. Patiently but firmly, I explained that I could not be responsible for all these charts just now. Could she please take them away? Oh, and by the way, could she also arrange for me to be transferred to a private room so that I could get some rest? Didn't she know I had cancer?

Not long after having that dream, I discovered that being someone diagnosed with cancer had certain powers. It gave me the right to ask for just about anything I wanted—like getting excused from attending administrative meetings and going home early or taking an afternoon off to interview prospective surgeons. It also liberated me from some of my own rigid, habitual behaviors, such as always being in a hurry and writing compulsively perfect medical notes. No one would find fault with me now, not even, I eventually realized, if I quit working altogether and went on medical leave.

So, one day, I did something I could never have imagined doing. I took off my white coat, hung it on its hook in my office and gave it a good long look. With my photo-ID badge pinned to its lapel, pens and a penlight stuffed into a breast pocket, and my stethoscope sticking its head from a thigh pocket, it embodied my doctor-hood. For a great many years it had announced to all who saw its white shape approaching, "Be reassured, a doctor is here!" It had made people listen to my words and bought me entrance into circles of power and influence in the hospital hierarchy. It had become such a part of me I wondered if I would know who I was without it. With that thought lingering in my mind, I left my office, knowing I would not return to put it on again.

As surgery and then chemotherapy began to take their toll, my perpetual be-in-charge, come-to-the-rescue, take-care-of-everyone-else self surrendered to letting others take care of me. There was no other choice. The energy required to resist was gone, swept away by the intensity of my treatment. At the same time, in the space created by the demise of my fierce independence, unexpected gifts began to appear. My husband, Charles, outdid himself with his loving kindness; our two teenaged children, Daniel and Kendra, matured overnight and touched me deeply with their concern; and good friends flocked around, offering their support.

Many gifts of kindness were given to me during those months. After years of looking into the eyes of people who were suffering and meeting those eyes with compassion, I now found myself looking into eyes of compassion that were focused on me. This was a profound experience. I discovered how powerful compassion truly is, how feeling truly cared about by others can inspire courage and hope even when illness is stealing away one's sense of wellness. Even my dreams became a source of compassion. One night, after lying awake for hours feeling ghastly ill from the effects of chemo and worrying about its toxic effects on my liver, heart, and brain, I fell asleep and dreamt that sparkling blue diamonds were flowing through my bloodstream. In the morning I awoke feeling completely refreshed and reassured.

Over the next weeks, however, the second and third rounds of chemo flattened me further with their destructive force, making it more difficult to find my footing again before each succeeding round came. Yet, strangely, I felt no fear. Instead, a sense of trust in all that was happening accompanied me, even as I grew weaker and more helpless. An inner certainty told me that cancer had not come to do me harm, but to teach me. It was waking me up and giving me a taste of death's inevitability, not staying for good. I believed that in my bones.

In fact, my patients had prepared me for this experience. The lessons I had witnessed them learn began to converge with my own. My memories of parents who had accepted and loved their children born with severe abnormalities encouraged me to accept the incompleteness and brokenness in myself. They helped me see that every one of us has our own quota of imperfection with which we must live. James, the drug dealer, and Randolf, the dying theater celebrity, inspired me as I sought to forgive myself for past mistakes and

failures, while my homeless, ex-addict friend, Paula, together
with Crystal, who tried to end her life four times, and Se-
nora Hernandez, whose son Hector was so brutally injured,
showed me how success can only be achieved by refusing to
give up. And Katherine, encased in her scleroderma prison,
showed me how gracefully some human beings can meet a
seemingly abominable fate.

Like elderly Hildie, and Sharon and Frazer, who lost their
beloved daughter, and like little Angel and his father, and even
crusty Leo, I saw how comfort could hide behind terrible ca-
lamity, only waiting to be found. Like Latwan, who never allowed the bouts of excruciating pain from sickle-cell disease
get him down, and like Taylor, with his advancing brain tumor,
and Terrell, after his amputation, I found I could stand back
from my body's hardship and remain grateful for every day.
Like Martin, whose young son drowned, and like Saul and Rebecca, who lost their first child to the ravages of neuroblastoma, and Migdalia, whose unborn baby died when she was
shot, I discovered I could feel deeply trusting of life, no matter
how excruciatingly difficult it might sometimes seem. I could
appreciate what an incredible gift it was to be alive—a gift so
precious that no price is too high to pay for it—just like Florine discovered as her death from ovarian cancer approached.
Most significantly of all, I was humbled to realize how vulnerable and strong I was simultaneously—how human, in fact, just
like every one of my patients.

I developed an interest in looking at myself in the mirror.
The face I saw there was both familiar and strikingly unfamiliar. It lacked eyebrows and was totally bald and pale as a
ghost, yet the presence in the eyes was astonishingly intense.
There were no adornments or artificiality about it. I felt as if
I were seeing my real self for the first time, and a feeling of
appreciation for this person I was flooded through me. I wondered how much more I could ask of her—how much more
she could endure.

Then, as my body struggled to cope with the brutal effects of the third round of chemo, I had another very clear dream. I was standing on a long, thin strip of dry, barren land far out in the ocean. My eyes could see nothing except dark, foreboding water stretching away in every direction, and my ears could not detect a single sound, not even that of the waves or wind— only silence. The sense of lifelessness was profound.

The next day, I decided I had gone far enough. Cancer had delivered its wake-up call, and chemo had hammered it home. I had broken free from old, constricting patterns of self-judgment and limitation and saw clearly what mattered most to me: love, kindness and gratitude. But three rounds of chemo had brought me so close to the boundary between life and death that I dared not have the fourth and final round. Every fiber of me warned it would be too much. I would have to trust that three rounds had done the job.

So, arm in arm with Charles, I went to see my oncologist. Sitting at the table in his conference room as we had months before, I told him my decision: I wanted to stop chemotherapy. My body was saying it couldn't take any more. I had come too close to the edge of life and didn't want to slip over accidentally.

As I held my breath, my oncologist gazed at me silently. Did he think I was crazy? Engaged in magical thinking? Deluded into believing that because I was a doctor, I was somehow exempt from the hard realities of cancer? Was he determined to talk me out of my decision?

I watched intently as he stroked his chin, evidently weighing his options. Then, as if reaching a decision, he nodded his head and picked up my chart, which had been lying open on the table in front of him, and closed it firmly. Leaning back in his chair, he gave me a thoughtful look and said, "All right, we'll stop here. Sometimes the patient knows best."

That was thirteen years ago—long, wonderful years in which I have continued to ponder the mysteries of life and death. To my great joy, Charles and I have also joined with friends to found and guide a small hospice residence on the island where we now live in the northwest corner of the country. There we create the perfect setting and support for people with terminal illness in our community to come to the end of life in the gentlest and most meaningful way possible for each one. I can't imagine a better gift to be able to offer in these later years of my life. For me it is the perfect way to honor the awesomeness of being human.

Acknowledgments

I COULD NOT HAVE written this book without a lifetime of support from innumerable sources. My profound gratitude goes to many: first and foremost, to Charles Terry, my husband, best friend and steadfast partner of forty-four years, whose never-failing help and unwavering belief both in me and in this book carried me the whole way, and to Daniel and Kendra, our two shining lights who have taught me so very much—Daniel, about the wisdom of valuing freedom and creativity as much as worldly success—and Kendra, about trusting one's intuition and never, ever giving up; to my mother and father, from whom I continue to learn, long after they have gone; to noble Casper, who lives in my heart still; to special friends and colleagues who shaped my career in powerful ways, including Rachel Remen M.D., Kathy Foley M.D. and the Open Society Institute Project on Death in America, and Michael Lerner of Commonweal; to the many individuals and groups whose support, friendship and wisdom have anchored me in this challenging world, including the intrepid ICIS community and our teacher Erling, all my dear Whidbey Island friends, the staff and leaders of Beth Israel Medical Center in New York City, the amazing Bravewell Collaborative, the folks of the Hollyhock summer gatherings, and the Whidbey Institute founders and community; to Hedgebrook, the unique retreat center for women writers that nurtured my muse while this book was being born and finally coming to completion; to Babs Small, M.D., who spent hundreds of Friday mornings writing with me; to my faithful and patient editor, A. T. Birmingham-Young; to Julie Glover, Christy Mack, Penny George, and Heather Ogilvy, who plowed their way through the manuscript and gave invaluable feedback; to Doug Hansen for his wonderfully generous help in getting me started on the cover, and to Christine Nyberg for her patience and skill in crafting the final, perfect one; to Sandy Welch, for her thoughtfulness and artful touch in designing the layout; to my sharp-eyed and caring proof reader, Carrie Wicks; to Joe Menth and Fine Balance Imaging Studios for stepping in with help at crucial moments; to David Trowbridge for his excellent work in creating Abiding Nowhere Press, and to all the Abiding Nowhere gang for our energizing and helpful meetings; to my indispensable iPhone, which has recorded innumerable sudden flashes of inspiration and been lost and found more times than I can count; to my MacBook—except when it scared me to death with its occasional quirks; and last but certainly not least, to all those intangible forces that have been helping me stay aligned with my soul's purpose while living in this world. Thank you all!

Index of Stories

Other books from Abiding Nowhere Press:

Bite into the Day: One Day at a Time,
a book of poetry by Miriam Sonn Raabe

Enso House: Caring for Each Other at the End of Life
by David Daiku Trowbridge

Abiding Nowhere Press
www.abidingnowhere.com

Made in the USA
San Bernardino, CA
19 September 2013